P9-CAA-556

109 WALKS
IN B.C.'S LOWER MAINLAND

Mary and David Macaree

THE MOUNTAINEERS, SEATTLE
AND MOUNTAINCRAFT, VANCOUVER

First printing May 1976

Copyright 1976 by The Mountaineers,
719 Pike Street,
Seattle, WA 98101.

Published simultaneously in Canada by
Mountain Craft,
P.O. Box 5232,
Vancouver, B.C. V6B 4B3.

Manufactured in Canada by Mitchell Press Ltd., Vancouver, B.C.

Library of Congress Catalog Card No. 76-19472

ISBN 0-916890-42-2

Design by Mary Macaree

Cover photo: Walking on Black Mountain Plateau (Walk 19). Courtesy of Bob Harris

Frontispiece: Great blue heron. Courtesy of B.C. Dept. of Recreation and Travel Industry

FOREWORD

After The Mountaineers (Seattle) and the British Columbia Mountaineering Club had collaborated in the 1973 publication of **103 Hikes in Southwestern British Columbia**, an acquaintance of Mary Macaree expressed disappointment at the lack of short walks suitable for family groups or for those whose physical state would not permit energetic hikes of the type described. The result of that casual criticism is the present book, which provides descriptions of over 100 hikes on beaches and dykes, lowland trails, mountain slopes, and to a few of the lower summits as well. Of course, some of these overlap shorter outings in the former collection; even where the destination is the same, however, the walks, with a few exceptions, have a different starting point or follow an alternative route.

As criteria for selection to its main list, the authors have taken into consideration distance, vertical height, and degree of difficulty, setting limits on these elements to ensure that no walk is more than an easy day's excursion. At the other end of the scale, we have included shorter outings because of some intrinsic interest or because these might otherwise remain neglected. In addition, we have listed, mainly for the benefit of visitors, a number of other walks with brief notes on access.

The main function of the book is, therefore, utilitarian, the descriptions representing as accurately as possible the state of trails and their approaches at time of printing; we cannot, of course, accept responsibility for changes that may occur subsequently. Despite the emphasis on usefulness, however, it is our hope that readers will obtain aesthetic pleasure from browsing through the text with its accompanying maps and photographs, so that the total effect is enjoyable as well as directive.

Naturally our book focusses chiefly on the lower mainland's population centres: Vancouver, and the municipalities bordering on the city. We do assume, though, that some readers will want to combine walks with drives into the country, while others will be glad to have outings described in the neighbourhood of campgrounds where they may be staying for a few days. The arrangement of contents, then, is Vancouver itself, the North Shore, Burnaby, and the lowlands south of the metropolitan area, mainly in Delta and Surrey. Following these, we give accounts of walks close to main radiating routes: Highway 99 to Squamish and Pemberton, with a foray across Howe Sound to the Sechelt Peninsula, Highway 7 along the north side of the Fraser Valley, and Highway 1 south of the river, the last two having as outer limits Yale at the beginning of the Fraser Canyon to the north of Hope and the Skagit Recreation Reserve to the south of it.

A compilation such as this does not claim to be exhaustive; in the nature of things it provides only a sampling — an attractive one, we hope. One sad feature, though, is the forced omission of certain walks because their approaches have been blocked off by the activities of developers, both public and private, accompanied by dissuasive "No Trespassing" signs. Controversy over the Ross Dam on the Skagit River makes doubtful one or two walks at the south end of that valley as well. It is easy to become emotional about such matters; it must be conceded, though, that indifference has been a contributory factor and, what is worse, so has user misbehaviour — ranging from simple carelessness and failure to respect privacy to deliberate acts of vandalism. The only way to offset the latter is through education in good trail manners, and in this respect parents may play a major role by impressing on youngsters this simple rule: LEAVE ONLY FOOTPRINTS; TAKE ONLY PHOTOGRAPHS.

It is particularly distressing to find instances of wilful damage in parks and recreation areas that have already been secured for public use, because here the vandal is destroying the property of all his fellow citizens. Not all of this can be attributed to walkers, of course; the trail bike is one of the most destructive agents of the recreational environment. The presence of these machines and their thoughtless riders is not only offensive because of the pollution they create with their noise and stench; the effects of their activity remain after them in the form of damage to trails, carved into deep ruts, and to plants, broken and twisted. When, in addition, it is considered that they waste non-renewable natural resources, it is difficult to understand why their users receive government encouragement in the form of exemption from licensing, exemption which renders identification difficult, even where they are in flagrant breach of the law.

A more cheerful note is the recent change in attitude of the forest companies towards multiple use of woodlands, resulting in the opening up of new areas to public access when logging is not going on. To encourage this more liberal policy, it should be hardly necessary to stress the need to respect the companies' property and to obey signs. Admittedly, routes through recently logged sections do not make for the most attractive walking; moves are now afoot, however, to retain treed corridors in scenic locations, and the availability of logging roads, even if only at weekends, does give access to new country. At that, lumbering operations are less messy than

Sign on Black Tusk Trail (Walk 105)

many downhill ski areas where summer debris and scalped slopes are little better than ecological disasters. And the attitude of ski resort operators is not particularly public spirited, witness the blocking of access to Dam Mountain in North Vancouver, so denying the use of its trails to summer visitors.

The most encouraging feature, however, is the increasing involvement of various levels of government in the establishment of parks and recreational corridors. One agency instrumental in putting people back on their feet is the Provincial Parks Branch. The activity of this body has created good trails in a number of recreation areas: Alice Lake, Garibaldi, Golden Ears, to name three. The only criticism — a surprising one, perhaps — is that some of them are too good with their easy grades and long zig-zags, leading to corner cutting and consequent damage. The B.C. Forest Service, too, has developed wilderness recreation sites, often in areas where logging is going on, and has marked various trails.

Close to main urban centres, the Greater Vancouver Regional District through its member municipalities has been promoting parks and walking routes. It has to be admitted, however, that some councils have been more active than others, with Burnaby's contribution being particularly noteworthy in its creation of "linear parks," a whole system of interlocking trails. Vancouver is just beginning a parallel development with the Parks Board attempting to put a girdle (of hiking and cycle tracks) round the city. Finally, creation at the provincial level of a new Outdoor Recreation Branch surely augurs well for the future, even if it does little more than expedite the transfer of crown land to allow regional districts room for expansion of facilities in such locations as Boundary Bay, Belcarra and Sasamat Lake, Iona Island, and Kanaka Creek.

Nor should the initiative of various outdoor clubs go unrecorded since these were, in many instances, the original creators of trails into scenic areas. Member groups of the Federation of Mountain Clubs of British Columbia have assumed responsibility for certain trails and these carry on periodic trail clearing bees. In this context, too, the Centennial Trail created by the Canadian Youth Hostels Association should be mentioned, several of the walks described herein being along stretches of that route to the interior.

Bunchberry with maidenhair fern

Similarly reference may be made to the Baden-Powell Trail along the North Shore, even though some parts of it have fallen on evil days because of hostility by various individuals while other portions have fallen prey to developers.

All in all, though, the picture is brighter than it was a few years ago. More people are walking and more attention is being given to requests for access to the countryside. It is our hope that this book will serve as an added stimulus to set more people's feet on the paths of this part of British Columbia. If we achieve this aim, our thanks must go to individuals like Joan Greenwood and Nancy Mason of the North Shore Hikers, as well as to officials of various government agencies, both provincial and municipal. The former supplied details of possible trails, the latter answered our questions and supplied us with data. To these and others go our thanks and appreciation for the patience with which they responded to what must often have seemed irrelevant questions. Last, a word of thanks to Mr. Howard Stansbury of the Mountaineers for his friendly encouragement during our struggle to work the material into shape for this publication.

David and Mary Macaree

SOURCES OF INFORMATION

Apart from the references listed at the end of this note, information is available from a variety of sources, public and private. The larger provincial parks have information centres that provide trail maps; in others, the ranger will help. All existing parks guides may be obtained on request from Parks Branch, Department of Recreation and Travel Industry, Parliament Buildings, Victoria, B.C. Notes on B.C. Forest Service recreational areas and trails in them are procurable at local ranger stations, while some municipalities of the Greater Vancouver Regional District supply descriptive booklets.

If you wish to build up a personal stock of maps, you may begin with the pocket maps of Vancouver, the Fraser Valley, and the Sunshine Coast published by Dominion Map Limited, 571 Howe Street, Vancouver, a firm that is also able to supply sheets of the 1:50,000 National Topographic Series and the 1:63,360 B.C. Provincial map of Garibaldi Park. Topographic maps may also be obtained from Information Canada, 800 Granville Street, or from Geological Survey of Canada, 100 West Pender.

Besides the sheer enjoyment involved in getting back the use of your limbs and escaping from your fellow human beings, your excursions outdoors should increase your awareness of nature in at least some of its manifestations: flowers and shrubs of summer, the trees of the forest and its wildlife, the record of the rocks, land features, and waterways. You will find brief comments on some of these topics in our descriptions of various walks, but these are to be considered only as appetite stimulators to send

Glacial scoring, the record of the rocks

you to the appropriate authority for more information. The same applies to human activity, even to the factors involved in giving names to places, a topic exhaustively covered in the first work listed. One unfortunate lack is a good, up-to-date, general history of the area; local groups have done studies of municipalities like Langley, Mission, Yale, and of course Vancouver has been well covered, but no overall survey exists. Surely here is a worthwhile project for some local historian.

USEFUL BOOKS

Akrigg, G.P.V., and H.B. **1001 British Columbia Place Names**, 2nd ed. Vancouver: Discovery Press, 1973.

Bowers, Dan. **Exploring Garibaldi Park**. Vancouver: Gundy's and Bernie's Guide Books, 1972.

Eisbacher, G.H. **Vancouver Geology**. Vancouver: Geological Association of Canada, 1973.

Kalman, Harold. **Exploring Vancouver: Ten Tours of the City and its Buildings**. Vancouver: University of B.C. Press, 1974.

Lyons, C.P. **Trees, Shrubs and Flowers to Know in British Columbia**, 2nd ed. Vancouver: Dent, 1966.

Matthews, W.H. **Garibaldi Geology**. Vancouver: Geological Association of Canada, 1975.

Morley, Alan. **Vancouver: From Milltown to Metropolis**, Revised 3rd ed., Vancouver: Mitchell Press, 1974.

Peterson, Roger T. **Field Guide to Western Birds**, 2nd ed. Boston: Houghton Mifflin, 1969.

Robbins, C.S., and others. **Birds of North America: A Guide to Field Indentification**, New York: Golden Press, 1966.

Vancouver Natural History Society. **Nature West Coast**. Vancouver: Discovery Press, 1973.

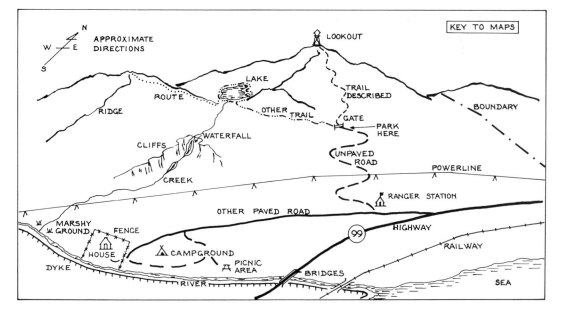

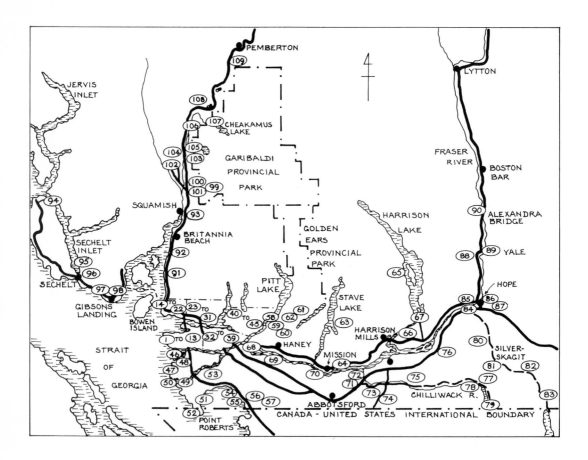

LIST OF WALKS

VANCOUVER

1   U.B.C. Gardens
2   Spanish Banks
3   Chancellor Woods
4   Endowment Lands Forest
5   Imperial Trail
6   Southlands
7   Quilchena
8   Shaughnessy Heights
9   Jericho Beach
10 Kitsilano Point
11 Stanley Park
12 Queen Elizabeth Park (Little Mountain)
13 Renfrew Triangle

NORTH SHORE

14 Whyte Island
15 Cypress Falls
16 Point Atkinson
17 Hollyburn Skyline Trail

18 Hollyburn Lakes
19 Black Mountain
20 Ambleside
21 Brothers Creek Falls
22 Lost Lake
23 Capilano Canyon
24 Mosquito Creek
25 Grouse Mountain Highway
26 Lynn Canyon
27 Baden-Powell Trail (Seymour Mt.)
28 Goldie Lake
29 Mystery Lake
30 Baden-Powell Trail (Deep Cove)
31 Old Dollar Mill (Cates Park)

EAST OF VANCOUVER

32 Harbourview Park
33 Burnaby Mountain
34 Simon Fraser University
35 Burnaby Lake
36 Brunette River
37 Central Park
38 Deer Lake (Century Park)
39 Robert Burnaby Park
40 Buntzen Lake
41 Mundy Lake
42 Coquitlam River
43 Pitt River Dyke
44 Minnekhada
45 Munro Lake

SOUTH OF VANCOUVER

46 Sea Island Dyke
47 Steveston Dyke
48 Richmond Nature Park
49 Ladner Harbour Park
50 Reifel Wildlife Refuge
51 Boundary Bay
52 Point Roberts
53 Burns Bog
54 Semiahmoo Trail
55 Crescent Beach
56 Redwood Park
57 Campbell River Park

FRASER VALLEY NORTH

58 Pitt Lake
59 U.B.C. Research Forest

60 Mike Lake Circuit
61 Gold Creek
62 Alouette Lake Viewpoint
63 Davis Lake
64 Hatzic Dyke
65 Harrison Lookout
66 Mount Woodside
67 Whippoorwill Point

FRASER VALLEY SOUTH

68 Barnston Island
69 Fort Langley
70 Matsqui Dyke
71 Sumas Peak
72 Chadsey Lake
73 Vedder Mountain
74 Teapot Hill
75 Elk Mountain Meadows
76 Cheam Trail (McNulty Falls)

CHILLIWACK RIVER

77 Lindeman Lake
78 Lower Post Creek
79 Upper Chilliwack River

SILVER/SKAGIT

80 Swanee Creek Falls
81 Hicks Creek
82 Rhododendron Trail (Skagit River)
83 Skyline Trail

HOPE AND FRASER CANYON

84 Bristol Island
85 Pebble Beach
86 Thacker Mountain
87 Coquihalla River
88 Spirit Caves
89 Historic Yale
90 Old Alexandra Bridge

HOWE SOUND

91 Harvey Creek
92 Furry Creek Valley
93 Stawamus Chief (South Peak)

SECHELT

94 Skookumchuck Narrows
95 Gray Creek Falls
96 Chapman Creek Falls
97 Sunshine Coast Recreation Centre
98 Soames Hill

SQUAMISH TO PEMBERTON

99 Paul Ridge

100 Four Lakes Trail
101 DeBeck Hill
102 Levette Lake
103 Culliton Creek
104 No-Name Lake (Tricouni Trail)
105 The Barrier
106 Brandywine Falls
107 Cheakamus Lake
108 Rainbow Falls
109 Nairn Falls

The trees encountered on a country stroll
Reveal a lot about a country's soul.

W.H. Auden, "Woods" c 1953 Random House Inc.

1   U.B.C. GARDENS

It is an unfortunate fact that the University of British Columbia, despite its superb setting on Point Grey, provides little inspiration in its buildings. For this reason, a walk on its campus is best described in terms of the various gardens, where art has managed, especially in spring, to harmonize with nature. In fact, the result is a kind of world tour embracing such diversity as a formal rose garden in the European style, a Japanese landscape in miniature, a park with totem poles and related westcoast Indian artifacts, and a cliff-top display of perennials and heathers, the last two set against a background of sea and mountains.

To make the most of this garden tour, park if possible in the visitors' lot by the gymnasium on University Boulevard, close to the bus terminal. Walk north along East Mall towards the University Library; just before you reach it, turn left, emerging onto a wide open space by the clock tower and facing the interesting underground Sedgewick Undergraduate Library. Continue past it on the Main Mall to the flagpole at its north end, where you will want to pause and enjoy the view up Howe Sound to the Tantalus Range as well as the sight of the rose garden at your feet.

Before you descend to inspect its charm at close range, however, make a short side trip along the front of the Faculty Club on your left to examine a fountain and its cast figures, **Transcendence**, by Jack Harmon, a group facetiously renamed "The Metrecal Maidens" by students. Now return to the terrace and walk down among the roses.

You should not be disappointed in the variety of exquisite blossoms of varied hues and scents, and here you will probably want to wander for a time sampling its beauties. But there is more to see, so eventually you make ready to move on across Northwest Marine Drive through what was once Fort Camp, a student residence of ex-army huts, now transformed into an anthropological museum where "The proper study of mankind is Man."

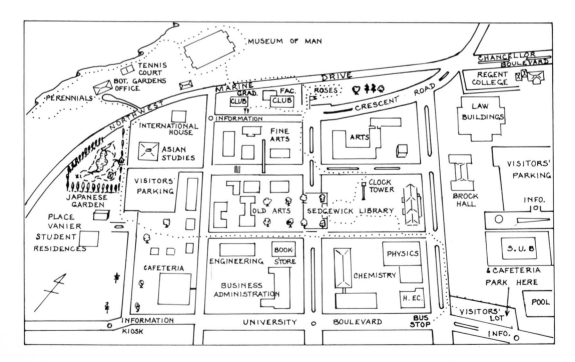

Lingering in the Nitobe Garden

What you will see on the seaward side of this edifice is hard to describe since it is still in the process of becoming. Suffice to say that the intention is to house the whole university totem pole collection in the grounds, with Burrard Inlet and Bowen Island as background. Similarly, it is planned to turn the garden of what was the President's House, next door, into a garden of perennials. In any event, you still have Nitobe Memorial Garden, a Japanese landscape (admission 25c).

For the Garden, recross Marine Drive somewhat to the west and follow the footpath into the trees to the right of the West Mall entrance. As you proceed, you become aware of a large building beyond the grove on your left. This is the pride and joy of the Asian Studies Department, the pavilion resited from the Osaka World's Fair of 1970. Your destination, though, lies to the right, through the ornamental gate into the Japanese garden.

Here is a miniscule rendering of a whole landscape: a river system from the mountain stream to deltaic marshland, complete with a lake stocked with large carp, and surrounded by trees that make a rare show in April with their blossom. There is a Japanese tea house as well, expertly reconstructed to depict a way of life very different from the North American.

This is your last stop. But how to get back to your transportation? You do not want to set off across the wasteland of a parking lot; turn right, therefore, at the gate and stroll towards the park-like surroundings of the Place Vanier Residences. Once there, cut diagonally left to a footpath that takes you up to West Mall, from which a further short walk uphill brings you out at the south end of Sedgewick Library and an easy return to your conveyance.

Round trip 2 miles (3.2 km)
Allow 2 hours
Sidewalk, mainly
Good all year

15

2 SPANISH BANKS

This circuit, interesting at any time of the year, and at its best when the tide is low, involves a beach walk in one direction with a park hike for part of the return trip along the top of the bluffs overlooking Burrard Inlet. In fact, though the area lies within the University of British Columbia Endowment Lands, it is administered by the parks branch of the Greater Vancouver Regional District, which has improved trails and also runs a refreshment concession and comfort station at Spanish Banks (East) should your body demand attention at the start or the finish of your walk.

Just at this spot on Northwest Marine Drive is Spanish Banks bus loop, terminal for a service that connects on Alma Street with Broadway busses and also with the Fourth Avenue service. To the west are carparks for some distance, but between these and the beach runs a corridor of grass and young trees to give relief from black-top. The beach at this point is a mixture of coarse sand and rocks with alternating bays and points: at high tide, that is. When the water is low, fine sand and silt stretch far out into the bay.

Set off along here, undeterred by the curious stares of those who enjoy nature from the seats of their cars; enjoy, instead, the view of Bowen Island rising to its high point Mount Gardner (2479 feet), with Point Atkinson and the North Shore mountains further round to the right. For those who appreciate the human comedy, there are kite-fliers to see, varied groups of picnickers, and clam-diggers with tall ships as background.

For the first half mile you walk parallel with the road. From here, however, Marine Drive begins to rise towards the university and you part company with it, staying on the path just above the beach.

Soon another track joins from the east parking lot, a little way up the hill, then you cross a creek on a footbridge, a great improvement over the slippery rocks or boulders that supplied till recently the only route. Thereafter the trail you have been using goes off to the left uphill and you leave it for the shore, saving it for your return journey. Stretching ahead of you now is beach, tree-lined on the landward side and with tidal pools and sandbars inviting you to remove shoes and give your feet an outing.

Take this section gently; it has a great restorative effect on jangled nerves. Even the two searchlight towers hint only at "old unhappy far-off things, and battles long ago." The more distant of them with the point behind suggests further possibilities for exploration round to Wreck Beach, but on this occasion, the nearer one is the limit of the walk along the shore, a trail from just behind it leading to a dark ravine with steps here and there on its steeper stretches. Ascend this track, one popular with students seeking respite from books in a walk to the beach, and you emerge on a very different scene

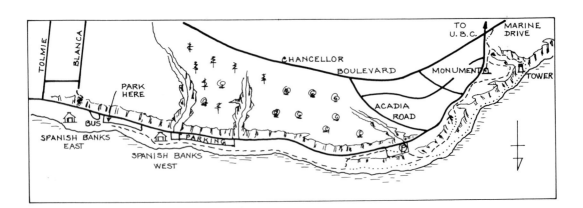

from the one below.

Here the landward side of Marine Drive is residential and academic. Uphill to your right are university buildings; downhill stretch the smart gardens of Endowment Lands homes. Only on the seaward side does nature — aided by man — still maintain itself. Wander downhill through the park, passing the memorial cairn commemorating Captain Vancouver's meeting with two early Spanish explorers and taking advantage of the numerous viewpoints along the cliff's edge. As you descend, the park first narrows where a deep gully bites in close to the road, then it opens out into a wide grassy stretch where you can get away from the traffic by staying close to the seaward edge. Finally, at the foot of the hill you come on the trail that drops down to the beach and your original route, this time with the towers of Vancouver's West End vying for attention with the mountains on Burrard Inlet's north shore.

Round trip 4.5 miles (7 km)
Allow 2.5 hours
Beach and path
Good all year.

3   CHANCELLOR WOODS

The northern section of the University of B.C.'s endowment lands — extending, roughly, from Chancellor Boulevard to North West Marine Drive — contains several walks. Mostly they are in forest, but in forest that is quite diversified, from impressive conifers of some age to quite young deciduous trees, with certain sections making no pretensions to being more than scrub timber. There are also one or two interesting ravines and, of course, the tree-crowned bluffs above Spanish Banks.

The trail system is such that it lends itself to circular hikes and the question is how to make the best use of the possibilities. Described here, then, are two walks starting from the same point and covering in part the same ground, but with the longer adding a stretch of beach to the

territory to be covered, along with a descent into a ravine. Several points of departure are possible; however, the one indicated has the advantage of being clear of all main thoroughfares while being convenient for trails, both in setting forth and returning.

From Blanca Street travel west along 8th Avenue. About a quarter of a mile along this, a barrier blocks further progress; park here. Alternatively, if coming by bus, take either a 10 (University) or a 4 (Fourth Avenue) to Blanca Loop and walk to the same spot. Just beyond the barrier, the new Chancellor approach links with the old alignment in a considerable bend. Cross here to the north side where a foot trail (Spanish Trail) goes off among the trees.

This part of the route lies in tall timber: second growth as the nurse stumps of the original forest show, but old enough to look satisfyingly mature in the eyes of city dwellers who may enjoy the sight of cedar, Douglas fir, and hemlock, with the last predominating. As it works its way north, the trail descends very gently until after about 20 minutes it ends in an open grassy space, with trees beyond, through whose branches you may catch glimpses of Burrard Inlet. Cross the "Plains of Abraham" as these have been named, apparently to commemorate an early settler in the location. The ruin of a concrete wall at the south end may give credence to the story but it is more likely to have been a wartime installation.

Cross this field to its seaward side, then turn left to find the path that heads off west close to the edge of the bank which drops precipitously to the roadway below. Now you have views across to the North Shore mountains, and, beneath them, to the numerous settlements across Burrard Inlet that make up West Vancouver, stretching west to Point Atkinson with its friendly light. Continue along this edge until further progress is barred (apparently) by a deep gully that drops steeply some one hundred feet or so to near sea level. Here the two trails part company; the shorter goes uphill to the left, the other descends into the depths.

To describe the shorter first: Its route follows the run of the ravine fairly closely even where it is forced away from the main valley by one or two deep washouts. One of these, the result of torrential rain at Christmas 1972, has gouged out a great gully in the clay and sand into which trees have tumbled in a tangled mass. As you continue inland, you begin again to hear the faint sound of traffic and eventually you step out of nature on to the Boulevard, to find yourself at some distance from your starting point. There is no need, however, to return along the road or by the cycle track on its south side. From this, the south side, a little left of where you emerged, a trail (Pioneer Trail) crosses the sidewalk and goes on into the woods.

Follow this some 300 yards until you come to a route crossing at right angles. Turn left. This new trail leads to "Little Australia," the residential settlement south of Chancellor and between it and the University Golf Course. From the woods you emerge onto Tasmania Crescent where, once more, your turn is left to take you back to your waiting vehicle.

Turning now to the longer walk, its track angles down into the ravine via a nicely groomed little trail. This brings you down to the stream at a point not far from Marine Drive. Make for the road, negotiate the deep ditch on its landward side, and cross it to the foreshore park. Once on the grass you go left again for about half a mile. Just after the road begins to climb, and before a parking lot on the seaward side, with a sign prohibiting camping, you will see a set of steps opposite, from the road level to the top of the bank (Admiralty Trail). Ascend these in spite of their awkward spacing and you find yourself on a narrow trail heading back east.

You return parallel with the outbound route; the only difference is that you are now walking among small trees on top of a bluff that is high enough above the road and the beach to give you a sense of remoteness from the creatures below. The trail is a little tricky here and there because of small washouts, but it is easily negotiated if you keep the inlet in sight on your left. Eventually you return to the ravine but you are now above it and on its opposite side. Nor need you descend into it. A trail continues to the right and slightly uphill and you follow it, the water-course a landmark on your left.

From this side, too, the great gouge in the opposite bank is visible and the main valley is impressively deep. As you progress, however, it speedily shallows and the further you go, the smaller it becomes. Finally, after staying left at

an intersection, you travel over a great fallen tree — indicative of the size of the old forest — then descend a little to cross what is now a demure little creek. Now, you hear traffic also and soon pavement comes in sight by a large sign board. The last part of this hike is identical with the short one: across the road, into the woods, then left to emerge on Tasmania Crescent. And what would have happened had you gone straight on at that last intersection? You would have emerged on the golf course.

Short Circuit 2.2 miles (3.9 km)
Allow 1 hour
Long circuit 3.5 miles (5.5 km)
Allow up to 2 hours
Forest paths
Good all year

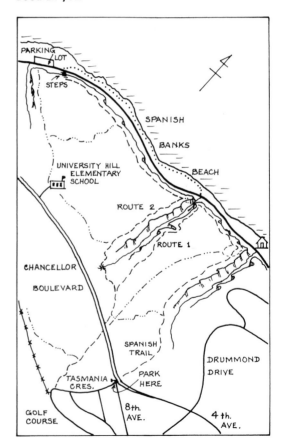

Woodpecker holes in cedar

4 ENDOWMENT LANDS FOREST

As a woodland walk in U.B.C.'s Endowment Lands, this circular trip should be satisfactory for the harried city dweller with an hour or so to spare. The only lack? Distant views to please lovers of the spectacular.

The outing begins on West Sixteenth Avenue at the point where Tolmie Street joins it in the 4500 block. Here a built-up trail (Sasamat Trail), the result of efforts by a devoted citizen group, goes into bushland in a once-cleared area that now supports a luxuriant growth of broom, that immigrant from Britain that has established itself on Vancouver Island and the Lower Fraser Valley. This soon gives place to small alder as you emerge by a reservoir and walk along its western edge towards a mixture of larger trees.

About ten minutes from your start, fork left at a major Y-junction just beyond the reservoir's southwest corner. Now the trail continues, skirting the edge of an aspen grove, something of a rarity in the coastal forest zone.

In about half an hour, just after another route (Council Trail) has joined from the right, you sense that there is a clearing ahead, forewarning of the approach to Imperial Trail a little south of 29th Avenue. Cross Imperial on the line you have been following and take the trail that plunges into the bush on its east side. Stay on this as it first turns a little downhill then resumes its original line, eventually emerging on an open space, once the site of horse stables. Turn right here on another major route (Clinton Trail) and head south in the midst of quite impressive second-growth timber.

By so doing, you emerge eventually on a large open space just north of S.W. Marine Drive not far from its intersection with 41st Avenue. Turn right again just as the bush opens out and, back in forest once more, travel north on Salish Trail for the next half mile before stepping out once again on Imperial, a considerable distance downhill from your original crossing and just opposite power-pole No. 55. Go left here, passing three more power poles; then, on the right of the road pick up another trail leading into woods to the right, just before Imperial itself turns left.

On this trail you remain, crossing Council Trail once more, till you come to a major T-junction just to the right of a footbridge. Turn right on this new path (Hemlock Trail) and proceed uphill till you arrive back at the original Y-junction just south of the reservoir. From here, simply retrace your steps to your setting-off point, your woodland outing over.

Round trip 4 miles (6.4 km)
Allow 2 hours
Forest paths
Good much of the year

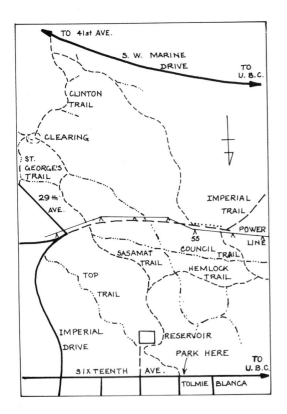

5 IMPERIAL TRAIL

Among hikes in the U.B.C. Endowment Lands, this one offers the greatest set of contrasts — ranging from trails in deep woodland to a one-time road, now a lane, with sight of TRIUMF and the B.C. Research Installation for good measure.

To reach the start point at Imperial Drive and West 29th, follow West 16th Avenue to its meeting with Discovery Street at the northwest corner of Camosun Park. Turn south here along the road with woods on the right hand and the park itself on the left for a short distance. As you approach a housing development south of the park, the road begins to swing left, further progress forward being blocked by a low wall. This is the start of your hike so leave the car as close as is convenient but clear of the travelled portion of the highway.

For a start, cross the wall and head downhill on the surfaced track parallel with a line of power-poles, a track that is closed to vehicles except service trucks. At first you bear a little right as you descend but one advantage of the power-line is that trees have been cut back to accommodate it so that you are in the open. On your way, note the trail that comes in from the right just after the start; it should be the one you return by. Thereafter, as you proceed, you will see one or two trails going off into the woods to left or right, but leave them for now and enjoy the open lane.

At the foot of the hill, the lane and power-line separate, the latter continuing straight on while the former swings left; just as well, the right-of-way is very wet. Now the forest deepens and the trees on either side press in more closely, several large hemlocks looking particularly impressive. Here, too, the evidence of human interference with nature is being nicely obliterated, with small bushes and shrubs re-establishing themselves on what was blacktop not so long ago. Finally a chain across the road indicates a change in its status, one that is signalled by a great open drainage ditch and the sight of buildings nearby.

Here, a short distance off on the right looms the ugly bulk of TRIUMF (Tri-Universities Meson Facility); fortunately it is far enough back

to be less intrusive than might otherwise have been the case, but its appearance still comes as a shock. Stay with the track for two or three hundred yards further to a road that crosses it at right angles close to a hideous, large, tar-paper erection that U.B.C. students of an earlier generation will recognise, probably with more loathing than nostalgia, as the old fieldhouse that graced the East Mall and provided at one time a chilly place for examinations.

At this point, anyone who is keen for a side trip with a view of Georgia Strait may continue straight on to the end of Imperial where it is blocked off at Marine Drive. Cross the latter

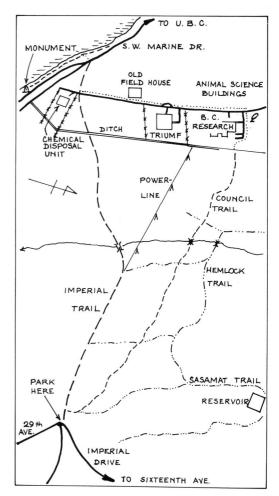

(being careful of traffic) then turn left along the grassy track on its seaward side to where the Musqueam historical marker commemorates the arrival of Fraser's party at the mouth of the river that now bears his name. Here is a fine spot to look south over the log-booming grounds to the delta lowlands with the islands of the gulf behind. This diversion, however, adds a mile to the hike and is suggested only for those who are avid for experience. The main route itself turns right in the direction of TRIUMF at the intersection by the old fieldhouse.

Walk along the front of this structure and proceed to the next building, one which houses B.C. Research. At its north end, almost opposite the new agriculture complex, go right on a road that leads to a car-park, fronting a field, noting on your left the large radio telescope as you walk past it. At the road end, cross the grass and make for the centre of the clearing. Here at the edge of the trees is your return trail.

The COUNCIL TRAIL, as it is appropriately named, leads straight into an impressive forest of large second-growth cedar, Douglas fir, and hemlock, with the great stumps that yet remain of the original cover indicating what giants were felled here in the early days of B.C.'s logging industry. On this trail you now remain, ignoring the two or three intersecting routes that you come across as you proceed. And your route is not without interest. At one point a footbridge over a creek; at another, small cleared areas as evidence of unofficial campsites; at yet a third, an avenue of alder bearing mute testimony to the line of an old forest right-of-way.

Finally, the trees thin out, your trail joins another broader one, and soon you step out on to Imperial just south of the wall. Apart from the many cross routes, the return poses no great problem. Even if you do go off the line, little harm is done; you will only emerge into the open at a greater distance from your transportation.

One final word for those of you who use this route in the near future: If you have enjoyed the hike, support the efforts being made to keep this area as a regional park for future generations.

Round trip 3 miles (5 km)
Allow 1.5 hours
Dirt road and forest path
Good all year

6 SOUTHLANDS

Here is a walk for a short winter day or for a summer evening, involving as it does only a short drive for Vancouverites to the southwest corner of the city, where the Point Grey district abuts on the north arm of the Fraser River. This area, rich in riding stables, paddocks, and golf courses, lies south of S.W. Marine Drive between Dunbar Street and 49th Avenue and is sufficiently free of traffic to make road walking a possibility. The outing described, however, keeps off pavement altogether, giving the walker opportunity for uninterrupted mountain and river views.

To reach the eastern end of the trail, turn south off Marine Drive on Blenheim Street, go right for one block at the next intersection, then left along Carrington Street to the road end at a wooden bridge just by the river. To the right as you face south a large sign announces Southlands Bridle Path and indicates that its use is limited to horseback riders and pedestrians. The curious walker will, of course, want to stroll to the wooden bridge at the end of the road and he is likely to be rewarded for his effort by sight of the many fishing craft that use the little backwater as home, just downstream from Celtic Shipyard.

The trail itself takes you downstream along the river bank, with Point Grey Golf Course (private) on your right behind its various barriers. Over in the south, the roar of a huge jet betrays the location of Vancouver International Airport. On the opposite bank of the river, various squat buildings indicate the location of Vancouver's sewage treatment plant on Iona Island, a fact attested to by the great cloud of birds that rises in company with the jet plane's take-off. The river itself is busy with commercial and pleasure craft. A tug may be pulling a barge or a log raft, a fishing boat may be returning home from the grounds, or a log salvage operator in his small boat may be towing a prize or two behind him.

The path goes steadily seawards but the most interesting views are over the lowlands to the south, or north over the golf course to the North Shore mountains. Finally, the Point Grey course ends with a track running inland along its western boundary. You may make the circuit — rectangle would be a better name — but much of it is on road and it is probably more pleasurable, though shorter, to continue westwards. By so doing, you find yourself with another golf course, a small public one called Musqueam, to which is attached a driving range. Between this and the river goes the track until eventually an inlet blocks further progress westward.

This area is part of Musqueam Indian Reserve and there is at present some development going on so that it is difficult to walk round the Musqueam Course. It is therefore better to return by the outbound route, enjoying now the view upstream perhaps with the distant sight of Mount Baker away to the southeast.

Round trip 1.5 miles (2.5 km)
Allow 1 hour
River path
Good all year

Near Celtic Shipyard

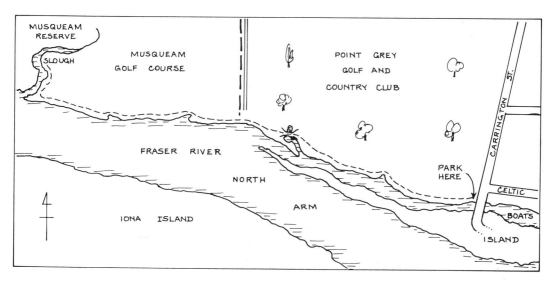

7 QUILCHENA

For those days when the weather has cleared too late for venturing far afield, or when time is otherwise limited, here is an unpretentious walk within minutes of downtown. This walk combines charm and variety, involving as it does two parks — small ones, admittedly — and the connecting thoroughfares with their varied residential architectural features. There's even a stretch of railway thrown in for good measure.

Drive, or take the bus along Arbutus Street, to Valley Drive, the second intersection south of West King Edward Avenue; turn east here opposite the Standard gas station. Beside the white Byzantine Greek Orthodox Church (St. George's), you will see Quilchena Park right ahead where the road forks. Here is your starting point; before setting off, however, take a little time to examine the handsome church with its dome and panelled doors, the more so because it will serve as a landmark for your return.

The park itself, once part of a golf course of the same name but with the golf activity now confined to a small putting green, stretches ahead rising gently to the B.C. Hydro railway that forms its eastern boundary. Stay near the northern limit of the open space as you tread turf, heading just to the left of the park keeper's house and the toilet facilities and coming on to a little tree-crowned knoll with a bench just short of the rail right-of-way. From here you look across to the highrise apartments of Kerrisdale and the smaller single-family dwellings of MacKenzie Heights as you continue on the grass along an avenue of fine trees, presumably a one-time fairway. On your right, grassy slopes extend down to Valley Drive, and you may want to pause at West 33rd Avenue to look back over the great sweep of Burrard Inlet and the mountains beyond.

Now your outing changes character, for the next stretch is over roads; but they are quiet roads in a residential area, so you have no worries about traffic once you cross 33rd. First follow Quilchena Crescent; then, where it is intersected by Cypress Street, take the latter uphill by turning sharp left. At the head of the rise is a familiar sight, the railway, but just below it Linden Street swings right again for a few yards until, as it starts to descend once more, you see on the left a lane with DO NOT ENTER (actually, the sign is a warning to motorists). This lane contours just

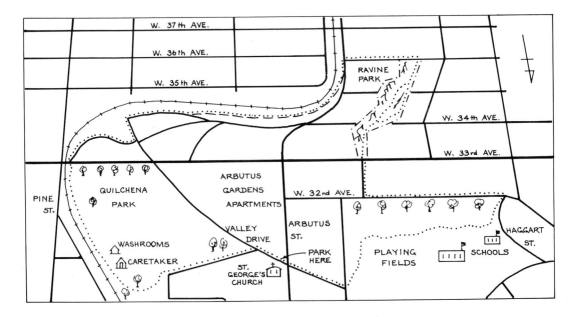

below the railway and gives views of the houses above the tracks, notably one recent conversion in stained wood that juts out boldly from the hillside.

The lower side is less striking, the backs of houses lacking the interest of their street faces. The views between them to inlet and mountain more than make up for any architectural short-comings in the foreground, however. By this time you have risen quite appreciably above your point of departure and the buildings of Kerris-dale look a good deal less imposing than they did from the park. Meanwhile the lane gradually turns from west to southwest, finally emerging on Arbutus close to 36th Avenue.

Cross here and follow the avenue for about half a block to a wooded gap between houses with the sign RAVINE PARK. Turn right here and begin descending the slope of this narrow sylvan corridor as the trail winds among tall trees, to emerge finally at 33rd Avenue some distance west of your crossing on the outward trip. If you wish, you may return to Quilchena Park from here by turning right, crossing Arbutus at the lights, then going left at Valley Drive. However, there is no need to do this, for a little more exploration is still possible.

Go straight forward across 33rd and travel one more block before turning left and heading uphill between two rows of architecturally diver-sified dwellings to the point where you meet Haggart Street just above a children's playground and the sports fields of Prince of Wales High School. Descend diagonally across this towards the white dome of St. George's in the distance, aiming for a point about midway along the eastern fence where there is an opening. From this point the last little stretch of road is visible and your urban peregrination is over.

Round trip 2 miles (3 km)
Allow 1 hour
Grass and blacktop
Good all year

In Ravine Park

Houses on Alexandra Street

8   SHAUGHNESSY HEIGHTS

This picturesque section of Vancouver gives you a chance to stroll the quiet tree-lined avenues fringed by elegant dwellings that stand aloof in their own grounds, gazing somewhat disdainfully, it seems, at mere foot travellers in Shaughnessy. But what's in a name? For, though its original possessor ended his life as a peer of the British Empire, plain Thomas George Shaughnessy was a simple American citizen when, in the early 1880's, he was recruited by the C.P.R., the company of which he eventually became president. In this capacity he controlled not just a transportation enterprise but a great amount of real estate, a small part of which was developed as this high-class residential section in the early years of this century and was given his name just as the streets commemorate lesser luminaries of the company.

Undoubtedly the focal point of the district is The Crescent, the simple unadorned name underscoring its importance even if it is oval rather than crescent-shaped. Because of its shape, though, roads radiate from it in a number of directions giving you a choice of routes; thus, the walk described here is by no means the only one possible through such an interesting area, and you may work out various alternatives. To heighten interest by adding to your knowledge of the properties passed, try to obtain Harold Kalman's **Exploring Vancouver**, which describes a number of these and supplies photos of some of the most striking houses.

One possible starting point is the new Arbutus shopping centre south of West 25th Avenue. The Arbutus bus service from town passes it and there is, of course, plenty of available parking. At the south end of the parking lot opposite the Arbutus Club, cross Arbutus Street on Nanton Avenue and head uphill across the BCE Railway and for three or so blocks to Angus Drive. Turn left here and walk north noting how the houses become larger and more ostentatious on the north side of West King Edward. Particularly pleasant are the great deciduous trees that line the roadway, set as these are in front of imposing residences in their own grounds.

The only break in the tranquillity comes with the crossing of Granville Street, that thoroughfare demanding a quick eye, a fleet foot, and some nerve. East of it, however, all is peaceful and soon The Crescent is reached. Traverse this in a clockwise direction, taking a look north along McRae Avenue and perhaps walking down the hill a short way to view the University Women's Club building, "Hycroft." Continue eastward following the bending line of the road and, by all means, complete the 360 degrees before cutting across the central park area, with its benches and its varied trees.

To begin the return trip, start on Osler Street, the dual carriageway that heads off southeast from beside the "Villa Russe" with its locked gates and warnings of ferocious dogs. Along here are more homes to enjoy, both the originals and, in some cases, modern replacements of these. From Osler you may head back west either by Matthews or by Balfour one block south; each is peaceful and has its points of architectural interest. Once again Granville has to be negotiated; then, if you have chosen Balfour, comes a short dog-leg right to Matthews on which you remain to Pine, one block west of Angus Drive. Turn left here and head for West King Edward Avenue.

To complete the trip you may cross King Edward and make for Nanton again or, if you wish, turn right at the through street for the sake of the view over Arbutus Village towards MacKenzie Heights; the view over the water towards the northwest is also inspiring. And so, return to your transportation on Arbutus, enjoying the realization that although your home may not be so roomy as the ones you have seen, it is probably a lot less trouble to maintain.

Round trip 3.5 miles (5.5 km)
Allow 2 hours
Sidewalks
Good all year

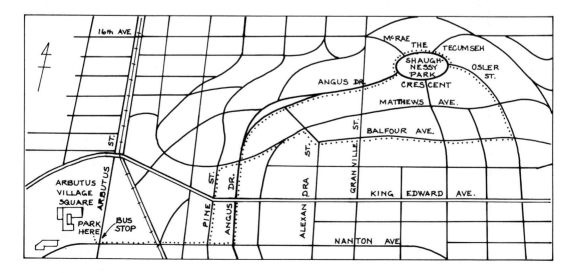

9 JERICHO BEACH

Now that Vancouver Park Board has acquired from the Department of National Defence the property north of West 4th Avenue between Wallace Street and Marine Drive, a whole new stretch along the shore of English Bay is opened up to walkers. Nor are you confined to one route; possibilities exist for walks of varying length, even for round trips.

To make the most of what this area has to offer, begin not in the park proper but at the little Hastings Mill Store Museum at the end of Alma just north of where it meets Point Grey Road (the nearest bus stop is 4th and Alma). The unpretentious wooden building is a relic of Vancouver's earliest days for, built in 1865 by Captain Ed. Stamp, it served as the first post office, community library, and recreation centre on Burrard Inlet.

Starting here, then, you cross its little park and head west past the Vancouver Yacht Club and Jericho Tennis Club before swinging past an old people's centre (once an R.C.M.P. headquarters) towards the beach and a small Park Board pavilion.

From now on, you have the bay on your right with Point Atkinson and Bowen Island more or less ahead as you step, on the seaward side of a small lagoon, towards what is left of the old Jericho army base. Make for the large white building that faces you and you find as you near it that it is Vancouver's Youth Hostel. Once past it, continue half right to keep clear of Marine Drive with its traffic, and now you come to your second pavilion at Locarno Beach.

This may serve as destination of a short walk (round trip about one hour); however, if you wish to go further, there is nothing to stop you. Make your way, then, to Spanish Banks East with its refreshment counter and changing rooms. Here, too, you may turn round; an interesting alternative presents itself, though, if you do not wish to return by your outward route.

This involves crossing Marine Drive close by the bus loop and ascending the flight of steps up the steep bank on its landward side. These bring you out at the foot of Blanca Street, and a short walk uphill leads to a left turn and a descent on Belmont Avenue or, if you wish, along Bellevue and down West 2nd, passing "Aberthau," the one-time officers' mess, now a Community Cultural Centre. From here, recross Marine Drive and return across the embryonic park, this time taking the track south of the lagoon then turning half left to reach the end of Point Grey Road once more.

Round trip 2 miles (3.2 km) or more
Allow 1 hour or longer

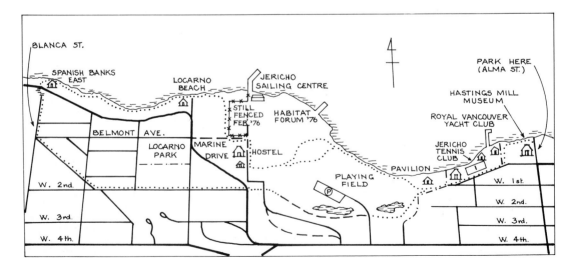

Gull tracks in the sand

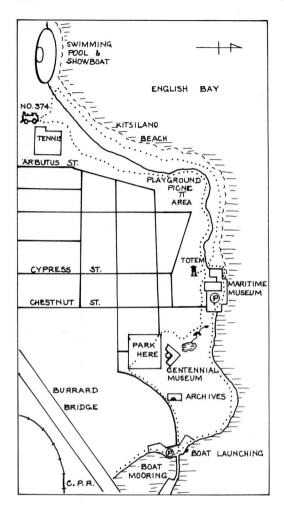

10   KITSILANO POINT

This point, the tip of the small peninsula jutting out into English Bay west of the entrance to False Creek, forms the pivot for a walk that may embrace such diverse attractions as the sight of small craft scurrying to and fro, under power or sail, the tall buildings of a modern city viewed across a narrow stretch of water, museums and records of B.C.'s past, beaches, forests, and mountains still relatively unspoiled, an open air swimming pool, and a concert area; a walk that, into the bargain, covers three city parks: Vanier, Haddon, and Kitsilano.

From Cornwall Street just west of Burrard Bridge, turn north on Cypress at the traffic light and follow the Centennial Museum signs (the MacDonald bus service stops at the intersection). Though some parking is available near the marina on False Creek, space can be at a premium on a summer day; it is probably best, therefore, to use the Centennial Museum lot, noting that building's inspiring lines with their upward sweep and resolving to visit its collection some day.

First set off towards the mouth of False Creek. Have a look at the Major Matthews building, home of the city archives, the low profile of which suggests the weight of the past in contrast to its lofty neighbour. Then come the marinas, a confusion of small craft at their slips with the span of Burrard Bridge to the southeast providing a frame for them as well as for its more distant neighbour, Granville Bridge. Across the creek squats the new swimming-pool building; fortunately it blends with its background, for it is no thing of beauty.

Now, as you head north, Stanley Park begins to show itself, stretching behind English Bay, itself the anchorage for larger ocean-going ships. Behind, on the north shore is the high country above West Vancouver rising to the summit of Hollyburn Mountain, while further west are the peaks round Howe Sound. On rounding this first point, too, you see closer at hand the Maritime Museum, home of the **St. Roch**, that pioneer ship of Arctic exploration which now sits demurely above the water, sheltered from the elements that she once braved.

Stay on the seaward side of this building, for just beyond it you may drop to the beach and

Historic engine

enjoy part of your walk on it for the rest of the outward journey. Now you continue into a small bay on which is situated the open-air pool with Kitsilano Showboat, the home of summer concert parties, and the yacht club just beyond it.

This is a suitable turning point, so walk up from the beach into Kitsilano Park. Here you may pay your respects to old CPR **No. 374** which, unlike the **St. Roch**, is unprotected and serves mainly as a children's plaything, more favoured frequently than the swings and apparatus furnished by the parks board. This time, pass the Maritime Museum on its landward side, stopping en route to have a look at the hundred-foot totem pole carved by Chief Mungo Martin to commemorate B.C.'s Centennial year, 1958. Note also that you are now in Haddon Park, Harvey Haddon having donated the land to the city.

Now comes your return to your original parking spot, your best route being by the ornamental bridge that spans the outflow of one of the small ornamental lakes to the north of the Planetarium. The actual distance covered on this hike is not great, but its variety of interest will ensure that you will not hasten round the point whose name commemorates an Indian chief of the Squamish Indian Band. But the white man's past is also commemorated, for the Major Matthews Building, named for the city archivist, is itself a centennial memorial to B.C.'s entering Confederation in 1871.

Round trip 2.2 miles (4 km)
Allow 1.5 hours
Surfaced path, beach, and sidewalk
Good all year

11 STANLEY PARK

For a circuit embracing a number of different surroundings while keeping clear of other users as much as possible, try this walk. It begins in the park's southwest corner from one of the parking lots located close to the Park Board Offices just north of Lagoon Drive or, if you are coming by bus, from the Denman Street terminal of the No. 5 or No. 8 service.

From here, make for the sea wall to get your sampling of what it has to offer in one of its most picturesque sections, the one running north along the shore of English Bay past Second Beach. At the same time, you surely do not wish to plod mechanically round the whole length of this walk, crowded as it is with pedestrians as well as cyclists. For that reason, ascend the steps at Ferguson Point to emerge on top of the low cliff opposite the tea-room run by the Vancouver Parks Board. Stay close to the edge, keeping the sea on your left as far as possible, a rule to follow on the whole of this stretch to Prospect Point.

The first point of interest is the roughly hewn stone monument to Pauline Johnson who loved the park in her lifetime, gave Lost Lagoon its name, and was thus commemorated following her death in 1913. Having paid your respects to

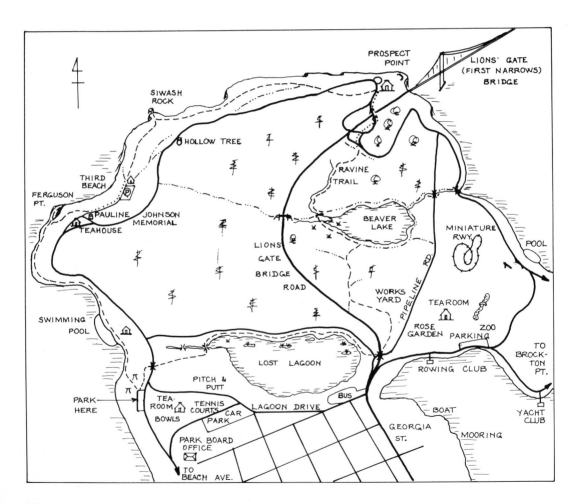

her, continue along the sidewalk of the access to Third Beach Parking Lot. At the beach, remain on the land side of the pavilion and pick up the Merilees Trail that runs along the top of the cliffs between 100 and 150 feet above the water. From here various viewpoints give glimpses across the bay and over to Point Atkinson and Bowen Island. Particularly spectacular is Siwash Rock seen from the old coast defence platform which now serves as a lookout point; you may even see the cormorant that often uses the rock as a perch if the seawall walk is quiet.

After the rock, stay with the trail as it works its way round to the northeast in a forest of mixed fir, cedar, and hemlock, finally rising via a flight of steps to a higher level and eventually coming out at the road a little south of Prospect Point. Even now, you have no need to pound the sidewalk; cross the road and follow a trail north through the bush to emerge opposite the cafe. Here you may pause either to refresh yourself, or to look down at First Narrows 247 feet below you, or to examine the walking beam of the old S.S. **Beaver**, or to contemplate the basalt dyke that helped create the headland by resisting erosion.

On resuming, you must stay with the sidewalk on the north side till you have crossed the bridge over the main road. Very soon after, however, cross back and follow a trail south parallel with the road and intersecting the two connections with the Lions Gate highway. Beyond the second of these pick up a service road going south and giving access to a works area. From here a footpath, Ravine Trail, continues along the left side of a small creek and you stay with this till you come to Beaver Lake. This is a particularly pretty stretch and the skunk cabbage in spring can, with some exercise of the imagination, be thought of in terms of Wordsworth's Daffodils — if only their name weren't against them.

From the southwest side of the lake follow the trail to the right and continue along it when another fork joins from the same side. Soon you arrive in the garden area south of the works yards and now all you have to do is to continue downhill past the rose garden and make for the underpass that will bring you out on the shores of Lost Lagoon. The more rewarding route back is along the north side, where you view the buildings of

the West End from a respectable distance and can enjoy the great mixture of bird life that haunts its banks and waters.

Finally, at the western end, cross the footbridge over the lagoon's extension that looks like an inlet, though it isn't, and seek your transportation once more.

Round trip 5 miles (8 km)
Allow 3 hours
Park trails mostly
Good all year

Siwash Rock from Merilees Trail

Quiet corner of the arboretum

12   QUEEN ELIZABETH PARK (LITTLE MOUNTAIN)

Anyone can drive to this city landmark, park the car (providing there is space, no certainty on a summer weekend), admire the view from the summit 410 feet above sea-level, give a brief glance into the Sunken Garden, look into the cafe and gift shop, then depart having "done the park," But there is far more to Queen Elizabeth Park: the arboretum on its lower slope, the rose garden, the lily ponds and waterways that are all free for the visitor to enjoy; not to mention the Bloedel Conservatory, for which there is a small admission charge.

To best sample the wide range of possibilities, a good point of departure is not in the park at all but at the foot of the hill on its northeast side where Midlothian Avenue runs towards Capilano Stadium. To get there, turn east off Cambie Street at 29th Avenue and drive for some two blocks past the Vancouver Curling Club and the apparently misnamed Hillcrest Park, with its soccer pitches, nestling beneath its more illustrious neighbour.

Here you leave your car and start walking back west on the grass of the park among stately trees and past a series of ponds and connecting waterways. At this stage the park road is still above you on your left; your route gradually rises, however, and finally crosses the blacktop as you work round the slope past the main entrance at Cambie and 33rd Avenue and cut across the top of the small parking lot.

Resist at this stage the temptation to take one of the trails leading uphill; instead, keep working round the flank of the slope towards the recreation area. Before you reach this far, however, you come on the rose garden, a blaze of summer and fall colour and well worth a leisurely inspection. Next you will see a notice announcing the existence of the Vancouver Lawn Bowling Club and now you take the footpath up and to your left to gain access to the summit area near its southeast corner.

Here you will surely want to pause and savour the view that stretches southeast to Mount Baker, south over the delta lowlands and Boundary Bay, southwest to Point Roberts and the Gulf Islands, and west to Vancouver Island. And the outlook is no less attractive as you head back west along the perimeter track then turn gradually to the mountains on the North Shore. Finally, you come to the roof garden area with fountains, wooden walks and espaliers plus the massive metal piece, "Knife Edge," by Henry Moore. These walks are cunningly arranged to give changes in direction, each one with its own attraction; and it is difficult not to linger at one point or another.

At the north end, however, is the great glass dome of the Conservatory and this prize-winning structure becomes the next objective even if no visit to it is intended for, just beyond its entrance, is a viewpoint overlooking the Sunken Gardens. Here, from just below your feet, a stream drops 50 sheer feet over the rock wall to the garden floor, where its waters form an ornamental pool in the midst of flowers and lawns. Nor should the rock plants be forgotten in the catalogue of attractions for they provide colour when other plants are off-duty.

Descend to the garden floor and stroll across the lawn, then pick up a path heading east below the rock wall of what was once a quarry and becomes, in fact, Quarry Garden, smaller and

quieter than its neighbour, but no less attractive. This display dates only from 1961 when it was created as a memorial of the seventy-fifth anniversary of the city's founding in 1886. And perched on a rock overlooking the garden is Quarry House Cafe and Restaurant, giving promise of internal refreshment for those who require it.

From here, the route is all downhill; first to another little pond situated just above the park drive and at the foot of a slope ornamented with tall trees and with rhododendron bushes. Next, cross the road, silently despising the weakling drivers and continue to journey's end at Midlothian, conscious that you have "done the park" — properly.

Round trip 1.75 miles (3 km)
Allow at least 1.5 hours
Grass and footpaths
Good all year

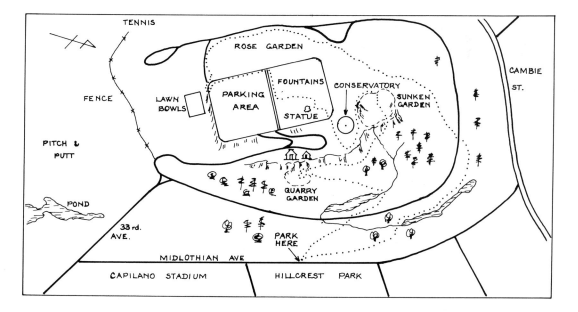

13   RENFREW TRIANGLE

This is a fairly literal description of a route that takes you east, then south, then northwest along the hypotenuse of a right angled triangle. For good measure, it gives you three parks and an abandoned railway right-of-way, with, as bonus, some striking clear-day views of The Lions, Crown Mountain, Seymour River Valley, as well as the tall buildings of downtown Vancouver. Best of all, it is close in, requiring little outlay of time in driving to its beginning.

One good point of departure is the northwest car park in John Hendry Park just past Victoria Drive. Travelling east to the 1900 block on 12th Avenue, turn south on Victoria then go another block east on 15th. Now you are looking across Trout Lake, its swimming area to the south on your right, a point to remember for a warm day if you want to top off your activity with a dip. For the present, however, you set off eastwards on your journey of discovery, making for the softball diamond on the opposite park boundary, picking up 15th again, crossing Nanaimo Street, then making a short jog half right to 16th and Beaconsfield Park.

Once again, turf beneath your feet rather than city pavement, you make for a softball diamond, this one in the southeast corner, then walk along 18th for a block, just north of the Children's Hospital. Now you cross Renfrew Street and you find yourself in your third park of the outing, Renfrew Ravine, a change from the first two, with its stream running north beneath shady trees and a children's playground above you on the left. A little south, too, is Renfrew Community Centre which you reach via a flight of steps, though the more usual approach is by a high bridge across the creek.

Now, as you look south, you realise that you must cross Renfrew Diversion to stay with the ravine, even though there is at present no trail in it on this stretch, so that you have to work your way along it on its eastern rim using lanes and little trails to stay with it. Finally, a footbridge takes you across to its west side at Atlin and 28th and from here one more block south brings you to the old B.C.E. Railway right-of-way for your return to base.

As if attempting to cover up old scars, Nature has been lavish with flowers and shrubs, the latter including blackberry bushes (abundant)

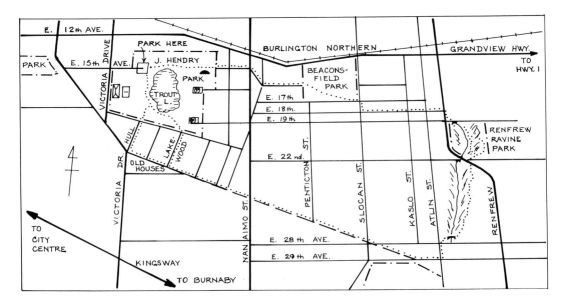

Renfrew ravine

and thimbleberry, while among the former are morning glory and foxgloves, with sweet peas and delphinium that have run wild. On this stretch you have tall downtown buildings laid out in front of you with a screen of mountains as background, providing a whole range of views. Finally, however, you drop down to Nanaimo Street again, John Hendry Park visible to your right. Stay with the right-of-way a little longer, though, at least until Lakewood Drive, where you may go north a short way to give yourself a longer walk in the park via Trout Lake's swimming area.

On the other hand, if your interest is old buildings, continue a block or so further to see one or two relics of Vancouver's past when variety of window shapes and sizes made up for box-like walls and roofs. Eventually you must turn half-right, however, to get back to your car, perhaps reflecting that there is a good deal of beauty and variety in East Vancouver.

Round trip 3 miles (4.8 km)
Allow 2 hours
Good all year

Whyte Island

14   WHYTE ISLAND

Though this rocky knoll is island by courtesy only, being accessible on foot via a boulder causeway when the tide is suitable, it makes a satisfying destination for a walk that includes a rocky spine of land overlooking Howe Sound, a wander through a pleasant little seaside park, and a stroll along a beach past a small-boat marina. Of course, you can drive to Whytecliff Park but doing so cuts the walk in two and is not nearly so rewarding.

Travelling west from the city along the Upper Levels Highway through West Vancouver, take the Squamish fork at Horseshoe Bay junction. Almost at once, however, turn left and cross the overpass, following the signs for Marine Drive. From the STOP sign a little way beyond, go straight ahead for just over half a mile to Hycroft Road, second turn-off on the right. Take this road, undeterred by the DEAD END sign, and very shortly go left uphill to the road end in a small circular patch. Ahead, among the trees, lies the trail. One warning, though; parking space is limited, so do not block a driveway.

Once in the trees the trail forks; it does not matter greatly which one you take, however, as they reunite later; perhaps the one to the right is best saved for return because of its spectacular views of the Howe Sound Mountains. In any case, you can enjoy the mixture of trees, conifers and arbutus predominating, as you wander along the ridge with its little rocky viewpoints to the right.

At its western end, the trail descends quite steeply by a flight of steps, to emerge on the overflow parking lot for Whytecliff Park, located just across Cliff Road. Cross the road and go down Rockland Wynd, then left along Arbutus Road, at the end of which a gate gives entry to the park. Once inside, head for the ornamental viewpoint where you will want to linger a little to enjoy the outlook over Howe Sound before continuing to the objective. To do so, walk along the rocky cliffs, cutting back inland a little to avoid an isolated promontory, then descending by a track and stone steps to the marina dock with its wooden jetty, once a pier of the old Union Steamship Company which ran ferries from this point.

Pass along the landward side of the mooring

slips and head along the little shingle beach, one frequented by skin divers in the open season, which happens to be winter, as diving is banned between April 1 and October 31. At the far end of the beach is the causeway, a little slippery perhaps, but easily negotiable with care by anyone who is properly shod. The same caution applies to the island rock also, though it is not too steep; ten minutes or so will put you on the summit so that you may say like another celebrated islander, "I am monarch of all I survey," and such a survey is rewarding. Point Grey looms across the inlet southwards, Bowen Island to the

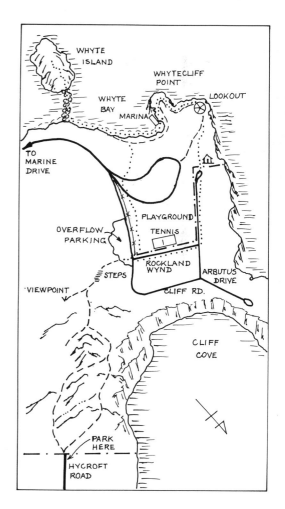

39

west, and Howe Sound again stretches north. And don't forget to look up from the rocky shores of Batchelor Bay to the bold headland of Eagle Bluff on Black Mountain.

To return, you may follow the same route exactly or vary it in detail by walking directly up from the beach into the park's grassy area, stretching diagonally to reach the overflow car park in the northeast corner. And, of course, you will take the other route back along Panorama Ridge, probably stopping often to admire the majestic peaks. Just one point though: don't bring Fido. No dogs are allowed in the park.

Incidentally, if you are wondering about the "Y" in Whytecliff, it commemorates a long dead land promoter, Colonel Whyte. The Colonel induced the old Pacific Great Eastern Railway to spell the name of the station this way rather than following the standard spelling which the British Admiralty survey had given to White Cliff Point because of its light-coloured granite rock.

Round trip 4 miles (6.5 km)
Allow 3 hours
High point 250 feet (76 m)
Good all year (but watch the tide)
Forest path, beach, and rock

Gazebo in Whytecliff Park

15 CYPRESS FALLS

No, this isn't a new name for the provincial park in Cypress Bowl; Cypress Falls Park is a relatively small recreation area situated only a stone's throw from the Upper Levels Highway, administered by West Vancouver Municipality, and still carrying a good deal of its original forest cover. Hitherto it has not enjoyed — or suffered, according to your point of view — much in the way of development though there is now some mention of putting a footbridge across the creek and locating a trail from the northeastern corner towards its younger namesake following the hydro power-line right-of-way uphill. That is all speculation, however, so let us consider the park

Sword fern

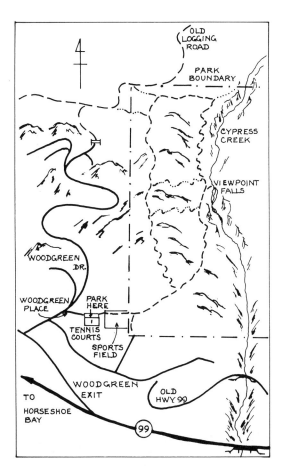

as it exists at present, not at some unspecified time in the future.

For a shady trail on a hot summer day within earshot of cool falling water, or for a pleasant winter hike when the stream is mute and icicles grow on its rocky banks; in fact, for any time of the year, this is a park to keep in mind, the more so because of its location convenient to the city. To reach it when travelling west along the Upper Levels, turn off right at the Woodgreen Drive exit, a short distance past the highway's new crossing of Cypress Creek. Take the second road right after you turn uphill, Woodgreen Place, a short dead-end with limited parking by some public tennis courts beside a West Vancouver Parks Board sign.

Enter the sports field that lies just beyond the tennis courts and walk along its edge towards the trees at its northeast corner where you pick up the trail. This leads gently upwards into forest with the rush of the creek gradually making itself more evident the closer you get to the falls. On this stretch, stay right at all trail junctions, ignoring the routes that point upwards and to the left. After walking for some 15 minutes, you arrive at the first series of falls though you are kept back from them by a wire fence; the reason for the fence becomes obvious when you peer down into the narrow gorge with its leaping spray. Especially on a winter day, the spot is dark and eerie, so after paying your respects to the scene, head uphill again.

More views of falls and rapids follow, but gradually your trail begins to turn left and, finally, as you begin to see the backs of some of the houses of Cypress Park Estates, you start your return journey. This time you stay higher on the hillside where the trees are thinner and the light a little better until, just before the end, you drop down to join the entrance route again and retrace your steps to your starting point.

Because of the strong forest growth — there are stately Douglas firs and some cedar — the ground cover is light. On the other hand, the dampness favours mushroom production so the fungus collector may have a field day. Also in evidence are little tree squirrels while a dominant sound is the sharp tapping of the woodpecker, the effect of whose activity is evident in the holes drilled into many of the tree trunks.

Round trip 2 miles (3.2 km)
Allow 1 hour
High point 990 feet (275 m)
Elevation gain 250 feet (76 m)
Forest path

Point Atkinson lighthouse from historic cairn

16 POINT ATKINSON

Even the urban troglodytes who emerge only infrequently from the built-up sections of Vancouver must be aware of this landmark where the waters of Howe Sound mingle with those of Burrard Inlet, if for no other reason than that its lighthouse sends friendly beams of light over the waters during the hours of darkness, and its foghorn bellows out its warning during periods of gloomy overcast. But Point Atkinson is well worth a visit for its own sake, located as it is at the southern tip of Lighthouse Park with its mixture of coastal forest, rocky headlands, and narrow bays, the haunt of varied wild life from the humble organisms of the intertidal zone to majestic birds.

To reach the park, drive west along Marine Drive from the north end of Lion's Gate Bridge for a distance of just over six miles a little past Caulfeild, to where, after a short rise in the road, Beacon Lane lies on the left. Turn along it for about a quarter of a mile to a designated parking area at the end of which a gate bars further progress, though a service road does continue beyond it. If possible, park a little north of the gate, close to the big information signboard on the right as you enter. This points to a main trail that goes off through tall conifers towards the northwest.

Very shortly comes the first stop at a viewpoint just to the right of the trail where large rough-looking nests in the forks of trees are visible. These are the homes of the bald eagles, those birds that mate for life and return year after year to the same habitation, carrying out repairs and additions as needed. After this break, stay with the left fork where the trail soon after branches; then, at the next divergence, go right and descend gradually to the coast at an attractive cove with dykes of igneous rock penetrating the granite and contrasting with it. A little further south, another short diversion right, marked with a signpost, leads to Jackpine Point with views across to Bowen Island and with all the beauty of a combined marine and forest landscape in the surroundings. Here, note the grooves in the rock, mute evidence of past glaciation.

As the trail turns southeastward towards the point, you have your first sight of the 60-foot white lighthouse tower rising among the trees. Do not make directly for it, however. It is surrounded by a high fence and the rock rising outside is steep and may be slippery. Stay on the trail, therefore, as it rises to the top of the rock, emerging into the open beside the historic cairn describing the naming of the point and giving the history of its beacon, now in its second century, though the present tower dates only from 1912. Also recorded is the birth here of the first white child on the North Shore.

For the return journey, go east to the service road to find a trail that parallels it, more or less. Postpone the inevitable, though, by making a

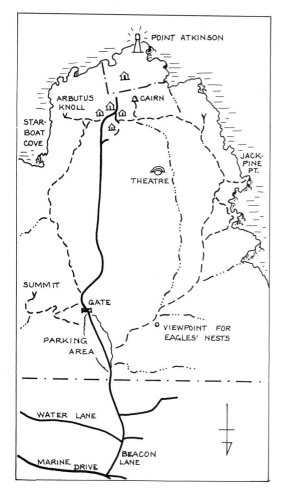

short trip to Arbutus Knoll, a rounded bluff looking over Steamboat Cove, a deep indentation in the coast that those with time and energy may scramble down to. The route back, however, rejoins the service road just before the gate and for most this will mark the end of an enjoyable outing. Those who wish more may take a sharply rising trail on the right, one that emerges at the park's high point, 390 feet above sea level.

In passing it may be recorded that West Vancouver Parks Board has provided information signs along the trails, identifying a variety of natural features. The serious naturalist, though, will want to obtain **Nature West Coast**, that exhaustive study of the park compiled by the members of the Vancouver Natural History Society. Thus armed, virtually nothing can escape your identification.

Round trip 3 miles, longer with diversions (5 km)
Allow at least 2.5 hours
High point 390 feet (120 m)
Good all year
Forest paths

17   HOLLYBURN SKYLINE TRAIL

Those of you who don't mind a little rough going in spots will find that the views from this trail on a clear day more than offset any unevenness of footing that you may encounter. The Skyline Trail, in fact, is one of the most rewarding of the local walks because it is over open country for a good part of its route, hence its views; even where it is in forest, it runs through mature timber with good footing and attractive alternation of light and shade.

To reach a convenient starting point, drive from Upper Levels Highway in West Vancouver up the new Cypress Provincial Park Highway for about 3.5 miles to a viewpoint with parking space at a major bend. Just to the right of the road where it turns back west, look for a rough track heading straight uphill among trees. Follow this for 100 yards or so then take a footpath left. This angles upwards in a westerly direction until it turns back north as you stay right at the next junction, located a short distance below the point where you cross an old logging road and continue uphill to the B.C. Hydro power-line

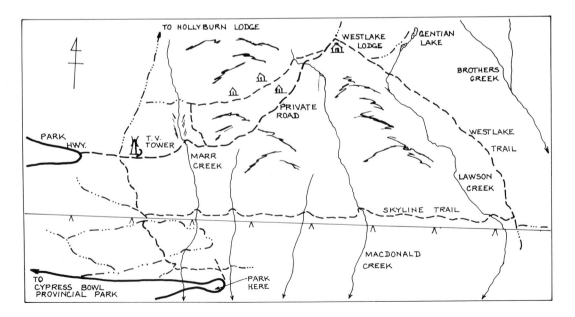

running east and west close to the old chairlift right-of-way. The trail, now marked with orange and blue triangles lies parallel with the power-line and, at this point, is a little above it as you go right to head east.

On this trail — sometimes in the open, sometimes in the forest — you walk for the next two miles in the direction of Grouse Mountain, the lower slopes of which are visible ahead of you except when you plunge into the various ravines that carry creeks down to lower levels, and cross these streams over fragile footbridges. Thus you continue till you have traversed the third of these, Lawson Creek; then, emerging from its gully, you come to a junction with Eyremount Drive — Westlake Lodge trail.

On this you go left, uphill, following yellow markers as your route parallels the creek you recently crossed. Now you are in a forest of tall trees, pleasant walking on a hot day as you eventually come to one or two cabins and arrive at the lodge with its promise of refreshment. Thus sustained, drop downhill on the right of the building to pick up the hiking trail westwards. This again takes you into forest but now you have for company various wooden cabins rejoicing in such titles as "Times Square," "The Glass House," and so on, each with its picturesque little outhouse.

Finally you arrive at another clearing; just ahead is what was the upper terminal of the old chairlift, but your way is now downhill, keeping the right-of-way on your right. A short distance below, you join the vehicle access road to Westlake Lodge and you turn right on it as it gradually descends westwards. Next you see a microwave tower on your right while you have sight of the highway ahead; however, you are not going to join the highway yet.

Just a little beyond the tower, you come on a trail sign on the left of your route, this one marked with an orange triangle. Again you plunge into forest, picking your way among trees of pretty fair size, as you discover when you have to navigate past a fallen one. Ignore the first old road that crosses your route and continue downhill till you reach a logging road heading downhill left. Follow it and in a very few minutes you should recognise the point at which you embarked on the Skyline Trail, leaving only a short descent to your waiting car.

May Day on Hollyburn

Round trip 6.5 miles (10.4 km)
Allow 4 hours
Forest paths and old logging roads
High point 2500 feet (780 m)
Elevation gain 900 feet (280 m)
Good June to October

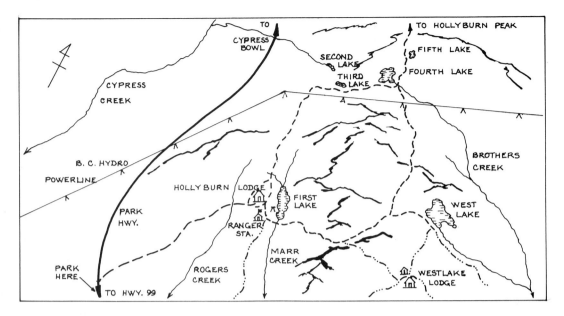

18   HOLLYBURN LAKES

Though the Provincial Government's ill-conceived plan for a downhill ski development in Cypress Bowl has probably ruined much of that once-scenic area for summer recreation, Holly-burn Ridge to the east, all that is to be left for cross-country skiers and snowshoers in winter, still has possibilities for walking at other seasons. The outing described here has for its objective a series of pretty little lakes dotted along this ridge in surroundings that are particularly attractive after the first frosts of fall have turned the bushes and shrubs to rich gold and russet. And it is best later in the season on yet another count: in some places, snow remains into July and the melt makes routes wet and muddy.

To reach your point of departure, go up the new Cypress Provincial Park Highway for almost seven miles to just below the spot where the signposted Hollyburn Lodge fire access route leaves it on the right. Park in the lot on the left of the road, cross the highway, and angle a little uphill to reach the lower end of this track. By the lodge is your first lake, appropriately named

First Lake. From it, follow the path north along the ridge, a cross-country ski route in winter, fringed on both sides by tall trees.

This pleasant sylvan setting is rudely interrupted by the wide Hydro power-line clearing that you must cross about a half mile beyond the lodge. An added misfortune is that removal of the natural vegetation has also wiped out the trail. So, having crossed to the north side, turn right and continue there a short distance to the east till you see another small lake on your left within the tree fringe. This is Third Lake — Second is close to it. You should now be able to find the route again as it begins to approach — guess what? — Fourth Lake, a footbridge at its eastern end allowing you to continue north to Fifth Lake.

From this spot, the route itself continues to the summit of Hollyburn Mountain, more than a mile further and 1000 feet higher. So unless you are a "peak-bagger," perhaps this is as far as you will want to go. You can, however, turn this walk into a circular tour if, back at Fourth Lake, you follow the trail that forks left (yellow triangular markers) for Westlake Lodge. This takes you down the ridge on its east side, finally bringing you to a T-junction where the trail to the right goes back to Hollyburn Lodge. But if you wish to add yet one more lake to your collection, go a few hundred yards to the left instead and emerge above West Lake.

Set against a background of tall trees with Dam Mountain and Goat Peak rising behind in the distance, this lake is one of the prettiest on the ridge. Now retrace your steps and follow the track from the T-junction back to the outlet to First Lake, with the West Vancouver Forest Service building straight ahead as you cross the footbridge, and the lodge to your right providing a marker for your return to transportation.

The beauty of this little trip is the immunity you enjoy from the sight of the disaster area that is Cypress Bowl. Screened from that by trees, you are in country reasonably unspoiled by man — except for the Hydro line.

Round trip 4 miles (6.4 km)
Allow 3 hours
High point 3200 feet (990 m)
Elevation gain 600 feet (190 m)
Good July to October

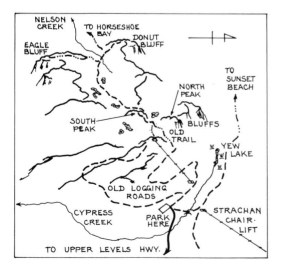

19   BLACK MOUNTAIN

The summit plateau of this mountain block above West Vancouver is so picturesque that its new accessibility from the chairlift in Cypress Provincial Park is bound to make it popular for walking even if the approach involves a climb of some 1,000 feet should the lift not be operating for some reason.

Drive the Cypress Provincial Park Highway from the Upper Levels Highway to its end at the chairlift parking lot. From here, Black Mountain is to the west of you, Mount Strachan to the northeast, and Hollyburn to the east. If you intend making the ascent on foot, your easiest route follows a logging road up, one that takes off from just above the lot on its west side. This first leads south towards the mouth of the upper valley with fine views out over Point Grey and the Strait of Georgia. Next it swings back in dog-leg fashion and ends on a knoll not far from the upper terminal of the chairlift.

From here the two summits are close at hand with an old wooden building in the dip between them. The south knob has a trail on its west side for the short drop to the summit plateau, its picturesque lakes and rocky outcrops. A walk across the marked route allows you to traverse the sub-alpine meadows (beautiful in Fall) till you emerge on its western edge at Donut Bluff with Horseshoe Bay and Howe Sound far below. Do not descend beyond this point; it's a long way back up. Return instead to the twin summits with their views of both Lions and the Tantalus range before retracing your route back to the carpark.

For those of you who do not desire such elevated prospects, a walk north from the parking lot towards Yew Lake is pleasant and non-demanding. Pass between the lower terminals of both chairlifts and continue close to the creek to the little lake among its trees; the distance is not great. One warning, though: the area round the lake may be wet, especially in early summer when the snow has just gone.

Round trip up to 5 miles (8 km)
Allow 3 hours
High point 4000 feet (1200 m)
Good July to October

Breakers in English Bay

20   AMBLESIDE

Enter the park from 13th Street after turning left on to it at its intersection with Marine Drive in West Vancouver. Cross the B.C. Railway track and park as far to the west as possible. To walk eastwards, use either the sea-wall or the beach facing towards where Vancouver Harbour is framed in the span of Lions Gate Bridge. On your left are playing fields and the swimming pool; to your right, the waters of English Bay beyond the main shipping track seaward through First Narrows.

Close at hand there is much to enjoy: beach-combing if your tastes lie that way; feeding wild-fowl in the pools that are a feature of the garden between the road and the little public golf course; further round is the fitness circuit with its jogging track and its exercise stations for the keep-fit buffs. Now the east-west line begins to give way to a northeast-southwest axis as the mouth of the Capilano River comes into view, barring further progress towards Lions Gate but permitting a short walk along the river bank. Thus, you turn your back for a time on the view across to Siwash Rock and Prospect Point and look instead at the great heave of Crown Mountain to the north, or closer, at the dark tower that marks the southeast extremity of Park Royal and overlooks the hurrying waters of the stream.

Once past the B.C. Railway underpass, follow the trail through the bush, then bear right along the outside of the parking lot towards the river. Just as it seems that further progress is barred by the tower, a narrow passage between it and the stream opens up leading to an underpass of the road bridge. Here, during most of the year, the Capilano shows the effect of the Cleveland Dam on its flow, for it by no means fills its stream bed; its shallows, too, are the haunt of great numbers of birds, notably crows and seagulls, both congregations of which keep up a continuous chatter. This stretch, in fact, is bedlam when the salmon run upstream is taking place, that run which provision of the salmon hatchery below the dam has done so much to reinstate.

Shortly after the road underpass, further progress appears to be barred by the outfall of Brothers Creek into the river. The obstacle, however, is minor; in summer, you may ford the creek, but when the water level is high, simply climb the few feet to the road on top of the bank and use the bridge that leads to Beacon Hill Lodge, an old people's home. On its north side a footpath goes back to the river and a path stretches along its bank to a new high-rise building complex and under another bridge. Here the Capilano is most pleasant and the view of Crown Mountain is striking. At present the trail ends shortly after the underpass but you may continue on the rocks to a point where the current sweeps close to the west bank and blocks further progress upstream.

Return, of course, is by the same route, along the river side of Park Royal and back into Ambleside Park with the view now being towards Point Grey and across the Strait of Georgia to Vancouver Island.

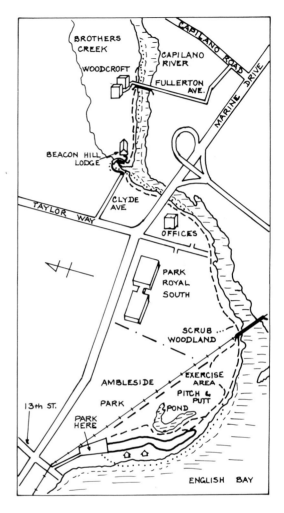

Round trip 5 miles (8 km)
Allow 2.5 hours
Good all year
Beach and dirt path

21   BROTHERS CREEK FALLS

This walk is feasible during most of the year; only when snow is well down to British Properties does it present problems. It is, however, more attractive in spring and fall than at other times: in spring, because the water from the snow melt above gives a spectacular element to the normally placid creek, sending sheets of white spray thundering over a 50-foot cliff to disappear into the gorge below; in fall, there are quiet pools reflecting the gold leaves in the limpid waters. The falls are readily accessible in a morning or afternoon hike.

One way to reach them is via the regular trail to Westlake Lodge from the end of Eyremount Drive in British Properties. Another, less well-known perhaps, follows a power line right-of-way from the intersection of Millstream Road and Craigmohr Drive just before the Glenmore electricity substation. To reach this start, the most direct route is via Highland Drive with a left turn onto Eyremount followed shortly after by a swing right on Crestline Road. Take this to its link with Millstream, from which the power station is visible, with a line of wooden poles coming downhill to it from the left. Park close

to where the line crosses the road and look for the orange and blue triangular markers that indicate the route uphill.

This is rather steep and rocky at first, but shortly the grade eases off and after about ten minutes an old road crosses the power line. The trail, however, still continues upward following the right-of-way which now runs between quite high trees. Eventually it angles right and into the forest just about the time that you become aware of a steady rush of water. Next, you get a first sight of the gorge on your left and the path starts dropping quite steeply to emerge just below the main fall beside an interesting looking pool, whose placidity in autumn contrasts with its agitation in spring.

For those with limited time, this makes a satisfying destination. If you wish a longer hike, however, you may continue across the creek on the footbridge, scramble out of the gully by the steep path on its west side and join the main Brothers Creek trail at the top of the bank. Go right here, following the orange markers, and staying above the stream's west bank as you ascend through the forest. Travelling thus, you come to a trail junction at a bridge where you go over to the east side. From here the Lost Lake

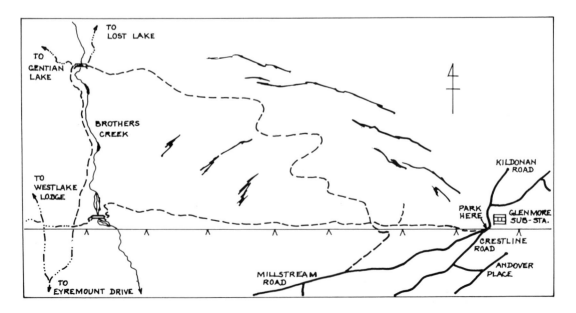

route proceeds upstream; your business, however, is with an old road going downhill to the right through the trees.

This is the old road which you saw intersecting the Falls trail on your outward journey. Although the road is clearly defined and easily followed, it has no triangular markers so that you are in a sense on your own. Certainly you should not venture on it late in the afternoon. The route, though, is particularly appealing on a warm day, being among tall trees that temper the sun's rays; it gives you a nice circle trip as well, if you do not wish to retrace your steps.

Round trip to falls 2 miles (3 km)
Allow 1 hour

Long circuit 3.5 miles (5.5 km)
Allow 2 hours
High point 2,300 feet (700 m)
Elevation gain 800 feet (260 m)
Foot trail and forest road
Good April to November

Lost Lake

22   LOST LAKE

This objective allows for the pleasant variations provided by a round trip; it also gives views of two or three attractive woodland lakes in addition to a tramp through open forest on marked trails, with Brothers Creek for company part of the way.

Travel up Highland Drive in British Properties by going left at the estate office. Follow it uphill, then go left on Eyremount, remaining with it to a point where further westward progress ends at a gated road by a lookout point.

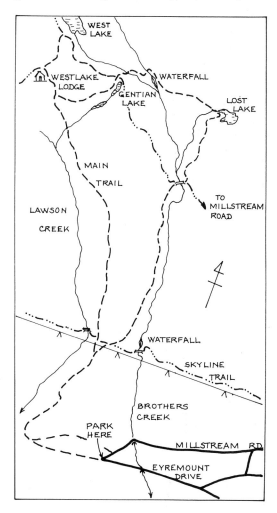

Park here and head west for a short distance to where signs on the right point uphill to Westlake Lodge and Hollyburn. Take this trail as it goes fairly steeply upward for about twenty minutes to where another trail diverges on the right with a pointer for Brothers Creek. This is your route; follow it.

Very soon, it emerges into the open on a power line right-of-way, crosses it, and continues into the forest beyond. Shortly thereafter the sound of the creek is heard and you may see its waters tumbling downwards, particularly in spring. The trail, marked with orange triangles, follows its west bank past alternate gentle stretches and romantically dark canyons, with a handrail to prevent the impetuous from too close contact with the waters.

After about an hour, you come to a wide wooden bridge crossing the stream; there is also an alternative trail, leading away from the stream to the left, and going to Blue Gentian Lake (red triangles). It is, however, more interesting to cross the footbridge and follow the trail with orange markers to Lost Lake. Here nestled in peaceful forest with an old picnic site on its south side is a little lake, from which, turning west, you cross the outlet on a bridge that is somewhat in need of repair.

This trail eventually recrosses Brothers Creek and shortly thereafter arrives at the northern tip of Blue Gentian Lake, intersecting the direct route from the bridge. Stay with the orange markers and make for the main Westlake Lodge trail, negotiating the swampy ground at the lake's western end as best you can. Another possibility, if time permits, is to follow instead the red markers northwest to West Lake itself, with its wooden dam and its open slopes giving glimpses of Crown Mountain and Dam. From here a short walk south leads back to Westlake Lodge from which the main trail down (yellow markers) takes you back to the power line and the route back to Eyremount Drive.

The creek and lakes are most impressive in early summer when their levels are highest and the ineptly named skunk cabbage at its most luxuriant. Later, though, the water lilies on Blue Gentian Lake are notable, and the going is less apt to be muddy. Fall, too, has its rewards; bunchberry in the forest and the blaze of gold, bronze, and red foliage in the open areas, even if the spectacular water effects are lacking.

Round trip 5 miles (8 km)
Allow 3.5 hours
High point 2,900 feet (880 m)
Gain 1,700 feet (520 m)
Forest paths
Good May to November

Skunk cabbage

23 CAPILANO CANYON

For the most pleasurable route on this walk, ignore the regular entrance to Capilano Canyon Park and instead proceed an extra mile up Capilano Road as far as the parking lot at Cleveland Dam, the barrier which holds back the water of the river, creating Capilano Lake as storage for thirsty Vancouverites. By starting thus, you have the view of the Lions standing up in the northwest and forming a fitting background for the lake and the valley. And you may savour, as well, the delights of the canyon with its great vertical walls created by the waters of the river on its way to tidewater near First Narrows at the entrance to Vancouver harbour.

To reach the suggested start of this hike, drive north on Capilano Road for about 2.5 miles from Lions Gate Bridge. Here, the gardens associated with Cleveland Dam become visible on the left with a car park just beyond. Park as close as you can to the top of the great 100-foot barrier with massive concrete spillways on its south side, and its lake on the north.

To begin with, you may start your descent on the works road that begins close to the side of the dam, or you may walk over to the trees on the left at the south end of the parking area near the ornamental gates and go down the steep Towers Trail. In either case, after about 10 minutes you must switch to the Palisades Trail which zig-zags down into the canyon, the roof of the salmon hatchery being visible below. One word of caution here: don't cut corners; you aid erosion when you do.

By the canyon floor the salmon hatchery is to your right; it certainly demands a visit with its illustrated account of the salmon's life cycle from spawning to the last return to the home waters. In fact, this final act, inevitable as any Greek tragedy, may be watched at the appropriate time of year when the fish, urged by instinct, struggle back to their own spawning ground before death and are directed via a fish ladder into tanks where one generation ends its days in propagating its successor.

On leaving the hatchery, continue downstream on the bank of the river as it approaches Cable Bridge, a structure from which you may have fascinating views of the canyon. Do not cross by it, however, for it is more rewarding to stay on the east side because of the views of pools and the rock walls. Here the river makes a right-angled bend to the west at the end of which another bridge, called Pipe-line Bridge for obvious reasons, takes you over to the other bank.

From the crossing, take the widest trail, ignoring both the footpath on the left (which leads to British Properties at Rabbit Lane) and a right fork. The trail goes straight uphill for a short way before bending right, and it is away

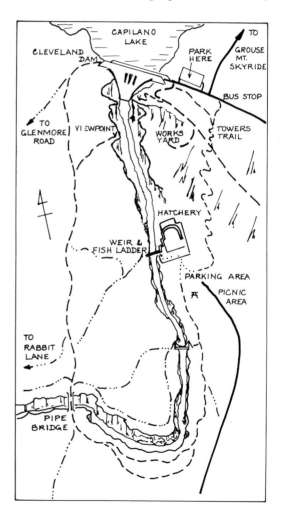

from the river for part of its route, perhaps because of the dangerous precipice on this side. For the best view of the great spillway, take a second right fork. This is a dead-end but the short detour is worth it for the spectacle, especially when the water level is high.

Return to the road and climb back up to the top of the dam on its west side, preparatory to crossing the spillway. On the way, note the orange markers of the Baden-Powell Trail which uses this connection between Hollyburn Mountain and Grouse. Finally, back on the east side, you may want to spend a little more time in the gardens and by the lake viewpoint before returning to your transportation.

Round trip 2 miles (3.2 km)
Allow up to 2 hours
Park trails
Good all year

24   MOSQUITO CREEK

This short walk has something to suit almost any taste: a stretch of forest, an open track along a power-line, a creek with footbridge erected by Boy Scouts as a part of a Centennial project. It is close in too, so it makes a perfect outing for a short winter day, or for an afternoon at almost any other time of year.

Besides the power-line right-of-way and the Baden-Powell Trail, the route makes use of part of the so-called St. George's Trail, which links the Upper Lonsdale area of North Vancouver with the old Grouse Mountain Highway and provides access to Mount Fromme and Kennedy Lake for hardy outdoors types. To reach your departure point is a trifle complicated, so follow these directions with care. Drive up Lonsdale to Osborne, turn right for one block, go left on St. George's to Balmoral, right again here for one

more block, then left on St. Mary's. All is now plain sailing. Drive to the top of St. Mary's even where it narrows and becomes steep, and park in the cleared space by the power-line to the left of the road.

Looking due west, you see the track running along the right-of-way with another coming downhill half right. Note this in passing; you'll descend it on your return route. Now follow your nose in the direction of the distant summits of Hollyburn and Strachan, pausing, though, to enjoy the view over city and harbour from 1200 feet up. The further you proceed, the more you become aware of houses and gardens below on the left; finally you see a dirt road angling across towards you. Descend to the road and walk right towards two large green water towers close to the bank of Mosquito Creek. As you near them, you will see the orange markers of the Baden-Powell Trail pointing upstream. At the same time, another part of the trail, visible just behind the towers, descends the hillside from the right. This will be part of your return route, but first take a short walk alongside the creek to the footbridge installed by the Scouts. Here the water descends, splashing over large stones in a setting that is utterly peaceful, so that you could be miles from the nearest dwelling instead of on the outskirts of a large city.

Retrace your steps to the trail where it ascends behind the water towers. The grade remains reasonably gentle and you are now among trees that provide welcome shade on a warm day. This is the sylvan part of your walk, and though the forest consists of second-growth timber, its trees are sufficiently impressive. In spring, too, the open banks are clothed with yellow violets, giving a touch of colour. As you progress, you may also applaud the industry and ingenuity of the Scouts in bridging small creeks and in building steps to aid upward progress.

Finally, you reach a trail junction. Ahead of you the Baden-Powell Trail continues eastward, but at right angles to it and running up and down the slope is St. George's Trail. Go right (downhill) on it and in a few minutes you will see a tall radio mast (CKLG). Next you emerge on a dirt road angling downhill from the wired enclosure; following this soon brings you in sight of the power-line and your car.

Round trip 2.5 miles (4 km)
Allow 2 hours
High point 1700 feet (520 m)
Elevation gain 500 feet (160 m)
Forest path and dirt track
Good most of the year

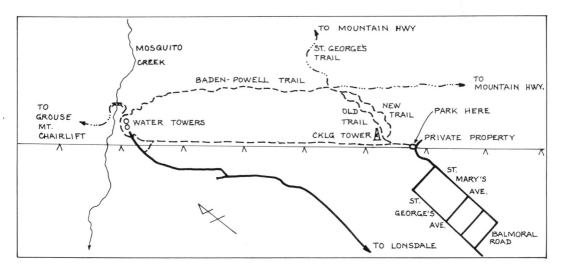

Bridge over Mosquito Creek

25 GROUSE MOUNTAIN HIGHWAY

You may actually spend very little time on this old access road to Grouse Mountain Ski Area if you so desire. The approach via St. George's Trail brings you out on the road near the point where it swings into the valley of Mosquito Creek, and your return may be by the same route. You may, however, expand this walk considerably, turning it into a circular trip into the bargain by using the road for one part of the return trip.

The approach for this walk is the same as that for Mosquito Creek (see page 54); but take the right fork where the power-line trail goes straight on. Then to the right of the radio tower, look for your path as it starts heading uphill. At its intersection with the Boy Scout trail, continue straight ahead on a route, rough in spots but perfectly clear, that rises steadily with few concessions to weakness or obesity. Mostly it lies among trees, but here and there these thin out and give tantalizing glimpses over the city. Notice the ground cover in these areas, too: salal, fern, and small shrubs. Finally, after some 45 minutes you step out on to the road, now much eroded and seamed with small channels here and there.

No walk is complete without a view, so turn left and head uphill on the highway. After a short distance, this turns and suddenly you come into the open at a point where the road forks. Go along the left branch a short way and you may enjoy all the scenery you want. Ahead are the slopes of Grouse Mountain — far enough off, however, for the scars of the ski operation to be softened. Below is the deep trough of Mosquito Creek, its valley working back to your right as you stand. Further off to the west and southwest lie West Vancouver and Burrard Inlet, with Point Grey behind and, on a clear day, the Vancouver Island mountains across the Strait of Georgia.

For your return, you may drop off the highway at the top of St. George's Trail again and follow your outward route back. But if you have time and lots of energy, you may continue down the road with its screen of trees on either side. At first you travel in a fairly straight line, but you finish up with three steep zig-zags where you may see, among trees, the road far below you as you descend. Finally, you pass two water towers on the right and shortly after, where a creek comes in from the right also, you will see the familiar orange triangles of the Scout trail going

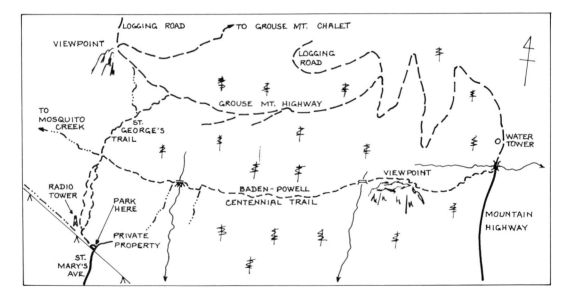

off uphill. Follow these westwards.

Once on the trail, travelling west, you find yourself again in tall timber on what is quite a steep slope, with occasional viewpoints from little bluffs. Thus you proceed, crossing streams on interesting bridges, and always among trees. Ignore two trails that you cross; you are going back to St. George's. And finally you come out on it quite unexpectedly. Turn sharp left here and go downhill for a few minutes, the sight of the TV tower indicating that your hike is almost at an end.

The long circuit just described makes a nice snowshoe trip late in the winter; in fact, the road is best with snow on it to keep the motor-bikes away.

Short trip 2.75 miles (4.4 km)
Allow 1.5 hours
Forest trail
Altitude 2200 feet (680 m)
Gain 1000 feet (300 m)

Long trip 6.5 miles (10.4 km)
Allow 4 hours
Forest trail and old road
Good April to November

Scout-made bridge

26   LYNN CANYON

This North Shore beauty spot is so popular, especially on summer weekends, that many visitors are unable to make the most of its varied attractions because of car parking difficulties and the press of numbers in the central area round the suspension bridge. The object of this hike is to avoid the worst of the crowds while visiting the main points of interest in a reasonably energetic walk that also includes less frequented sections of this miniature wilderness. The hike embraces both banks of the creek and covers much of the surrounding woodland as well.

To reach the starting point from the city, go north across Second Narrows Bridge, then take the Keith Road exit from Highway 1.

Follow the signs for Lillooet Road and travel on it uphill to the right as it rises between rows of timber town houses. Continue uphill past First Memorial Chapel and the North Vancouver Cemetery, staying with Lillooet Road after it narrows and becomes a private thoroughfare (still open to the public, however). After just under two miles from the turnoff, a large Centennial Trail sign on the right of the roadway announces the starting point for the hike. Some parking is available a little further up the road on the left opposite the point where the trail follows a pipe-line uphill, heading east towards the Seymour area.

Take the path that goes westward from the left hand side of the road, following the distinctive Boy Scout orange triangles. The route first

Winter in Lynn Park

descends, but soon levels off and traverses open forest along a high bench that opens out to give views of Lynn Creek two hundred feet below. Though the descent may seem steep, the trail is nicely graded and provides no difficulty so that there is every chance to enjoy the upstream view. Once by the creek, the route travels over a wooden footway across a marshy stretch where a main-pipe traverses the water, making a kind of small barrier that may provide a crossing in summer.

The main trail, however, stays on the east bank, rising gradually as the valley walls converge and become steeper. Finally, after ascending a series of steps, the hiker comes to the first bridge crossing, Twin Falls, a lovely, dark, mysterious spot where the stream is pent in its miniature canyon and the route on the west bank approaches the footbridge down a steep flight of steps. Cross here, and having ascended, come out on an open terrace at a Boy Scout Trail sign. Turn right and continue upstream, keeping an eye open for the first sight of the suspension bridge; it is, to say the least, interesting.

By this time one is close to the park centre. The main drive with its parking is on the left hand, the refreshment concession is straight ahead, and the bridge is to the right. Before experiencing either of these, however, the visitor should take time and visit the Ecology Centre a little way up the road on the left. Here both ear and eye are catered to in varied displays in the well-designed building. There is also a self-guiding Nature Trail (booklet 10c) that well repays the twenty minutes or so that it requires. Many of the park trees are identified by metal tags, and it soon becomes simple to distinguish red cedar from balsam or Douglas fir by noting their distinctive features.

Now is the time to approach the suspension bridge. Before crossing, however, note that the Baden-Powell Trail also uses it, coming downstream from the north to this point on the west bank and swinging to the other side here. Once over, the hiker should notice the orange markers; they are the guides for his return route. Before setting off south, however, check the trail to the left; it leads in a short distance to a clear pool, very popular for swimming in summer; unfortunately this route stops by the creek and the only way back is via the suspension bridge.

Continuing downstream again, the hiker is continually tempted to linger at various viewpoints that give glimpses of the creek, its falls and rapids with their potholes scoured out from the stream bed by the action of water power on stones that act as grinders. There are also beautifully clear pools to stimulate the imagination. Soon, however, comes Twin Falls once more, after which the trail descends to the creek before beginning its rise uphill for the return to your point of departure.

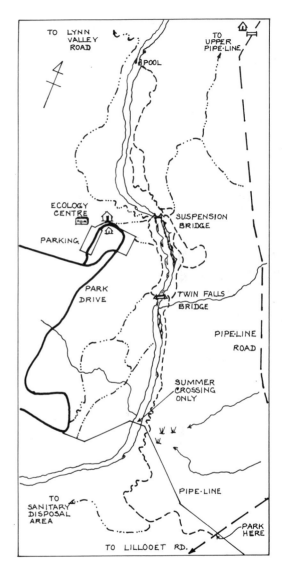

Distance about 4 miles (6.5 km)
Allow 3 to 4 hours
Forest path
Good all year

27 BADEN-POWELL TRAIL (SEYMOUR MOUNTAIN)

Those who have driven the highway in Seymour Mountain Provincial Park must be aware of the large wooden archway on the west side of the road just below the power-line right-of-way. The stretch of trail thus announced provides a pleasant woodland walk in its own right; it also gives the chance of return along the service road for the aforesaid power-line as an alternative to retracing your steps.

Drive up Seymour Highway for about 1.5 miles from the park entrance to the small parking area and picnic site opposite the sign, cross the road, and you are on your way. At first the trail gains only a little height as it heads west; later, however, it links up with an old logging road and from now on it rises steadily in open forest of the usual second-growth timber. The trees, however, are tall and well spaced, and the ground is relatively open.

Finally, through a tunnel of trees, the wires of the power-line become visible and now comes the parting of the ways. A re-routing of the trail takes it off west in the forest; you, however, want to strike forward to the open right-of-way. As you reach the cleared stretch, you find that you are actually beyond the highest point and that your view is westwards over Lynn Valley to West Vancouver and out across the harbour to Point Grey in the distance.

The dirt service road is just on the up side of the pylon so now you turn back on this road, rising at first to the high point of the ridge, then gently descending eastwards. Now your view is towards Eagle Ridge over on the other side of Indian Arm. Let it be conceded that although power-lines are no things of beauty, in this instance the wide swath cleared for them does provide far more extensive views than would otherwise be the case.

Next comes your return to the highway at the hairpin bend where it turns back on itself. The road you have followed ends just above the thoroughfare, but it is easy to scramble down from just beside the last pylon. Watch for traffic, though, as you turn downhill towards your original starting point, the ornamental trail arch.

For any who want a longer and more invigorating walk than the described route gives, an extension is possible. This has its beginning and end not on Seymour Highway, but on River Road below it and to the east. This provides more interesting forest walking, again following the orange markers of the Boy Scout trail, and introduces you to a different section of it.

To reach the start, turn right off Seymour Highway just below the park sign and traffic light on a dirt road bearing a NO EXIT sign.

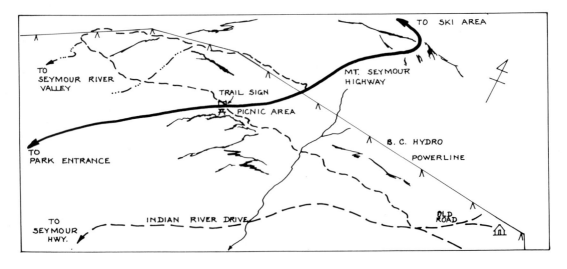

From the turnoff, drive 1.9 miles to where the trail goes off on the left at the summit of a small rise just before an old logging road. The start is not too clear so look carefully for triangular markers. Once on it, however, the trail presents no difficulty, as it winds along on wooden bridges over creeks, with walkways across marshy stretches as an added convenience. The forest is deep and cool so this is a good stretch for a warm day. Even the picnic table up at Seymour Highway is shady and the Baden-Powell Trail sign already mentioned is just opposite. Thus you add 1.25 miles to the round trip and treat yourself to an attractive piece of forest trail into the bargain.

Short round trip 2.75 miles (4.4 km)
Allow 1.5 hours
High point 1500 feet (460 m)
Elevation gain 400 feet (122 m)
Forest paths and dirt road
Good March to November

Long round trip 4 miles (6.4 km)
Allow 2.5 hours
Elevation gain 750 feet (230 m)

Trail sign at Seymour Highway

28   GOLDIE LAKE

"What do you know of Seymour, who only Seymour know?" Such a question may well be asked of the many visitors to Mount Seymour Provincial Park who drive to the upper parking lot, wander up the main trail with an ugly chair-lift crowding the ridge and the lack of ground cover giving mute evidence of savage treatment, then depart wondering what all the fuss is about. As a more attractive alternative, this hike, through cool forest to the picturesque little lake below the upper parking area and about three-quarters of a mile to the east of it, has a

great deal in its favour, including perhaps an increase in knowlege of what Seymour has to offer.

For the start of the Perimeter Trail, popularly named the Escape Trail, drive to the parking lot on the hairpin bend at Mile 7 on the Seymour Mountain Highway, the ski-jump platform across the road providing easy identification. Once on foot, cross to the east side of the road just below the corner and pick up the trail as it angles off slightly downhill to bypass the foot of a ski run. After this, the forest asserts itself and the only signs of human activity are the elderly log cabins among the trees, survivors of the days before this area came under the control of the B.C. Parks Branch.

The trail, designed for straying skiers as its name suggests, is clearly marked with parti-coloured diamond-shaped signs. To give the Parks Branch its due, it has carried out many improvements without making these too obtrusive, providing footing in wet spots and bridging creeks in a number of instances where such aids are needed. At Scott-Goldie Creek, the first you reach, another branch of the trail joins from the right, one that has come up from a lower point still. Pause on the little footbridge here to enjoy the creek in its miniature canyon before you continue your journey northwards; it's a pleasant spot.

After an hour in forest comes the parting of the ways. The main escape trail swings right at a large rock, but a subsidiary route, not sign-posted at the time of printing, is the one to Goldie Lake. Go left here, then, and proceed for a short distance until on your left appears a body of water attractively ringed with water lilies in Fall. An even smaller lake is on the right, and just ahead is Goldie with a trail running right round its shore line.

In Fall particularly the spot is most attractive with the lake grasses and water lilies contrasting with the vivid reds and orange of the ground shrubs. There are flat rocks where one can sit; in fact, all is as it should be in this peaceful basin cradled among tall trees with cliffs behind.

Return may be by the same route, but an alternative suitable for clear days can turn this into a circular trip with spectacular views. Continue westwards from the lake, then rise

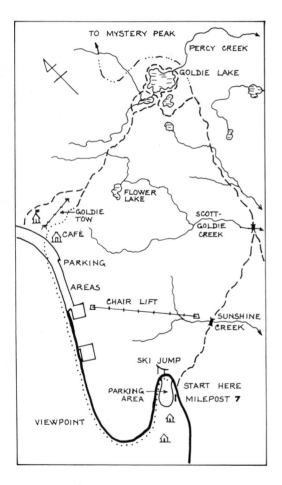

Morning mist near Goldie Lake

gently uphill, keeping rocky bluffs on your right. Soon your route comes to the foot of Goldie rope tow and from here a short rise brings you to the upper parking lot with all its signs of human activity, including a cafe and a comfort station.

Thereafter, cross the west side of the parking lot and head south down the side of the road, savouring the great sweep of scenery from the Gulf Islands across the Strait of Georgia to the other mountains of the North Shore. Traffic on the road may be annoying, but the shoulder is wide and perhaps the view is compensation. After some twenty minutes the bend and parking lot come into view, ending a trip that gives you contact with the less public side of Mount Seymour.

Round trip 4 miles (6.4 km)
Allow 3 hours
High point 3300 feet (100 m)
Elevation gain 300 feet (92 m)
Forest trail and black-top
Good June to November

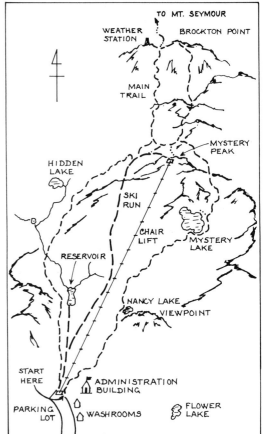

Mystery Lake

29 MYSTERY LAKE

What mystery gave this attractive body of water its name we are not now likely to discover. In any event, the lake provides a pleasant stop-over point on what may be a circular hike or a straight there-and-backer starting from the upper parking lot in Mount Seymour Provincial Park.

Drive the eight miles of the Mount Seymour Highway to its destination at the lower terminal of the main chair lift. When the snow has gone the area does not look particularly appealing at first sight, with the towers of the lift stretching uphill in the middle of the picture; but these are not going to be visible for long. Begin by dropping into the little basin to the right of the chair, and opposite its first pylon you will see a narrow trail going off half-right into the trees. Follow this.

After 20 minutes or so of walking you come to the tiny Nancy Lake with its rocky outcrop above it to the south. A brief visit to this is rewarded by views of the city of Vancouver right round to Burnaby Mountain, with Mount Baker dominant in the southeast. Take the trail to the west of the lake; then turn a little round the north end of it, ascending along a nice ledge with small cliffs on the left hand and forest cover elsewhere. Thus, you progress; the trees gradually thin out and the country becomes sub-alpine. Then comes Mystery Lake at 3950 feet in its rock basin.

Here is a spot for contemplation. Although one of the chairlift towers does spoil the view to the east, human activity is minimal here and it is pleasant to sit on the clean rock and let the peace wash over you. But then comes the moment of decision: you may return by the outward route; continue uphill and on to Mystery Peak with its upper chair terminal; or, if you are really energetic, go further north still — round the back of Mystery Peak and up to Brockton Point with its panorama.

For the last of these suggestions, work your way gently into the saddle behind Mystery Peak until you come on the trail heading for the great rock wall. Turn right on it. At first the ascent looks steep but it is easier than it appears; and soon you are on Brockton Point and on top of the world — almost. Actually, the main summit of Mount Seymour is to the north, but you are on top of your own immediate world looking down on the Fraser lowlands and over the Strait of Georgia to the peaks of Vancouver Island away to the west.

To return from here to the parking lot, follow the main hiking trail down on the right of Mystery Peak, leaving the main ski run by a footpath on its right shortly after it starts to descend. But do not stray too far to the right in looking for Hidden Lake, for that way lies Suicide Bluffs, well-named and sinister. Eventually you emerge above a small reservoir and, keeping it on your left, return to your transportation.

Bunchberry

One final note: the chairlift parking lot is also the beginning of the hike to Dog Mountain, described in **103 Hikes**.

Round trip 4 miles (6.4 km)
Allow 3 hours
High point 4200 feet (1280 m)
Elevation gain 700 feet (220 m)
Trail
Best June to October

30 BADEN-POWELL TRAIL (DEEP COVE)

It is not often that the destination of a hike is visible from its start (or nearly); but that is the case here, with a power-line pylon on its head-land above Indian Arm standing above the trees that lie between Deep Cove and the objective. In fact, the view from the parking lot at Panorama Park gives indication of what is to come in its glimpses of small craft on the water with treed bluffs around, to the sides of which cling houses in a variety of architectural styles.

Panorama Park is actually a little south of

the trail's start, parking on Panorama Drive's 2500 block being very limited. In any case, the view from the park makes a stop here worthwhile, stretching as it does along the shore of a picturesque little bay. Reaching it is not difficult either, the most direct approach being over the Mount Seymour Parkway, carrying straight on at the point where the park highway goes off left, descending the hill, then turning left at the stop sign where Dollarton Highway intersects the road. From here, head along Deep Cove Road, veer right on to Gallant Avenue, then swing left on Panorama Drive, and your parking is just off the blacktop on the right.

From the parking lot descend to the little path that heads north across the grass, passing a picnic site, and rejoining the road just at the spot where a large sign announces the existence of the trail with the further information that Mountain Highway is 1.5 hours off. And there *is* the trail, going uphill between houses on the left of the road. Indeed, this first stretch is a good lung-opener as it leads inland and uphill among the trees of an old second-growth forest before turning right once it has made enough height.

Along its route, the path crosses a number of creeks, descending into their ravines then re-emerging on the other side after a crossing by means of Scout-made footbridges. Thus you progress for more than a mile until, just to the right of the trail, a rock provides a chance for

a seat with a view south down Indian Arm and across to Burnaby Mountain and the brooding buildings of Simon Fraser University.

Finally the trees thin out and the open right-of-way of the B.C. Hydro power-line shows itself ahead. However, there is still one more creek to negotiate before turning right and heading down an old dirt road towards the bluff where the last great pylon flings its wires out across the Indian Arm to Belcarra; the best viewpoint, however, is the higher bluff to the right of the one crowned by the pylon. Here the outlook is across the Arm to Buntzen Ridge with Eagle Ridge behind; to the southeast there is also the view up the main valley of the Fraser.

Those who wish to travel further may head uphill to River Road along which the Baden-Powell route travels for one-fifth of a mile before continuing uphill to Mountain Highway. That stretch is better incorporated with the Seymour section, however, since the forested part can then be walked with no necessity to tramp along a dusty road, as is the case if you start from the power-line.

Round trip 3.5 miles (5.6 km)
Allow 2 hours
High point 500 feet (145 m)
Forest trail
Good most of the year

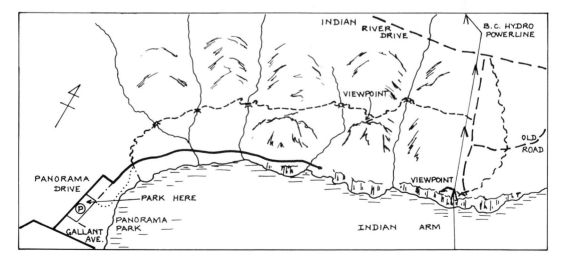

Old furnace room

31　OLD DOLLAR MILL (CATES PARK)

This hike may be short on distance; on the other hand, it is long on points of interest that include a cedar grove, Indian relics, and the foundations of the old mill. Add to these a beach walk, a swimming area, and an abundance of harbour and mountain views and you have an outing with enough variety to give an hour's enjoyment, or a day's.

To reach the beginning of this walk, travel east along Dollarton Highway to a point three miles from the Second Narrows Bridge exit. Here, on the right a sign announces Cates Park.

Turn towards the park and drive downhill looking for a parking spot as far to the west as possible without getting mixed up with the boat launching traffic. Note also that dogs are not allowed in the park between May 1 and October 1, an indication of how busy the area is in summer, especially at weekends. Unless a swim is on your agenda, therefore, this hike may be saved for an off-season when peace reigns and the beauty of the park can be savoured in solitude.

Standing at the wooden jetty by the launching ramp and looking west, you see the buildings of the Matsumoto Shipyard a little way off, with a relic of the seas, the Island Prince, tied up at a pier, its days of service long past. Across the harbour stands Burnaby Mountain, its sides disfigured by the paraphernalia of oil refiners but pleasant enough otherwise. Here is your departure point and from here you set off eastwards along the beach, the footing consisting mainly of clean grit, though here and there rounded boulders have to be negotiated with some care.

At Roche Point with its beacon, the waters of Indian Arm join with those of Burrard Inlet and now your route swings north, giving views across to Belcarra Park and to Buntzen Ridge, with Eagle Mountain looming behind to the northeast. But here, too, there is a closer point of interest. On the grassy stretch just above the beach a metal figure of a dolphin disports itself a few feet above its natural element. And there is a change in the character of the coastline: little bays alternating with small headlands, the first of these being set aside for swimming while further along the skin divers disport themselves in the clear water.

Finally, at a pile of boulders a sign announcing a private beach bars further progress along the shore. Scramble here over the rocks to the bank above where swings and a jungle gym announce a children's playground. And just a little to one side is a low concrete structure much overgrown with moss — all that now remains of the sawmill furnace room, a memorial of sorts to the Scots-Canadian founder of an American shipping line, and developer of the mill towards the end of World War One. Round the installation grew the company town of Dollarton, so to remain till the mill closed at the end of World War Two. From this time on the settlement has been residential though its most famous inhabitant, Malcolm Lowry, the novelist, left it with bitter memories, being evicted to provide space for this very park in which you stand.

The return is among tall trees on a track running parallel with the beach. Eventually this leads into the open by an Indian totem pole, soon to be followed by another, close to a fifty-foot Indian war canoe. This treasure was created in 1921 by Chief Henry Peter George after a year of loving labour and donated to the District by his widow; a more attractive memento than the mill foundation, and commemorative of an older culture. From here the back view of the friendly dolphin is visible beside Roche Point, giving warning that your little trip is almost over.

Round trip 1.3 miles (2.1 km)
Allow 1 hour
Beach and park trails
Good all year

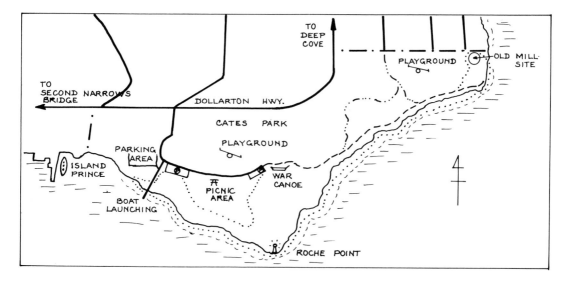

32 HARBOURVIEW PARK

Feel like a good lung opener on a winter's day, or some exercise on a summer evening with a glorious view for reward? This little gem of a neighbourhood park on the top of Capitol Hill in Burnaby will fill the bill admirably. The walk proposed here is partly on streets but they are quiet ones in a residential neighbourhood where traffic is minimal. Moreover, you begin the walk in a park and reach your destination in another park.

To reach the start of this walk, head for Confederation Park by driving north on Willingdon Avenue five blocks north of Hastings Street, then turning right on Penzance Drive. Go right again into the parking lot by the lawn bowling green and pause to survey the task ahead of you, across the park and uphill — steadily uphill.

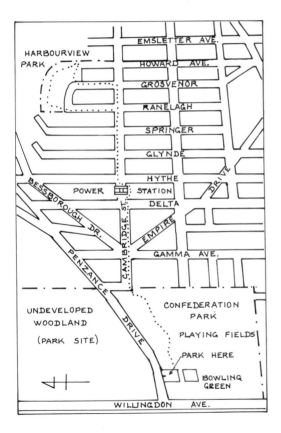

Still it is nice to have grass underfoot as you set off eastward, stepping out for the street that breasts the hill in front of you. Pick your way carefully, though. Some of the park drainage is not too good among the trees. You can avoid wet feet with a little care, however, by staying out of the low areas where water may collect.

Once you have reached Cambridge Street you start climbing, and the beauty of this route is that a small hydro sub-station in a grass plot splits it, inhibiting through traffic. To pass the hydro station mount the grass bank in front of it and take the little trail round its side, then continue upwards past Hythe Avenue. Three more blocks take you to the top of the hill and Grosvenor Avenue; turn left on it and a few minutes more brings your reward, the newly created Harbourview Park.

The park more than lives up to its name. Besides your having the unsurpassed view of Vancouver's Inner Harbour, you look directly across to Mount Seymour and up the scenic Indian Arm. Admittedly the oil refineries of Ioco are below and to the right; they are sufficiently low and far off to be innocuous, however, and it is easy to ignore them in enjoyment of the view over the whole stretch of the North Shore: Mount Fromme, Grouse, Crown, with Hollyburn and Strachan further off.

After you have had your fill of beauty and your heart and lungs are performing normally again, you may think about return. For this, work your way down and to the left to pick up the end of Ranelagh for the return to Cambridge Street. Now you get the full sense of the height that you have gained on your outward trip. Below you is spread out Confederation Park and, a little to the right, the full sweep fo the harbour is laid out for inspection and admiration, right from Second Narrows Bridge to the peninsula of Stanley Park and Lions Gate. And this view stays with you, diminishing as you descend but only disappearing once you set foot in Confederation Park again.

Round trip 2 miles (3.2 km)
Allow 1 hour
High point 700 feet (280 m)
Elevation gain 400 feet (120 m)
Grass and Sidewalk
Good all year

33 BURNABY MOUNTAIN

Everyone knows that Simon Fraser University is situated on top of Burnaby Mountain; not so many are aware, perhaps, that the mountain is also the site of Burnaby's Centennial Park which

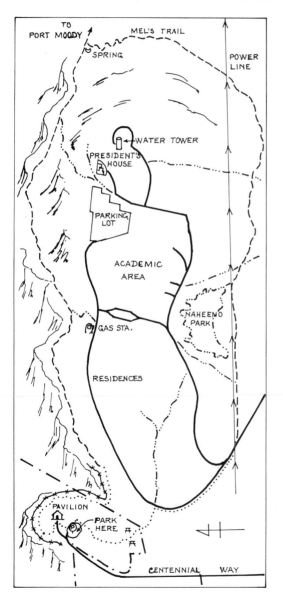

Trillium

lies about half a mile to the west of its illustrious neighbour. It is in the park, though, that this walk has its beginning and end, the two separated by a circle of about 5 miles circumference.

The easiest way to reach Centennial Park is to drive east on Curtis Street in Burnaby, using Sperling Avenue to get to it by coming north from Trans-Canada Way or the Lougheed Highway, or south from Hastings Street. Curtis starts rising as the houses thin out after a little more than a mile. At the intersection with Fraser Way, turn left and drive to the parking lot by the Centennial Pavilion, situated on a commanding spur overlooking Burrard Inlet, giving deference only to the proud mountains of the north.

From here set off uphill past the two presentation totem poles and keeping the wire fence on your left. Pass by the children's playground and emerge finally on a stretch to the left of the one-way road leading from Simon Fraser University. Here a well-defined trail strikes off to the left in the second-growth forest on the north side of the mountain, below the crest and out of sight of the university. This trail travels eastward dropping a little as it progresses, shaded by tall trees. The only drawback here is the possible presence of trail motorbikes; this nuisance, however, abates after a little less than two miles when, at a seat by a small spring, a foot-trail, "Mel's," strikes off uphill to the right.

On this trail you swing round the east side of the mountain, catching occasional glimpses of the works of man below, including the Port Mann Bridge that carries the freeway over the Fraser River. At one point the trail intersects a power-line running up the mountain; otherwise it remains undisturbed as it meanders along — now up, now down — crosses an old access road, then strikes the power-line again.

This is the point of decision. You may work your way past Naheeno Park and cross the university campus to return to your starting point by University Drive, or you can follow this power-line westwards downhill. This descends for about half a mile till it emerges on the Fraser Way just a little below the junction of its two branches. Go half right here and, staying on the grassy verge, follow the left hand fork uphill for about a fifth of a mile to where an old road comes in from the right. Now strike off to the left to make your way back to the parking lot past the Centennial Park picnic site.

Round trip 5 miles (8 km)
Allow 3 hours
Foot trails and road verge
Good all year

34 SIMON FRASER UNIVERSITY

Here is a walk that combines a visit to Arthur Erickson's architectural creation and a stroll in a peaceful forest park where a stretch of the university campus has been laid out in a circular trail of just under a mile in length. This piece of ground, Naheeno Park, has various attractions: a jungle gym, totem poles, plus a selection of the region's trees and shrubs.

Drive up Simon Fraser Way to the university and remain on the road to the south of the central complex of buildings, going straight on where a turnoff left leads to underground parking. As you travel east along Inner Road you will note in passing Naheeno Park on your right, a little beyond the junction; at this time, however, you continue beyond it till your road swings north at "B" parking lot and rises to the ridge crest. Stop in the free parking area as close as possible to the high point and begin your walk by heading due west towards the main university buildings.

This way, you approach the academic quadrangle from the rear instead of by the more conventional route with its awe-inspiring flights

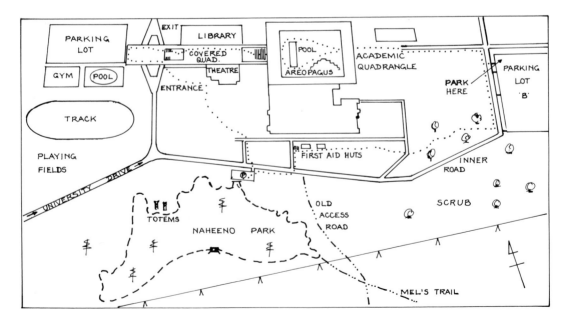

of steps to give you a sense of your own insignificance. Now you travel from quad to quad, descending from one level to the next but pausing on each stage to sample the views to north and south. Finally, where the access roadway vanishes beneath your feet, and you begin to run out of walking room, two fine viewpoints, one north and one south, invite your inspection before you return — literally — to earth at the roadway or just to the east of it.

Now cut diagonally across the lawn to Naheeno Park to begin your trail walk on its circuit, which is virtually self-guiding. The route, taken counter-clockwise, drops a little in a series of cunningly constructed S-bends with occasional views through the trees over the delta lands to the south and the islands of the Strait of Georgia. Among the trees you will come on the play area where any children hiking with you will love the climbing nets, the stepping logs, and Tarzan-like swings and slides. Further on the round, on the banks above a small stream, are miniature totems, examination of which involves yet another stop before you resume your circumambulation.

On completion of it, recross Inner Road and walk down a dirt road opposite for a short distance towards the university buildings. Very soon, though, you mount a flight of steps to the top of a bank on your right. Here the scars of construction are being hidden by new tree growth and the only immediate signs of human presence are a few first-aid trailer huts. Beyond them, you cross another road and walk through a copse of trees to emerge opposite "B" lot, but further down the hill than where you left your car. Thus ends your circuit of the groves of academe.

Round trip 3 miles (5 km)
Allow 2 hours
Forest path, roads, and quadrangles
Good all year

35   BURNABY LAKE

On some trails the sublimity of the scenery is sufficient to keep you speechless with awe; on others, the tranquillity of the surroundings acts as a soporific for ragged nerves; with a third category, however, consisting mainly of those in heavily populated areas, your reaction is one of

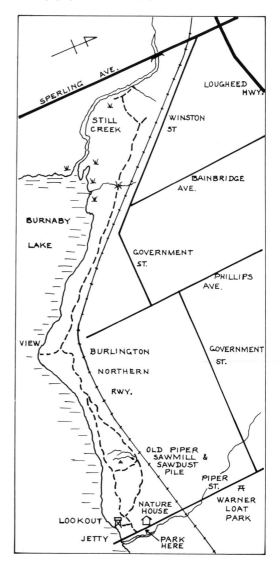

simple gratitude that a few people had the vision and the determination to preserve some natural beauty from the hand of the spoiler. The trail along the east side of Burnaby Lake belongs to this last class. Here a 1973 LIP grant has been put to valuable use by the Burnaby Outdoor Education Association for the creation of a nature trail, interestingly laid out and appealingly diversified.

To reach its beginning from Highway 1, turn off at the Cariboo Road exit, go north across the Brunette River and immediately after the Burlington Northern railway tracks turn left along Government Street at the T-junction. At Piper Avenue go left, once more recross the tracks, noting just before you do so the attractive little Warner Loat Park with its picnic sites and washrooms as a possible stopping point. Straight ahead is the lake, on the right is the little nature house, and just beyond that the entrance to the trail. The approach from Lougheed Highway is also along Piper Road, the turnoff being at the eastern end of Charles Rummel Park.

At the nature house copies of the trail guide are available and, thus armed, you may begin your exploration of the area. Before you do so, however, you may wish to stroll to the canoe launching jetty with its small slough, the haunt of duck, geese, and those comical coots, all of whom will welcome handouts. From the end of the jetty are interesting views up, down, and across the lake which, despite its built-up surroundings, manages to preserve a good deal of its rural character even in the presence of the

Beginning of the trail

rowing course on the water and the sports complex beyond.

Back at the start of the trail, you set off north, your attention directed by the guide to the natural fauna of the area, from tiny mosses to "the largest alder tree in Burnaby." On the way you note by the few remnants of the Piper Sawmill, and its sawdust pile already becoming overgrown, how evidence of past human activity is blotted out. There are more distant views, too. At one point near the beginning a short side trip to the shore gives a grandstand view similar to — but better than — the one from the jetty with Burnaby City Hall standing out clearly across the lake, and the high-rise buildings round Kingsway rearing up in the distance like giant watch towers. And, of course, your eye is drawn to the lake, for now you may see its great beds of water-lilies and the masses of purple loose-strife round its banks.

Further along, markers are less frequent and evidence of human activity is a little more in evidence. There is partial compensation, however, in the mountain vistas, the cleared trail between trees acting as a tunnel to direct the eye towards The Lions, rising in the distance above the valley of the Capilano River. At last, a turn left takes you close to the sports pavilion, though you are separated from it by the waters of Still Creek, waters whose darkness suggests the truth of the old cliché: still waters run deep.

Now comes the inevitable return, though part of the trail does divide, allowing for a change of route. Back at the starting point, don't forget a silent vote of thanks to the originators of the idea and those who had the energy to bring it to a fruitful reality; include, too, the members of the Grade 12 carpentry class of Burnaby Central School for the fine observation tower recently completed.

Round trip 3 miles (5 km)
Allow up to 2 hours
Woodland trail
Good all year

Brunette River below the weir

36   BRUNETTE RIVER

. For most people, the only contact they have with even the name of this stream is a small sign at an overpass on Highway 1 that they may or may not see as they speed between Burnaby and New Westminster on their way to the wide open spaces. Perhaps they may wonder idly at the unusual name, but that is about all. Well, one stretch of this river is suited to walking with the route described here having its destination at an interesting small park just inside New Westminster, one that can provide a picnic site for those who wish to combine alfresco lunch with hiking.

From Highway 1 eastbound, the approach to the starting point is via Cariboo Road, crossing on the overpass, then parking just a little north of the river bridge at a cleared space by two houses. If you are coming from Lougheed Highway, turn off on Brighton, go left on Government Road, then at right angles on to Cariboo road itself, just at a railway crossing. From the parking spot, the route runs along the river bank and is not too prepossessing at first, passing as it does a great mound of rubble on the left, part of an unfinished intersection for Highway 1. Once beyond the locked gate, however, matters improve greatly.

As you proceed, you have small second-growth alder on the left, with large bramble bushes sporting vicious looking thorns. Across the stream, on the right, are tall trees, but between you and them are road and river, the latter flowing in sprightly fashion at first then gradually becoming still, and a little sinister looking. The mystery, however, is soon cleared up: two successive weirs hold back the waters and are responsible for the silence. As you progress, you become aware of the railway on the left, screened though it is by trees and bushes; in fact, something of the thrill of rail-roads comes back if a freight or passenger train passes along.

Eventually, though, another kind of traffic becomes audible as a little ahead appears another gate, beyond which is the busy North Road. This need not be the destination of your hike, how-ever; at the road, turn right, cross the river on the bridge, then enter Hume Park to the south, a recreation area administered by New Westmin-ster Parks Board. At its entrance a flat grassy field with picnic tables and washrooms stretches ahead until it is enclosed by the old banks of the river, indication that the stream once made quite a bend here. To the right, a sign points to a nature path that contours the hillside, gradually rising to the sports field, getting on for 100 feet above your original level.

Stroll in this pleasant area heading towards the fenced off stretch extending almost to the river bank. At the very edge, however, a trail leads downhill, back to the lower level. From now, you are on your return trip, and once again North Road has to be negotiated. This is not always the simplest of matters, but there-after you have the peaceful road back by the river. At least it should be peaceful, but occasion-ally you may be annoyed by motorbikers on it, despite the efforts of Burnaby Police to keep them off. The police advice for dealing with motorbikers in places where they don't belong is this: report them as soon as you can.

To end on a pleasanter note, did you con-

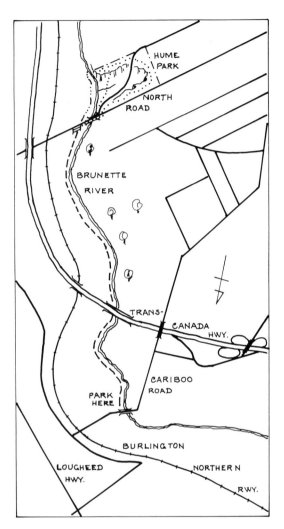

nect the dark hue of the water of Brunette River with its name or did you simply assume that the colour was the result of pollution? Well, there may be a little of the latter but the stream received its name, according to **1001 British Columbia Place Names**, from the peaty ground in which it originated near Burnaby Lake.

Round trip 4.5 miles (7 km)
Allow 2 hours
Dirt road and park path
Good all year

37   CENTRAL PARK

Anyone who has ever driven along Kingsway between Vancouver and New Westminster knows the north end of this park with its tall trees and its sports stadium: bus-riders because of the zone change at Boundary Road that involves a ticket inspection, automobile travellers because of the railway crossing that acts as a deterrent to would-be low fliers trying to prove that Burnaby's traffic signals are not set for 29 m.p.h. North-end parking is just east of the stadium and is approached by a road that turns right off Kingsway (for anyone coming from Vancouver) a little beyond the Boundary Road traffic light. The entrance is marked by a pair of tall stone pillars, a kind of ceremonial gateway. Once past them, drive a short distance to the parking lot between the stadium and a park picnic area set on treed lawns.

From here, various main trails lead deeper into the forest; the route described here, though, covers all the chief features of one of the oldest lower mainland recreation areas. To begin with, head away from the stadium to pick up a trail that begins just by the washrooms. This trail takes you off southeastwards though it does wind somewhat in the timber, second-growth forest as the silent stumps of once-great trees indicate. Stay left at the first main intersection but at the second, go right as you follow the path that takes you mainly south. Note after some fifteen minutes' walking the construction on the left: a new underground reservoir which is to have tennis courts on its roof.

At this point, close to the park's eastern boundary and Patterson Avenue, another trail joins from the west; just beyond, where Maynard Street unites with Patterson, there is yet one more route going off half right following the split-rail fence of the pitch-and-putt course that occupies the southeast corner. Follow this, pausing from time to time to feast your eyes on the views between the trees of the golf course, over the Fraser Delta, and all the way south to Point Roberts. A short distance along this trail another comes in from the right, but only those in a mad rush to get home need to take it; in fact, it cuts off one of the park's most interesting features, the pond just by the golf course entrance where model yachts are sailed.

Just by this body of water is another parking lot, this one approached from Imperial Street, so that you could reverse your walk if you wish and start it here instead. In any event, it is now that

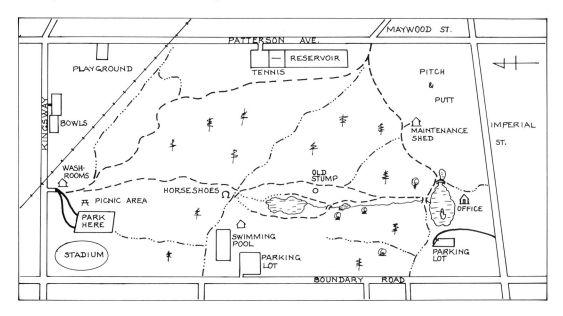

you turn north, using a trail that parallels the small stream which flows through a Japanese-type garden on its way to add its water to the model boating pond. Some fifteen minutes along this route is a larger body of water to the south of the Horseshoe Pitching ground, located just by the 45th Avenue entrance. From this point, the forest path runs directly back to the stadium and your car.

Obviously, on a walk like this a number of variations are possible. The section in the south-east corner may be lengthened, for instance, by following the outside fence of the golf course along Patterson to Imperial, then going west along that street towards the boating pond. The only drawback to this plan is the traffic on your left.

Round trip 2.7 miles (4.3 km)
Allow 1.5 hours
Forest trails
Good all year

Boating pond

38 DEER LAKE (CENTURY PARK)

Besides Century Park in Burnaby, there are few places in the lower mainland where you can, within a radius of 1½ miles, visit an art gallery, explore a re-created village, stroll through formal gardens, and walk across a grassy sward to a still lake nestled in a deep hollow. Here the city's art collection (admission 25c) is housed in a one-time mansion, its carefully preserved gardens providing a fit setting. Downhill to the east is Heritage Village, open to the public from early April till Labour Day (admission 50c for adults, 25c for children, phone 291-8525 for details). To the south lies the lake, the home of various waterfowl.

To reach these delights from Vancouver, make for Canada Way, turning left off Boundary Road a few blocks south of Grandview Highway. Follow the Way to the Municipal Government complex, swinging right, uphill, just past the Corporation Hall, then going left to park by the Art Gallery or by the Civic Theatre. From here you may choose your activity according to taste. A visit to the formal gardens is particularly re-warding in May when the rhododendrons are in bloom and the formal layout may attune you to the past that is waiting in Heritage Village.

But you will surely want to spend considerable time here so perhaps a visit to the old lake may come next. Stroll downhill on a grassy slope passing en route an architect's conception of the homes of elves and gnomes as part of a children's playground. The lake itself has a walk running along its bank for a short distance, giving a splendid view across the water to Deer Lake Park proper, a small recreation area with a sandy beach, cut off from you, however, by private homes. There are flowers by the shore as well, irises and wild roses, while water lilies stretch into the lake on either side of the little landing stage.

Returning uphill, bear to the right and follow the signs for Heritage Village, this wonderful evocation of the early years of the century, with its recreated stores, offices and homes. Here for older visitors, at least, nostalgia will take over at the sight of once familiar artifacts of everyday living. A model railway is also projected so youngsters may share the thrill that train travel gave to their elders in more spacious times when getting there *was* half the fun.

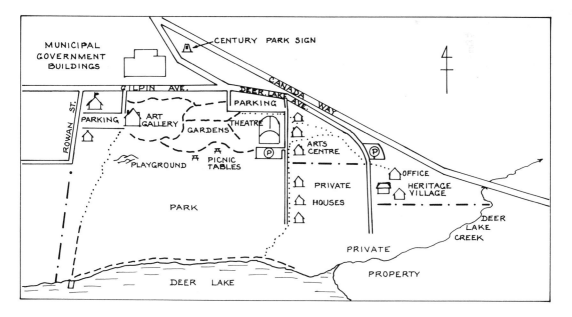

Burnaby Art Gallery

You will not want to tear yourself away from the Village in a hurry. Perhaps, though, another conundrum may send you back to look at the Art Gallery again. What do Century Park, Burnaby, and Stanley Park, Vancouver, have in common? Answer: possession of something associated with the Ceperley family. **Fairacres**, that family's home from 1909 to 1922, now houses the art gallery, while proceeds from its original sale were used, according to Mrs. Ceperley's will, to provide the children's playground in Stanley Park.

Round trip 1.5 miles (2.5 km)
Allow 3 hours
Gravel paths and grass
Good all year; best when Heritage Village is open

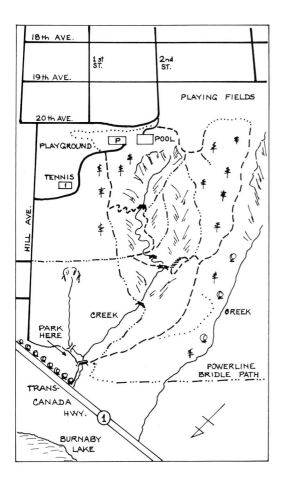

left here, follow Edmonds past its intersection with Canada Way, turn south on 6th Street for two short blocks, swing left on 18th Avenue and, after two blocks more, left again on 2nd Street. Now the park is straight ahead — but not the parking. For this, you must turn left again at the eastern end of the developed park and, on Hill Avenue, head downhill as far as you can drive to the large parking lot and picnic area just south of Highway 1.

On arrival, look about you. Uphill lies the park; down the wooded slopes in a picturesque ravine flows a small creek crossed here and there by footbridges. On the other side of Highway 1 looms Burnaby Mountain with the low-set mass of Simon Fraser University capping its top. Behind are higher mountain tops promising views once you get out and stretch your legs on the climb.

One route keeps to the right of the creek system, taking you uphill among tall trees with the little stream on your left and below you and with occasional cross trails coming up to join the main bridle path as it stretches upwards. Finally, by keeping right, you arrive on a small sportsfield at the edge of the park just above a notice warning of a dangerous ravine. Cut left from here towards the trees and soon a way opens through them, one that brings you out to the pretty little

Swallowtail butterfly

39   ROBERT BURNABY PARK

That this little gem of a park is not better known is probably due to its not lying handy to a main thoroughfare. Even though Highway 1 runs at the foot of the park, it does not provide access. So the hurrying vehicles rush past, their drivers unconscious of what they are missing: walks in well laid out ravine trails or forest glades with grassy lawns, even an open-air swimming pool.

To reach this spot from Vancouver is a trifle complicated, involving as it does a drive along Kingsway past Central Park and through Burnaby for another thirty blocks to Edmonds Street. Go

open-air swimming pool if you take the right branch at each of two successive forks. Just beyond is the upper car park and beyond that again is a children's playground imaginatively laid out among tall trees set well apart. From here, too, the view up the Coquitlam River to the mountain of the same name and the western side of Burke Ridge is truly impressive, particularly when, in spring, snow is gleaming in the sun.

There is still plenty to see, however, as you start wending your way downhill, this time starting on the right side of the creek. Now you look across Burnaby Lake in its shallow trough towards the mountain backdrop, while close at hand is the winding stream. Watch for a path dropping left on some steps into the ravine, then go right down the winding trail till it meets a major intersecting route. Jog right here, then left, climb or bypass another flight of steps, and continue downhill towards where your vehicle is located. Before you leave finally, however, take a wander over to the open grassy stretch among the trees to the west; it is a perfect little forest glade, especially with the sun streaking through the tall trees and on to the grass, creating patterns of light and shade.

Round trip 2 miles (3.2 km)
Allow 1.5 hours
Bridle and footpath
Good all year

Ravine in Robert Burnaby Park

40   BUNTZEN LAKE

At one time, this lake parallel with Indian Arm and separated from it by a long ridge rejoiced in the name of Lake Beautiful. In the early days of hydro-electric power, however, the lake, nearly five hundred feet above the inlet, seemed just the place for a storage reservoir from which the rush of its waters (supplemented by those of Coquitlam Lake) could drive the turbines for a growing city's power needs. In the course of this change from ornamental to utilitarian, the lake suffered a change of name as well, to Buntzen (after a power company official), a title that the ridge on its west side also acquired.

Despite this alteration, its surroundings still provide attractive walks along gated access roads, open, however, to members of the public on foot. The reward: views over the lake to the high ridges on either side and, at its north end the spillways and pipes that channel its waters. In addition, there is a recreation area by the start of the walk, where Buntzen Creek joins its lake at a tidy little park with beach and picnic tables.

From Highway 7A just north of Port Moody, fork left for Ioco. Turn right at Ioco School after about three miles then go right again on the Anmore road at the next fork (alternatively you may travel by Water Street and East Road). Just past the store in Anmore a road, gated but usually open to the public, turns right for Buntzen Lake Recreation Area. Follow this to the parking lot near the creek, beyond which further vehicle progress is barred by a locked gate.

Slip past this obstacle and continue along the road, among trees at first then emerging into open country. Now the lake is on your left and Eagle Ridge heaves itself heavenward on your right hand. A gentle wander along this rolling track brings you, via the intake from Coquitlam Lake, to the north end with its dam and its view over Indian Arm to Mount Seymour. For most this will be a satisfying destination but for those who want to go further an old logging road, forking right, leads to Buntzen Bay and Indian Arm. The track, however, is washed out here and there and creek crossings may be awkward.

A pleasant short alternative to the walk just described follows the west side of the lake from a gate just north of Anmore store at the point where the other road goes right. This west road is permanently closed to traffic since it gives access to a pump-house, but again Hydro does not object to its use by walkers.

By following this route you come out to the lake at a little treed headland by the pump-house; however, you may if you wish continue along a rough track on the power line uphill to a viewpoint overlooking the lake.

Round trip 5 miles (8 km)
Allow 3 hours

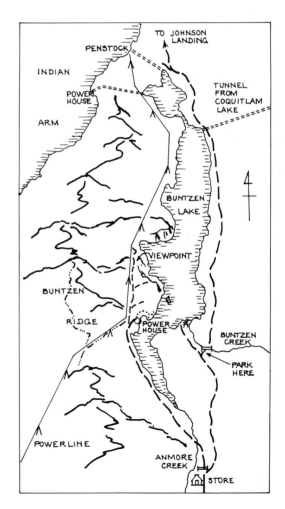

41   MUNDY LAKE

For a pleasant afternoon stroll on well laid out forest trails, with intriguing glimpses of small lakes, try this delightful park near the eastern edge of the developed section of Coquitlam Municipality. Part of the fun, too, consists in the getting there, for though the journey is not long, finding the objective requires a little care, especially for those travelling east from Vancouver on the Trans-Canada Highway.

From Highway 1, turn on to Brunette Avenue North, cross the overpass, and then, at the intersection with Lougheed Highway, take Blue Mountain Street uphill and north for about three-quarters of a mile to its meeting with Austin Avenue; here turn right. Continue on Austin for about a mile and a half, go sharp left on Hillcrest Street — and suddenly there it is, the destination. Park in the first lot between the street and the sports fields, with a small picnic area to the south and restrooms on the north,

beyond which is another parking area with an access road leading into it.

Walk in this direction, taking the track along the east side of the lot, then passing the small ornamental lakes and the swimming pool. Next comes the senior sports field followed by the intersection with a main gravel path; ignore this and continue north behind the school to the point where a path goes off sharp right at a T-junction (continuing north here will lead to Como Lake Avenue). Take this right hand trail and follow it eastwards, crossing two main gravel paths while wandering through a fine forested stretch in the course of which the route gradually swings south, then gives tantalizing glimpses of a small lake in a forest clearing.

Where the trail crosses a gravel path, go left on the latter for better views of the shore, attractively ringed as it is by lily pads. There is a small picnic area not far off providing seats for resting while you are contemplating Lost Lake, as it is called.

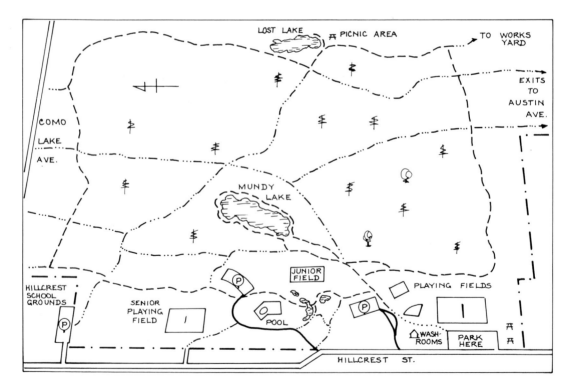

On resuming, continue south on the gravel path, then swing sharp right at the first T (going straight on takes one into the Municipal Works Yard). Stay with the trail over two intersections enjoying the fresh wood scent of the sawdust path that it has now become. Soon the sports fields come into sight again, but the hike is not yet over; the climax is Mundy Lake itself.

To reach it walk north along the east side of the playing fields until the path emerges at the lake's south end. There is a trail right round this oval body of water and the circumambulation of it is well worth while for its varied views as well as for its flowers and plants: Labrador tea, tiger lilies in particular. Thereafter, return to the car park.

Round trip 3 miles (5 km)
Allow 2 hours
Park trails
Good all year

42   COQUITLAM RIVER

This outing, amounting in all to nearly six miles, is on a river path which provides a view northward along the great glaciated U-shaped valley that the stream flows along. It is of interest, too, in demonstrating the changes that a waterway undergoes within a relatively short distance. As you head upriver, the still water of the lower reaches is replaced by a wide braided stream bed with shingle banks separating its numerous channels; then come higher banks and larger boulders washed by a current of some force.

Turn east off the Lougheed Highway as it passes Essondale at the Pitt River Road traffic light. Cross the bridge and park on the north side of the heavily-travelled road (Note: highway improvements are being made here). The treed dike leads north from this spot; set off along it. The trail is in the midst of alder and willow and it is most attractive when leaves hide the highway opposite and deaden the noise of car engines. Then comes the garbage dump, separated by a thin screen of trees, though the activity associated with it is unfortunately manifest in a number of ways.

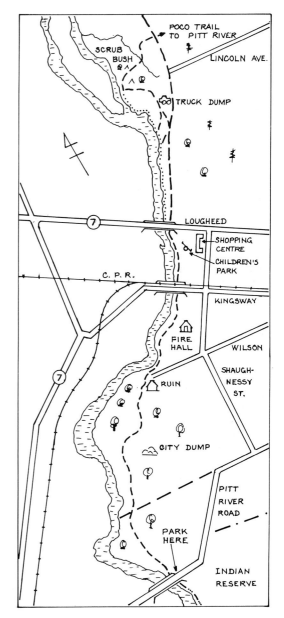

Next you have more woodland where you may see a kingfisher darting if you are lucky, but then the possible sound of a train whistle announces your approach to the railway crossing of the river, with a highway bridge just beyond.

Looking upstream

A pair of underpasses take you past these ob-
stacles with their colonies of nesting pigeons; an
intriguing sight, if somewhat nerve-wracking.
Now follow a pleasant little park north of the
road, another possible starting point should you
want a shorter outing.

The last crossing to be negotiated is Lougheed
Highway, but this also can be made by using an
underpass. And now comes the most attractive
part of the river, if you can blot out from your
consciousness the city works yard on the right.
Above on the right is Burke Ridge forming one
boundary; on the left hand is Eagle Ridge,
forming the other. Between them, dwarfed by
its glaciated valley, hurries the river as though

anxious to reach the Fraser.

Find a piece of river beach here to rest;
though the land has been designated as a municipal park, nothing has been done to develop it
as such, and no local citizens' group seems
anxious to press for its improvement, not surpris-
ingly, perhaps, in these days of high municipal
taxation, though a riverside park with tall trees
would make an attractive destination.

Round trip 5.75 miles (9.2 km)
Allow 3 hours
River dyke
Good all year

43 PITT RIVER DYKE

Despite its destination at a slough, this walk from Wild Duck Inn on the dyke that runs north and south along the west bank of Pitt River provides sublime mountain views, especially to the northeast. The river bank is popular with picnickers too, and determined hikers on the Poco Trail stride purposefully along it while attempting to complete as much of the circuit of Port Coquitlam as they can. You may meet horses as well, and motorcyclists make a nuisance of themselves despite the ban on wheeled vehicles.

Travel east from Port Coquitlam along Lougheed Highway to its crossing of the Pitt River. Because of construction on the north side connected with the widening of the bridge, it is best to park on the south near Wild Duck Inn and get across to the dyke as best you can where it stretches away northwards. On your right as you walk, you have peaks of the Golden Ears group rising up behind U.B.C. Research Forest, and these remain as companions on your outing.

Between them and you, however, is the flat polder country on the east side of Pitt River, the name indicating the Dutch origin of the settlers who drained the area and created a little bit of Holland amid mountain surroundings so different from their own lowlands. But, inevitably, the peaks are the chief attraction, with your view of them extending north as you progress to their culmination in what, well into

Canada geese mate for life

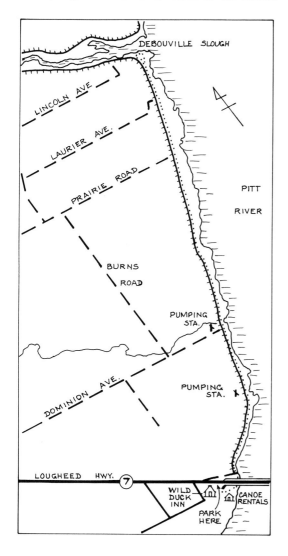

summer, appears as a great white wall, distant and majestic, the aptly named Remote Peak.

The closer scene has attractions also, even if they do tend to be dwarfed by the backdrop. The river flows gently along and plays host to duck, coot, and gull; overhead, you will see a blue heron winging its way along with great thrusts of its powerful pinions. Upriver is an attractive rounded headland where Pitt Lake narrows and its outlet begins its short passage to the Fraser. And over to the front of Golden Ears is a lower ridge, part of the U.B.C. Research Forest north of Haney, while away to the east is a classic example of a crag-and-tail formation, Grant Hill, mute witness to the power of long-ago glaciers.

At the two mile mark the dyke turns from north to west at the mouth of De Bouville Slough and this is probably as far as most will want to go. For the return, you have Mount Baker as a distant companion, heaving its great bulk to more than ten thousand feet. Still, it is difficult to resist a backward glance at the mountains you are leaving behind you as you wander back downstream towards the bridges that carry highway and C.P. Railway across the river that you have been in communion with for the last few hours. In fact, you may have the added interest of seeing the bridges open to permit passage of barges and tugs.

Round trip 4 miles (6.4 km)
Allow 2 hours
River dyke
Good all year

44   MINNEKHADA

"Quiet Waters," the destination of this walk, is, unfortunately — like Eden after the fall of man — forbidden territory. In other words, this walk ends perforce at the dyke gate which would give access to Minnekhada Farm were it not locked and festooned with NO TRESPASSING signs, backed by the noise of hounds baying. Actually, if you have walked this far, the enforced turn around will come as no hardship since you have been enjoying the still waters of the sloughs behind the dyke all the way along, as well as the more active current of Pitt River for a considerable distance.

From Lougheed Highway in Port Coquitlam, turn north on Coast Meridian Road for two miles then go right on Victoria Drive at a gas station. Where the drive splits, stay on the right fork and continue downhill to Cedar Drive just where a dyked waterway heads off east. Park here by the gate on its north side (on the south is a stretch of the Poco Trail).

You are now walking along the north bank of De Bouville Slough, the waterway being quite a small stream with wide verges clad in coarse grass and contained by dykes set quite far back. Nor are they dead straight; instead, they curve attractively, giving an artistic effect heightened by the still waters behind the dyke on your side, pent in its channel with the dense tree cover of marshy bottom land alongside.

As you continue downstream, you pass a small boat-launching ramp on the south side, where a road comes up to the dyke, and this is followed by a few boat shelters, also approached from the opposite bank, your side being pleasantly unspoiled. Then comes the main river with its log booms and sand banks, and you turn northeast along it leaving most signs of human settlement behind you as you walk upstream with Sheridan Hill across the river on your right. Here you are on Chatham Reach, the name a compliment to Thomas Pitt, Earl of Chatham, and elder brother of Britain's Prime Minister during the Napoleonic Wars.

Now birdwatchers come into their own. Waterfowl are plentiful; the great blue heron wings its way across the water, while on the dyke and its sides the flicker dines off insects or makes

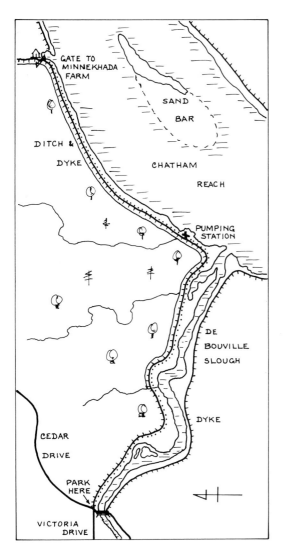

for the trees as you near him. Thus you wander along till you reach the gate that bars future progress — if you choose to walk that far. Of course, return is simple with no possibility of losing your way. And this time as you walk upstream along the slough, you have the slopes of Burke Mountain ahead of you and, stretching away to your right, the continuation of the ridge north towards Widgeon Peak.

Round trip 4.75 miles (7.6 km)
Allow 3 hours
Dyke top
Good all year

45   MUNRO LAKE

The objective of this invigorating hike is an attractive little lake on a shoulder of Burke Mountain at a height of 2750 feet. It is invigorating because the trail, ascending quite steeply, makes few concessions to human frailty, so it is not for those who are not in fair shape. On the other hand, the walk provides a good test of fitness, plus inspiring views across Pitt River lowlands to Golden Ears, with Mount Baker and the Fraser delta for the return journey.

Driving east on the Lougheed Highway through Port Coquitlam, cross the Coquitlam River and continue to Coast Meridian Road. Turn sharp left here and continue north for two miles to Victoria Drive. Go right at this junction; then, after a mile, take the left branch of Victoria Drive just at the top of a hill and follow it in a northeasterly direction as it becomes Quarry Road and loses its blacktop surface, becoming somewhat pot-holey thereafter. On your way along this stretch, notice a rarity on the left of the road: a drystone wall of a type common in Scotland but not often seen in British Columbia. After nearly 4.5 miles from the turn on to Victoria Drive comes the parking place, a wide stretch on the left of the road where an old logging track comes downhill to join it.

Follow this old road for about five minutes, then go right on the narrow footpath that rises steadily, a creek on its left. Now it is that conditioning begins to tell. The trail goes up quite steeply, heading mainly northwest with few alternations of gradient for something like 2000 feet. Markers are few on the lower stretches — apart from a few exhortations in red paint to repent before it is too late — but the route is a well used one and staying on it should pose no difficulty. Part of the way leads through an old burned-over stretch, now in process of being hidden by vigorous second growth, but there are still viewpoints which give a valid excuse for resting while looking over Pitt River Polder — a striking contrast to the alpine country round Golden Ears Mountain and Edge Peak.

Finally tree cover reasserts itself as you reach the shoulder of Burke Ridge and from now on the walk is virtually on the level; however, since nothing is perfect in this imperfect world, the trail may now be muddy, especially in early summer. A little south of the lake, another trail joins from the left, this one coming from Burke Mountain Village. Just at the south end of the lake, yet another trail goes off left, this one to Dennett Lake, a mile farther on and another 400 feet higher.

To find a place to rest, follow the path along the lake's east bank to Munro Creek, the outlet, with its small dam, where drinking water is available providing earlier arrivals have not messed the area up. Remember: garbage breeds garbage; practise control. Fishing in the lake is a possible pastime for some; others will be content to contemplate the peaceful scene and enjoy the silence.

For the return trip, follow the same route, being careful to take the left fork where the Burke Mountain trail, marked with aluminum circles, goes straight on towards the southwest, while your path is the one to Quarry Road. Now there is no strain: the difficulty is in restraint, so stop occasionally to feast the eyes on the great expanse of country that stretches south across the Fraser away to the border, with Mount Baker as sentinel on the American side, its snowclad slopes contrasting with the lush green of the lowland valleys.

Round trip 5 miles (8 km)
Allow 4 hours
High point 2750 feet (840 m)
Forest trail
July to October

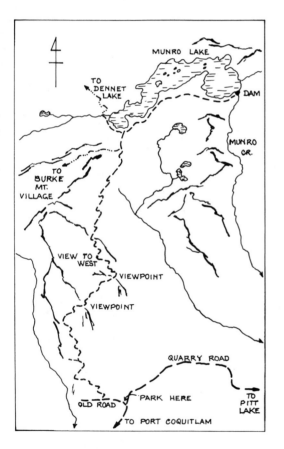

46   SEA ISLAND DYKE

If you wish to see what South Vancouver looks like along the stretch of the Fraser River between Marpole and West Point Grey, this walk will satisfy your curiosity to the full, covering as it does the whole North Arm from just west of the new Arthur Laing Bridge to the Iona Island Causeway. Nor need you confine yourself to cross-river views of the stately homes of Southwest Marine Drive; there is river traffic for interest and, over to the left, the noisy activity of Vancouver International Airport.

To reach the start of this walk, turn off Oak Street Bridge on Sea Island Way, cross the Middle Arm Bridge, and, at the traffic light immediately after it, go right on Airport Road. Follow this north until it swings left under the span of the new bridge and runs west as Grauer Road. About 200 yards beyond the Gulf Oil Company's storage tanks, there is an open spot to the right of the blacktop below the dyke and just before a gate on it. Park here.

As you head west along the dyke, you are made powerfully aware of the Canadian Forest Products mill and booming grounds across the river, which is here busy with pleasure craft as well as with log rafts and barges being towed along by tugs, all intent on their own business. Gradually, though, the scene changes; industry gives place to homes and these latter become steadily more stately as you continue downstream. Finally, after about a mile and a half and another gate, you come to a small slough on your right, beyond which lie the sand dunes that make up the so-called Wood Island. Here you may leave the dyke if you wish and follow the river round, your view now including a golf course with the B.C. Forest Service ship maintenance depot a little downstream.

This small detour ends at a public boat launching ramp and public park almost two miles from your point of departure; you may, therefore, decide to retrace your steps from here, perhaps staying with the dyke on your return route. You can continue westwards, however, via yet another gate by a pump house, traversing more dunes as you go. Even so, you must return to the track on the dyke to make further progress on this stretch, one that takes you along what becomes a slough facing Iona Island, the

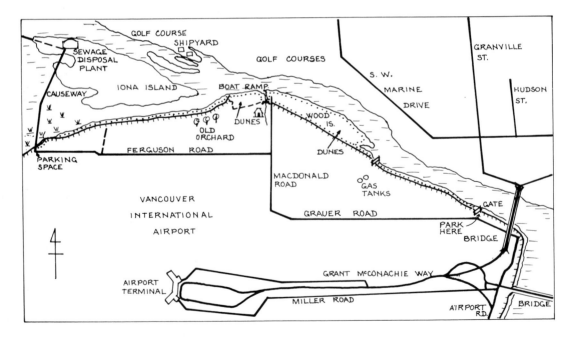

causeway to which cuts this channel off from the sea.

This area faces a threat of airport expansion; still, the dyke retains its attractions, white with wild cherry in spring and rich with blackberries in fall. The heron is a frequent visitor to this water as well and you may see an occasional cormorant on one or other of the wood pilings that line the channel; ducks, of course, are abundant.

Finally, as you look across to the sewage treatment plant that is Iona Island's chief claim to fame at present, you become aware of the causeway to it ahead of you and at last you step on to the road just where it turns from west to north at the extreme seaward corner of the airfield. Now you may look along the great Iona breakwater and on a clear day, have a view across the Strait of Georgia to the mountains of Vancouver Island.

Here, then, is the far point of your walk, fully 3.5 miles (5.6 km) from your point of departure. Note in passing that Vancouver Parks Board has ambitious plans for a marina and a recreational complex on reclaimed land here as an offset to sewage. However, these are for the future; there are no visible developments at present.

Now comes your return, a simple retracing of steps, perhaps staying on the dyke instead of straying among the dunes of Wood Island. This time, you are looking inland to the mountains that serve as the northern limit of the Fraser lowlands. You also have the chance to savour the clean lines of the new bridge as you march almost directly towards it on the way back to your waiting car.

One other note: If you wish to start at the seaward end, going as far as the little marina, continue west along Grauer Road beyond the parking spot already described; go north on MacDonald, then west on Ferguson to the spot where it turns sharp right to become the Iona Causeway. Park on the open space on the left by the locked gate. With so many alternatives, you should be able to find a walk to suit your mood; the river, anyway, is interesting at whatever season you travel along it.

Round trip 7.25 miles (12 km)
Allow 3 hours
Dyke and sandy beach
Good all year

47   STEVESTON DYKE

This is one of those accommodating walks that are capable of contraction or expansion depending on the energy of the participant and the amount of time available. At its longest, with the outward journey running from the seaward end of River Road in the north to the south arm of the Fraser River at Steveston in the south, the one-way distance is about 3.5 miles (5.6 km). However, access is also available at such intermediate points as the end of Westminster Highway, Blundell Road, and Francis Road, all of which are reached by right turns off No. 3 Road as it progresses south through Richmond.

To reach the start of the hike from River Road, turn off Highway 99 on the Airport exit at the south end of Oak Street Bridge and follow Sea Island Way for about two-thirds of a mile to its intersection with No. 3 Road. Turn left here; then, after a block, go right on Capstan Way for one block; turn left again on River Road and follow it along the south bank of the middle arm of the Fraser to its end opposite the runways of Vancouver International Airport. Park in the cleared space near the barrier.

At first the dyke is narrow, a little rough, and rather overgrown with brambles. After less than half a mile, however, at the access from Westminster Highway, a flood control project has made it quite a wide causeway, a character it will maintain from now to its end. Much of this walk's interest obviously lies on its seaward side where the marshes are the home of abundant bird life. Look out for the great blue heron and for the activities of various members of the duck and goose families. Also of interest on a clear day is the shipping out in the Strait of Georgia, ranging from small pleasure craft and fishing boats to great ocean carriers.

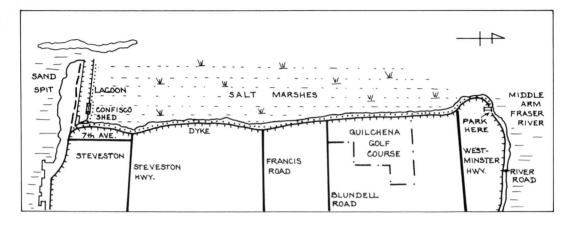

To landward the view is less inspiring. Quilchena Golf Course is quite attractive with its tree-lined fairways and healthy grass; thereafter, however, the view is of houses all the way. Even the sight of Mount Baker is not complete compensation for the loss of green fields.

Continuing south, you arrive next at a cluster of radio towers linked by walkways that march on stilt-like legs across the marshland. Then comes the end of the outward journey where a lagoon serves as home to a number of commercial fishing craft. To round out the trip, take the rough road that runs seaward parallel with the lagoon, eventually ending at its junction with the Fraser's south arm. From here, on the opposite shore, the woods and houses of Ladner are visible, with Reifel Island and its bird sanctuary just to the west.

After this, there is nothing to do but return along the dyke, an invigorating experience if there is a northwesterly blowing to bring the blood to the cheek and stimulate a healthy appetite.

Round trip up to 7 miles (11 km)
Allow up to 4 hours
Gravel dyke
Open all year

48   RICHMOND NATURE PARK

The motorist speeding south from Vancouver on Highway 99 is very likely unaware of the outdoor pleasure available to him only a few yards from the turnoff to No. 5 Road in Richmond. Here, fronting Westminster Highway, is Richmond Nature Park, the creation of a devoted group of conservationists.

To find this hidden treasure, leave the Throughway at the aforementioned turnoff, some two miles south of Oak Street Bridge, and turn right on Westminster Highway. A very short distance along this road on the right is the parking lot for the reserve, next to the park headquarters. In the office, various useful guides are available; so are bags of seed for the inhabitants of the waterfowl pond just a little way inside the gate. There is a picnic area for humans, too, if you wish to make a leisurely round and need sustenance afterwards.

Though the park covers only 108 acres, it is so skilfully laid out that a complete round of the inner and outer circuits comes to little short of two miles, with only a small stretch having to be covered twice. One way to cover the ground effectively is to turn left just inside the park, crossing the end of the bird pond, paying your respects to the pair of swans and the resident geese. The mallard ducks, too, will demand attention, if you are providing hand-outs. Next, work your way west along the southern boundary of the park past a stand of small birch, then into a more open area with a variety of shrubs and bushes, labrador tea being prominent, especially when it flowers in June. Salal is also found and it flowers about the same time, with the berries ripe by mid-August.

Where the outer ring meets the inner on the north side of the park, small pine trees exist in numbers. Though these are called Shore Pine in the guide, they have as alternative names scrub, or screw pine, perhaps because of their crooked twisted trunks and stunted forms. Unlike many conifers, this tree does not thrive in shade and it is usually among the first plants to re-establish itself after fire; in fact, the heat of fire helps to open the cones and release the seed.

Armed with the park guide you may spend much time identifying these and other plants and one result of your hike may be an enrichment of knowledge. But suppose you are still eager for exercise by the time you have covered the whole area. On the east side of the Throughway, the track corresponding to the one you have just been walking on is in process of being laid out in similar fashion; therefore, drive east along Westminster Highway to the first turnoff on your left, a cleared space on the east side of a short dead-end road, where you can park.

Here the circular trail is in place, a large pond has been bridged so nothing is lacking for enjoyment except, perhaps, identifying tags on

The swans, Cleo and Tony

some of the plants. The area is basically similar to its neighbour further west, both being peat bogs, and they both provide fine walks.

Round trip —
West park 2 miles (3.2 km) 1.5 hours
East park 1.5 miles (2 km) 1 hour
Foot trails
Good all year

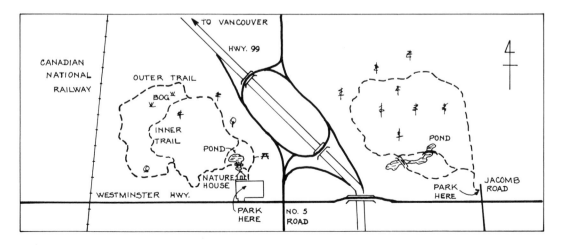

At the entrance

49   LADNER HARBOUR PARK

If you have never left Deas Island Throughway by the Ladner River Road exit just one-quarter mile south of the Massey Tunnel, you may be unaware of this pleasant little park, the municipality's centennial project, that fronts the Fraser River. To be more exact, the park is across from Gunn Island and the sloughs to the south of the main stream with their extensive mudbanks, the haunt of clouds of gulls.

Having left Highway 99, drive along River Road for 1.4 miles until you come to an interesting-looking bridge on the right of the road. A large wooden park sign hanging between two uprights confirms that this is where you turn off. You cross the deep ditch, then go sharp left between it and a big artificial pond — it's actually a sewage lagoon — and park in the designated space at the far end by the entrance gate. As you drive along the gravel road between lagoon and slough you might be lucky enough to see the heron, a frequent visitor.

Just ahead of you is a circular grassy stretch with a picnic shelter and, over to the right, a children's playground. The trail skirts the playground, and just beyond it, a wooden sign invites

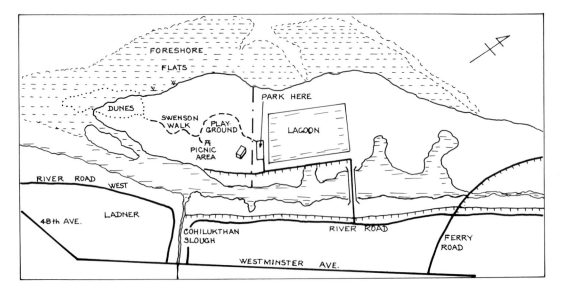

you to share Swenson Walk, a wide track among tall cottonwood trees, sweet-smelling in spring with their balmy fragrance. The trail is pleasantly curved, too, so that you travel with anticipation from one bend to the next.

Finally, the trees thin out, the vegetation dwindles to shrub-size, and you find yourself on sand. The slough reappears on your left, now providing moorings for pleasure craft and fish-boats. Walk across this open space stlll heading westwards until finally you discover yourself by the water's edge at the end of a spit looking over Ladner Beach to the flats with their gulls. And away in the distance to the north are mountains, clearly visible over the flatlands of the delta.

If you follow the water on your return, you come on all that is left of one or two old cabin sites and their bits of furnishing, perhaps an archeologist's midden in some future age. But there are willows too, and just ahead of you a great crop of bulrushes, along with various marsh grasses and numerous plants of the kind we used to call horsetails. As you wend your way back, you notice, too, that birch and cherry are in the wood beside the cottonwood.

One last thought: parks like this one have at least one distinct advantage; they are relatively undeveloped so that you may roam wherever the spirit moves you.

Round trip 1 mile or more (1.6 km)
Allow 1 hour
Woodland path and sand
Good all year

Entrance to Reifel Wildfowl Refuge from lookout tower (Walk 50)

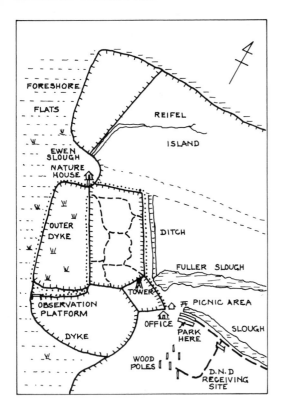

50 REIFEL WILDLIFE REFUGE

The only possible deterrent to this outing is the admission charge, 75c for adults and 40c for youngsters. But if one contrasts the tranquillity and the unspoiled surroundings of this estuarine marshland with the tidewater slums of Richmond, that is a small price to pay, taking into account that the B.C. waterfowl Society, which administers the site, is constantly expanding and improving the facilities. Although tours may be arranged, it is just as much fun to purchase the little booklet to identify the creatures of the area and make the walk into a self-guided nature tour. One can pick out the different species of birds, notably waterfowl, though shorebirds are not lacking either.

Reifel Island itself lies west of Ladner at the

mouth of the Fraser River's main channel, where it widens out into a delta with relatively dry land and sandbars alternating with various channels that rejoice in a variety of names: pass, reach, or slough. Actually, the sanctuary is located on part of the larger Westham Island with access from the mainland by way of a single-lane bridge leading off River Road West. To reach here from Vancouver, take the Victoria Ferry (Highway 17) turnoff from Highway 99 a little south of the George Massey Tunnel, and go south just a little over a mile to the intersection with 48th Avenue (Ladner Trunk Road). Turn sharp right at the traffic light and continue west till it becomes Westham Street, at which point go left one block, then right, to join River Road West. Continue west along this to the sharp right turn for Westham Island, a distance of three and a half miles from the traffic light. Once over the single-lane bridge the road crosses the farmland of the island, making right-angled turns at the boundaries of fields. Finally, after you have driven alongside a slough noisy with duck and geese, a small grove with picnic tables appears, and just beyond that is the car park. Straight ahead from here is the entrance to the sanctuary leading through the small park office where guide books are available. There are also packets of seed to offer those cheerful panhandlers among the resident population or the seasonal visitors.

Though there is a choice of routes in the sanctuary, the one described here covers the whole area as exhaustively as possible, taking into account the possibility that a few areas will have NO ENTRY signs at certain times of the year to avoid disturbing such seasonal visitors as the snow geese. First, follow the eastern boundary north along the treed dyke with its mixture of shore pine and Douglas fir, mixed with alder and blackberry bushes. Note the birds in the water of the marsh, or, in winter, congregated round the feeders: Canada geese, snow geese, various ducks, and of course those convivial creatures, the coots, with their uncanny ability to walk on water.

Turning west along the northern boundary one comes on the nature house overlooking Ewen Slough, then the other marsh with its treeless dyke and the tidal flats with their varied plant life: cattails and varied tall grasses being the most striking as these rise to six feet or more among the muddy channels. This track leads back south, giving fine views across the Straits on a clear day to the Gulf Islands. Closer at hand, one sees some of the more elusive visitors to the Sanctuary, like the trumpeter swans and the great blue heron which stands four feet tall and looks like a round-shouldered old person in the distance.

Before beginning the inner circuit, there may be time to visit the open platform that serves as observation tower for the outer marsh, approached by a narrow causeway and giving a fine panorama over the whole tidal area.

Back on the main dyke, go north outside the wire fence to the gate in the northwest corner. Enter by this gate and travel south on the bank that follows a sinuous course through the marsh, enjoying all the activity of the varied winged guests as they pursue their proper activities. Note what a noisy place the Sanctuary is; there are geese honking, ducks quacking, the beating of wings when a group rises from the water, and the continual chatter of the varied species.

This part of the trip makes a very irregular Z, quartering the marsh and ending near the main observation tower with its large platform. From here, the whole area is spread out from the entrance road in the south to the houses of Steveston across the river to the north, with the Reifel farm across to the east.

Round trip 3 miles (5 km)
Allow 3 hours (at least)
Dyke paths
Good all year

51   BOUNDARY BAY

This walk, partly on a dyke, partly on the beach itself, is interesting at any time of the year. When the tide is out, so are the clam-diggers; when the tide is high, the sparkling waters of the bay provide a fine foreground for the country to the east, with Mount Baker towering in the distance and with the North Shore peaks dominating the northern prospect.

To reach the start of this outing at Beach Grove, drive south along Highway 17 from the point where it leaves Highway 99 at Ladner

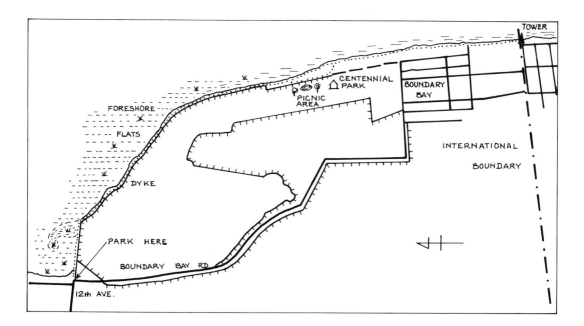

Interchange. At the second traffic lights about 4.5 miles from the turnoff, go left on Boundary Bay Road and continue south to Beach Grove as far as 12th Avenue. Turn left at the traffic light here and drive east to the point where the road turns sharp south at the end of a dyke. Park here by the Centennial Beach Park sign.

Set off along the dyke, going east at first and looking across the bay to Crescent Beach. Gradually this track curves round to the south and disappears among the bent grass behind the sandy beach itself. Here you may see various duck and geese, as well as numerous birds that nest in the fields beyond the dyke. By now, you are looking south towards the low cliffs of Point Roberts with the sweep of the San Juan Islands behind, their outlines softened by distance in contrast to the stronger lineaments of the houses in Boundary Bay, the little resort just ahead.

The homes here stretch right down to the beach and extend pretty well to the border between Canada and Point Roberts. Here the law-abiding citizen will stop, preparatory to turning north; the unscrupulous or the indifferent person will venture on to alien territory to enjoy more of the view of the islands as well as of Semiahmoo Bay to the east, with the houses of White Rock catching the light on the opposite shoreline.

Turning back at last you now see the full sweep of the North Shore mountains, particularly impressive when snow-clad. Nearer at hand, the masts of the radio station of the Royal Canadian Coastguard stand up across the bay, great red and white barber poles.

One final cheering note as you return to your vehicle: Greater Vancouver Regional District has recommended that the entire bay be designated as a recreation and conservation area. To that end it has already acquired some 65 acres beside Centennial Beach Park.

Round trip 4 miles (6.4 km)
Allow 2 hours
Dyke and beach
Good all year

52   POINT ROBERTS

Point Roberts, isolated from the continental United States by Boundary Bay and with no public sea link, draws most of its visitors from British Columbia. For these visitors the trip involves only a short car ride south across the 49th parallel to Lighthouse Park at the south-west tip of the peninsula, or to South Beach in the middle of its southern coast line.

Actually, the natural starting point for a beach walk such as is proposed would be Lighthouse Park, but since Whatcom County Parks Board has a $2 car-park charge for day use, perhaps the alternative beach access is preferable. Thus, the walk suggested here begins 1.5 miles to the east of the Lighthouse, giving you a chance to stroll either east or west as the spirit moves you, though the walk eastward is more interesting. Some advice, though: save this walk for the off-season unless you can bear humanity in the mass; check for low tides; and wear waterproof footwear (or carry shoes and go barefoot where the going is suitable).

To reach the walk's beginning from Tyee Drive, the main north-south access from the border crossing, travel to the point where it turns left at a right angle and becomes A.P.A. Road, noting as you pass it the right turn on Gulf Road with its sign for Lighthouse Park. Travel east along A.P.A. Road to its intersection with South Beach Avenue, go right here and travel for two blocks to the beach at a small grocery store. From here, you look south across the waters of Puget Sound to the San Juan Islands; just in front of you is the beach stretching east and west.

At first sight there may not be much to the choice; eastwards, however, has interesting-looking cliffs and a long stoney spit of land pointing south, while westwards there are only trailer parks and some modern beach homes. And eastward has Mount Baker as background, so eastward it is. If the tide is out, the fine sand close to the water gives nice footing if you are adequately shod (or unshod); otherwise you must pick your way along a stretch of rounded stones and shingles, which make for harder going.

On the way, admire the eccentric design of a

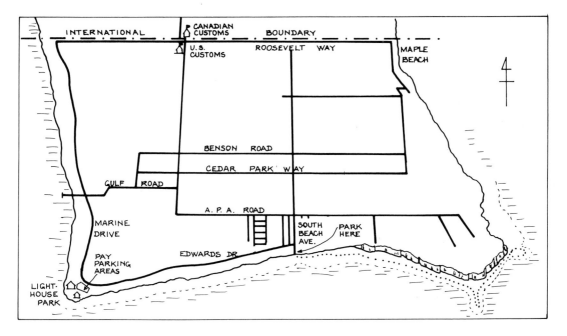

cluster of beach homes and the various routes that their occupants have created down the cliff, some of the ladders being hair-raising erections, to say the least. As you progress, the cliffs steepen and the effects of erosion on their uncompacted sand and clay become more and more visible; towards the point, some bluffs have fallen away altogether. And there is interest closer at hand, or at foot, as well: clam shells and scallops dot the beach, memorials to the many molluscs that have given their lives to satisfy human appetites.

As you near the gravel bar that signals the peninsula's southeast corner, you look across to Blaine and White Rock, while towards the left, Boundary Bay assumes the shape of a great bite out of the land. The spit itself makes a good turning point, though you may proceed northward round the corner if you wish; in any case, there is lots to supply interest at the spit and on your return from it.

By now you have turned your back on Mount Baker but you have the Gulf Islands spread out in front of you, with the San Juans away to your left. You may watch shipping in the strait from small pleasure craft through fish-boats and tugs towing barges and logs rafts, to great ocean freighters.

Round trip 3.5 miles (5.6 km) or more
Allow 2 hours
Beach walk
Good most of the year (but remember the summer crowds)

53   BURNS BOG

For a combination of exercise and education in natural history, this area would be hard to beat. Part of it, indeed, has been set aside by Delta Municipality as a Nature Reserve to retain some remnant of the once extensive peat bogs that covered considerable stretches of the lower mainland before the white man drained the land for farming, or, more recently, covered it with houses. To discover which plants thrive on what was once an extensive lake bed before it was swallowed up by the growth of sphagnum moss, Burns Bog is your laboratory.

Reaching it, however, poses something of a problem. You must make a circuitous trip from Highway 99 after leaving it a few miles south of the George Massey Tunnel to travel east on Highway 10. Leave this latter road by turning left at the traffic lights and travel north on 120th Street (Scott Road) as far as 80th Avenue. Go left again and head west till you reach 108th Street where again you turn left. By now, if you are not too giddy, you realise that you are going south; you are almost at journey's end, however, and this comes at the intersection of Monroe and Barrymore, where you should see the Delta Nature Reserve sign on your right (Note that this may change slightly because of housing developments). Park here.

First you walk downhill on quite a steep descent, emerging on a level road (it's called Sewerline) where you seem to have come to the end of the trail; look left, however, and there it is a few yards along. Next you cross the tracks of the Burlington Northern Railway, walk through a screen of trees — mainly spruce, hemlock, and cedar — and emerge by a footbridge spanning a deepish drainage ditch. Go over this, and you are on the edge of the bog. A glance north and south reveals the wooden piles that mark the reserve's boundaries, but trails extend on either side of these so you may follow any one of a number of paths. Take your sense of direction with you, though, for there are few landmarks.

As you leave behind you evidence of recent human activity, you find yourself in alternating stretches of trees and open country, the vegetation of the former being an interesting mixture of second-growth cedar and stunted pines, while the latter is dotted with a few dwarf trees mingled with a variety of ground shrubs, notably

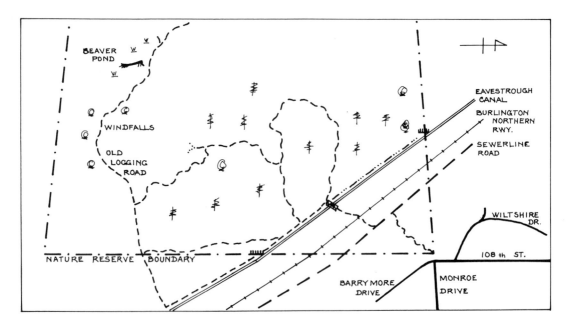

Summer in the bog

Labrador tea, swamp laurel with its pink star flowers, salal, fern — especially bracken — with black twinberry here and there as well. But the most interesting part of your lesson comes at the end of a walk to a beaver dam deep in the swamp. The approach, too is interesting, including as it does a very old logging site followed by a dive into jungle-like tangle of fallen trees, perhaps the aftermath of 1962's Hurricane Frieda.

Many signs of beaver activity are evident round the dam: gnawed stumps and trees stripped of bark. The large clearing to the north is also interesting, revealing yet another aspect of marsh environment. From here, retrace your steps as far as the old logging pile but beyond this continue directly to the deep ditch, your natural history lesson almost over.

One point yet remains: *the bog ecology is very fragile*. It is imperative that you remain on the trails; even sitting on the plants may flatten them and they take years to recover, so slow is the rate of growth on peat. This is dramatically illustrated by the stunted trees which have grown only two or three feet in nearly 20 years. An area like this is now a precious rarity in the lower mainland and it demands preservation, not alteration into a sewage lagoon as has been proposed in some quarters.

Round trip 2. 5 miles (4 km)
Allow 2 hours
Best in summer and fall

THE SEMIAHMOO TRAIL

This trail was an ancient Indian travel-way linking tribal villages in the south to salmon grounds of the Fraser River.

The first white explorers, led by Chief Trader James McMillan of the Hudson's Bay Company, passed here in December of 1824.

Using the Nicomekl and Salmon Rivers, they reached the Fraser and located the site of Fort Langley

— ERECTED BY —
THE MUNICIPALITY OF SURREY
DEPARTMENT OF
RECREATION — CONSERVATION
19   61

Historic sign

54   SEMIAHMOO TRAIL

The present state of this historic trade route is a mute reproach to building developers abetted by those who look on any piece of accessible land as a dump for their unwanted possessions; that part of it is the right-of-way for a power-line does not enhance its charms either. Admittedly, it is not all as bad as this; it still has woodland — second-growth timber but quite attractive — but a little care and attention in dealing with the trail would have left so much more of this relic of B.C.'s past that antedated the arrival of the white man. The Semiahmoo Trail, in fact, provided a route from the Indian villages in the south to the salmon fishing grounds of the Fraser River. It provided, too, the approach by which the early Hudson's Bay party (1824) travelled to survey the site of what was to become Fort Langley three years later.

Symptomatic of what has happened to the trail is the state of its northern approach, which lies just to the south of the Nicomekl River and is reached by a new bridge from Highway 99 immediately after its turnoff for Crescent Beach from the freeway to Blaine. Here, on a small triangular patch of grass, is a commemorative cairn and plaque, both dwarfed by a garish gas-station sign, the most visible landmark. From

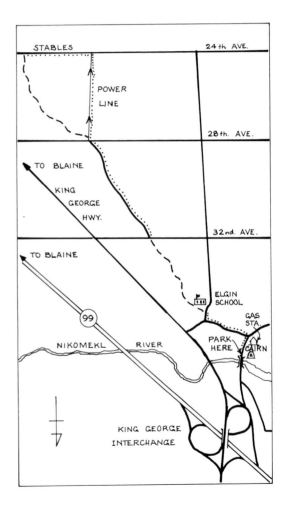

here, take the left fork south and cross Crescent Road to the footpath on its south side. Going left on the path, after about five minutes you reach the intersection with 144th Street and the little one-room Elgin Elementary School on the east side.

Cross 144th Street and follow the track that runs diagonally past the school and continues southeastwards in light timber, with occasional breaks giving views of the mountains on the north side of the Fraser Valley, notably the Golden Ears group. After a short time, however, a housing development greets you at 32nd Avenue and the trail, its glory diminished, crosses this and continues for the next half mile as a road with more suburbia on either side, a state of affairs that endures to 28th Avenue.

Here the road section ends again and the trail continues south, first along a power-line for a short distance; soon you take the left fork that leads you again into a wood, working its way along the contour of a gentle slope. On this traverse, it crosses a wide cleared area and one suspects that yet another stretch of it is going to be swallowed up some day. Eventually, it emerges into 24th Avenue just west of 152nd Street, and here, to all intents and purposes, it ends, a short southward extension having been virtually obliterated by a horse stable development on the avenue's south side.

As a slight variation on the return route, walk west on 24th to 148th Street and follow the power-line right-of-way back north through the wood to 28th, then along the road to the housing development on 32nd. Hence, it is back to the school and the Esso gas station that is the trail beginning.

The fate of this route, so rich in historical associations, is surely a warning; not only is our environment endangered by the outward spread of the city into once rural areas, so is our heritage of the past.

Round trip 3 miles (4.8 km)
Allow 1.5 hours
Footpath and country road
Good all year

55   CRESCENT BEACH

Here is another of those instances where you have a choice of outings from one starting point: a fairly short one north to Blackie's Spit, and one that goes south towards Ocean Park and White Rock which may be as long as you wish. Both are mainly beach walks along the east shoreline of Boundary Bay; the former introduces you to the inelegantly named Mud Bay, while the latter enables you to look into the more poetic sounding Semiahmoo Bay on which White Rock is situated.

Coming from Vancouver, leave Highway 99 at King George Highway Interchange and take Crescent Road west. This lies on the south side of the Nicomekl River at first; then, as that opens out into Mud Bay, the road crosses the railway tracks on to Beecher Street and ends finally at the beach, a distance of nearly four miles from the throughway.

For the walk northward, go along the path fronting the shore for about 15 minutes to a small pier. To continue, make a jog to the right for about 50 yards or so, then go left again behind an isolated house towards the undeveloped sandy spit, passing various sporting facilities en route. The spit is without trails or paths so that you wander on it at will; in any case, fifteen minutes or so brings you out to the end of it.

As you look north across Mud Bay from the point, you have the flat delta lands of the Fraser estuary in front of you with the North Shore mountains off in the distance. Westwards is Boundary Bay, and eastwards the Nicomekl River, its mouth barred by the causeway that carries the railway track. As may be expected, there is little vegetation: a few small trees — willow, poplar, crabapple, and bitter cherry; the main interest is in seeing how this sandspit has been built up, presumably from river silt.

But what of the walk southwards from Beecher? Well, it is mainly along a shore that is either pebbly or rocky, though the sand gives a footing when the tide is out if you are properly shod for squelching. You do begin on a path, but it soon peters out; thereafter, the railway right-of-way is your landward boundary while you have the whole beach to play with as you

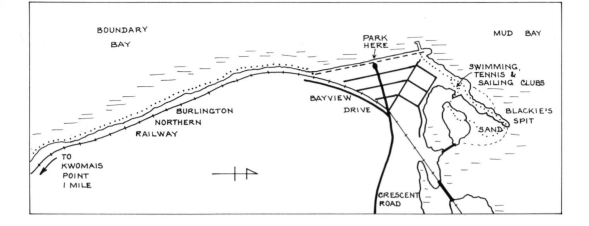

proceed towards the high banks of Ocean Park. And you need not confine yourself to walking; the area gives scope for clam-digging and searching for other shellfish.

For this walk, perhaps a convenient turn-around will be the corner at Kwomais Point, where the land turns eastwards towards White Rock and Semiahmoo Bay, with the point of the same name visible on the south side of the international boundary. With their outlines hazy in the distance, there are the San Juan Islands, their name attesting to one-time Spanish interest in this area. Here, despite the houses on the landward side of the track, the beach is often deserted and you can then indulge yourself in the feeling of being monarch of all you survey, at least as far as the shore is concerned. This is a nice spot for a picnic, too, but you had better carry provisions with you for the beach area is still unexploited by commercial establishments — and a good thing, too.

Of course, you must follow the same route for your return, but there are many worse things than strolling along a quiet beach, the late after-noon sun striking at your face. You have the whole sweep of Boundary Bay on your left hand and, ahead of you, the mountains north of Vancouver somewhat dwarfed by their distance from you.

Blackie's Spit
Round trip 2 miles (3.2 km)
Allow 1.5 hours
Beach path and sand
Good most of the year

Kwomais Point
Round trip 4 miles (6.4 km)
Allow 2. 5 hours
Beach
Good most of the year

56   REDWOOD PARK

Don't be put off by the small area of this park — only 64 acres. Because of its unique and attractive collection of trees bordering on shady lawns, you can easily cover two miles or more in following its varied trails.

Redwood Park more than lives up to its name. Its original owners, a pair of eccentric twin brothers, Peter and David Brown, made a hobby of collecting and planting the seeds of various trees. Among these are redwoods from California and, though there are such South American exotics as monkey puzzles in one of

Tree house

HISTORY OF REDWOOD PARK

REDWOOD PARK CONTAINS AN INTERESTING COLLECTION OF DECIDUOUS AND EVERGREEN TREES FROM MANY PARTS OF NORTH AMERICA, EUROPE AND ASIA. PROPERTY WAS OWNED BY PETER AND DAVID BROWN, TWINS, WHO CAME TO HAZELMERE VALLEY IN 1876. THEY LIVED ON THIS PROPERTY FROM 1893 TO 1958, PLANTING REDWOOD TREES FROM SEED OBTAINED IN CALIFORNIA. AN ORCHARD AND OTHER SPECIES OF TREES. AFTER TWO HOUSES BURNED DOWN, THEY BUILT THIS TREEHOUSE, WHICH WAS REACHED BY MEANS OF A RAMP. OVER THE YEARS, THE BROTHERS PLANTED 32 SPECIES OF TREES WHICH, IN ADDITION TO NATIVE FLORA, MAKE UP REDWOOD PARK. A LIVING MEMORIAL TO THE PIONEER BROWN FAMILY.

SURREY PARKS AND RECREATION COMM.

the groves, there are also more everyday conifers like cedar, pine, and fir. In fact, part of the charm of the place is the memory of the pioneer Surrey family that lived there, finally ending up in a large tree house that is still to be seen in a dense clump of timber.

The park is a little isolated considering that it is only 30 miles southeast of Vancouver. Probably the easiest approach from Highway 99 is to go south from it on King George Highway as far as North Bluff Road (16th Avenue) on the outskirts of White Rock. Turn left (east) on this to 176th Street (Highway 15), go left (north) for about one half mile to 20th Avenue, where you turn right and continue till you see the parking lot signs near the park's east side, facing the main area with its tables.

From here, head a little northwest to pick up a main trail (by the washroom) that will lead you into the forest. You will have a sense of the different trees in the park and identification of them will keep you guessing. By turning a little south you come out on one of the open grassy areas with trees on all sides except to the south-west, where you look out to the U.S. border and the San Juan Islands. Close to one of these clearings, too, is the treehouse with a short account of its building and function on a wooden signboard beside it.

In wandering thus you may put in a pleasant hour or so quite happily before returning to your car in the lot. There is, however, another possibility if you prefer climbing at the beginning of your hike to working your way back uphill at its end. Instead of turning off on 176th Street, continue east along North Bluff Road (16th Avenue) to a house numbered 17830, opposite which a trail goes off half left just inside the margin of the trees.

The path, actually a former railway grade, is the south border of the park, and after going along it for little more than a quarter mile, you see a trail heading uphill across a ditch. This takes you up to the lawn area below the tree house and you may fetch a huge circle east to the picnic area, descend the hill again and pick up another trail that joins the one you entered by. One warning, though: the ditch between the lane and the trail may be muddy, so be properly shod or step carefully.

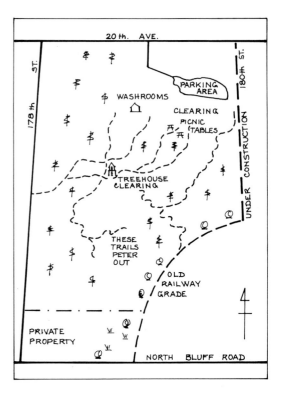

Round trip 1 mile at least (1.6 km)
Allow 2 hours
Forest paths and grass
Good all year

Meadows by the stream in spring

57 CAMPBELL RIVER PARK

No, we haven't got northern Vancouver Island mixed up with the lower mainland of British Columbia; we're dealing here with a stream that rises in the south end of Langley Municipality and flows gently westwards. It runs parallel with the U.S.-Canada border except for one hairpin-like swing to the north followed by return to its original line. Thereafter, it ends its uneventful course in Semiahmoo Bay, just to the south of White Rock.

On its northwards jog, it is crossed by North Bluff Road (16th Avenue), which you reach from Highway 99 via King George Highway by turning left off the latter after driving south on

it for about 4 miles. To accommodate the river crossing, North Bluff Road descends into the valley; just by the foot of the hill is an open space on the right opposite a sign for McLean Boy Scout Camp. Park off the road in this space.

Though there is no sign of development at present, it is the intention of the Greater Vancouver Regional District to turn this whole stretch of valley bottom into a park. For now, however, some of the land is leased for grazing so you should check if there are cattle around as you may have trouble with fences. Naturally you will remain on trails that stay clear of enclosures.

Begin your walk by heading south along an old dirt road in the bush. After ten minutes or so, you see a trail going off half left (the road itself ends at a fence with a NO TRESPASSING sign just beyond). Follow the footpath in attractively mixed bush, the ground ornamented in spring with trilliums. Please do not pick these beautiful flowers, though; they are not that common and others wish to enjoy them as well. The track continues close to the valley's eastern edge and you find yourself looking up at wooded slopes rising a hundred or so feet on your right hand, the whole composition making up a gentle sylvan scene that is infinitely soothing.

Finally, you come to a fence which is open enough to pass through, and you enter an open field where the course of the stream is marked by a line of bushes, the low ground round about damp and rich in spring with a luxuriant growth of skunk cabbage. Continue following the track which now rises gently up the side of the valley to a small field on top. The end of a road is just across from you behind a gate (actually Campbell River Road itself).

Looked at from this vantage point, the peaceful valley to the north is laid out nicely in front of you so that it seems a pity that you have to descend into it again to make your way back. The meadow below is, however, a pleasant spot for a picnic or even a little lazing; not spectacular, but placid. You may retrace your steps through the wood on resuming; however, you may take one of the other trails north staying parallel with the stream, for this also will bring you back to your starting point or near it.

Perhaps some day all this will be organised for recreation with trails and ponds. But that day is not yet; until then you may still enjoy a quiet walk along the valley of Campbell River.

Round trip 2.75 miles (4.5 km)
Allow 1.5 hours
Trail
Good in summer

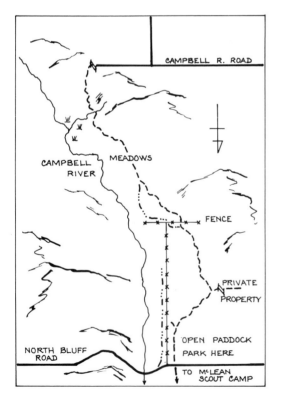

58 PITT LAKE

Choose a clear day for this walk to experience the full effect of the majestic peaks that enclose this beautiful body of water. The lake is situated only a few miles from Port Coquitlam, but is far removed from it in its attractiveness. Especially is this true in spring when peaks are still snow--clad and when your way is sweetened by the scent of balm from the surrounding cottonwoods. The area is rich in waterfowl, too, so birdwatchers are amply catered to.

To reach your jumping-off point, turn left on Dewdney Trunk Road just to the east of the Pitt River Bridge on the Lougheed Highway. Turn left again on Harris Road at the T-Junction, cross the Alouette River, then go right on McNeil. While passing Sheridan Hill, make a left turn onto Rannie Road, which takes you to your destination 11 miles from the main highway.

Here at the road-end is a public boat launching ramp; and here a dyke, the northern limit of a new polder, stretches eastwards ahead of you running along the south shore of the lake towards a wooded ridge that rises steeply to over 2,000 feet. As you make your way along the dyke you have plenty to occupy your attention:

the craft in Grant Narrows, from tugboats for log booms to tiny canoes; the numerous shore and water birds around; the mountain vistas on both sides of the lake. Small wonder, therefore, if you make slow progress.

At the dyke's eastern end is a wooded bluff with various rocky viewpoints looking out across the lake. Further progress, however, is barred by NO TRESPASSING signs marking private property in a little bay just beyond. From the rocks you look back across the lake to the ridge that forms the east side of Widgeon Creek valley; up to the north is Goose Island in the lake centre; along the east side, bluffs drop vertically into the water suggesting great depth beneath, indicative of glacier erosion that scooped out this great south-facing valley. Interestingly, though, because Pitt River is tidal, high water backing up from the Fraser is depositing sediment at the end of the lake, hence the narrow shipping channel that forces boats to head east before travelling north.

Round trip 3.5 miles (5.6 km)
Allow 2 hours
Dyke road
Good all year

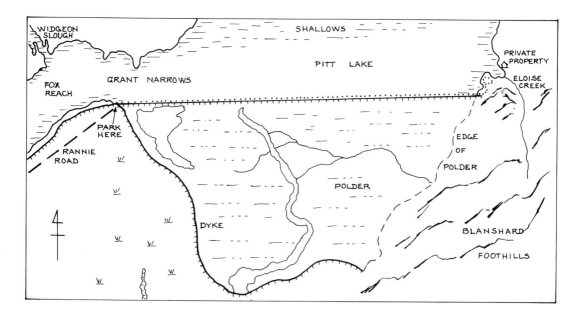

59   U.B.C. RESEARCH FOREST

If you wish to experience at first hand various aspects of foresty and logging, the installation near Haney administered by the Forestry faculty of the University of British Columbia provides the perfect open-air classroom. The forest exists to give practical training to students by providing space for a variety of experiments and studies, but though its function is primarily academic, it does not neglect the general public.

For even the casual visitor there is much to see and do — too much, in fact, to be taken in on one visit; you will surely want to return, therefore, either to walk the forest's roads and trails on your own or to participate in an open house with its accompanying displays of forest expertise. One more point: a moment's glance at the map will convince you that you can hardly cover the 50 miles of road and trail in this area of 20 square miles, even with repeated visits. All that is attempted here, therefore, is to suggest a short walk covering some easily reached highlights and to mention a few other possibilities.

To reach the parking lot from the Lougheed Highway in Haney, turn north on 232nd Street, following the Golden Ears Park signs for about 2.5 miles until, a few hundred yards beyond the bridge over the South Alouette River, you continue straight ahead on Silver Valley Road where the park access route turns half right. Thereafter you have only one slight jog to the right in the final mile or so to the barrier at the entrance. At the gate are displays, a large map, and a list of rules for visitors to follow: only hiking allowed, no dogs permitted (they worry the deer), Loon Lake Camp is off limits, remain on roads and trails. These restrictions excepted, the freedom of the forest is yours.

For those of you in family groups, perhaps the following short outing will serve as introduction to the forest highlights, whetting your appetite for a more active walk in the future. From the stone cairn on the grass, inside and to the left of the entrance, continue left towards the second wooden power pole by a hedge. Here a footbridge takes you over a ditch and, by crossing a road beyond, you come on a trail leading into the forest. This route takes you into a pleasantly wooded stretch; then, with the crossing of a second road, you find yourself on Second Century Trail, a route furnished with explanatory notes and signs.

Follow this through the forest, turning right when you come to the T-junction (the O.K. Trail to the left is a dead end at present). Finally,

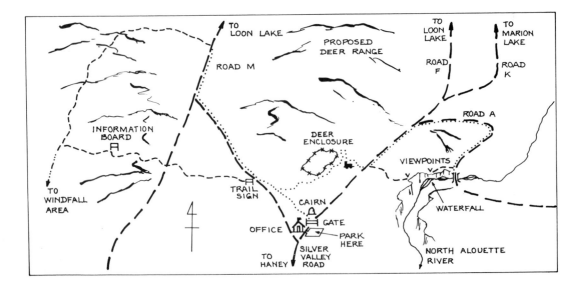

as you emerge on a road, go right again and stay with the road till you return to your footbridge and the gap in the hedge. Now follow the white marker sticks towards the deer park where a number of black-tail deer (subjects of an S.F.U. study) have the freedom of a large enclosure. All round this area, posts with horseshoe markers identify plants presented to the forest, including exotic conifers from China, Japan, and other far-off lands. Next comes a visit to an old donkey-engine, a relic of logging salvaged by U.B.C. forestry students from its resting and rusting place by Pitt Lake and transported to this spot by helicopter. Here it stands, in all the glory of a fresh coat of paint, just as it did during its days of active service that date back over 60 years to the time when its cheery whistle was first heard in the coast forests.

From this exhibit, head for the main access road and follow the power-line a short distance into the bush on its east side. At the top of a high bank, you look down on North Alouette River which here drops into a deep gorge a short distance below a substantial wooden bridge across it. Further progress is impossible from here, but if you wish to visit the bridge and the experimental areas beyond, go north a short distance on the main forest road, turn right on Road A, and stay right at the next junction. As you look downstream from the bridge, you see the river plunging over a rocky sill into the depths below; from here, too, some experimental areas are close so that you may put in an hour or so of browsing before returning to your starting point.

Part of the pleasure associated with the forest is the view of the Golden Ears group of mountains dominating the northeastern skyline, providing the forest with a fitting backdrop and giving you orientation on a number of hikes. Among these, the outing to Blaney Creek chum salmon hatchery may be mentioned; or if you want exercise on some crisp spring day, there is the 6-mile road circuit, on which you go north on F, west on E, and return on M. On this latter you have sight of a huge cedar, fenced off to give you a sense of its size. You may also, by a short detour north on road L, view certain education projects for schools: a model log cabin and a miniature skyline logging operation, for instance.

But perhaps the thought of 6 miles on log-ging roads is a little daunting; if so, you now have as alternative a new (1975) trail designed to give you close-up views of deer in their natural habitat, using the cleared area west of road F where feeders have been established to ensure a resident population.

All these and other possibilities exist; make the most of them. Heed one request, though: leave everything as you find it. These research projects represent much time and effort on the part of their originators and, in many instances, the expenditure of public money. Study, therefore; don't touch.

Round trip 1 mile or more
Allow at least 1 hour
Dirt roads and forest trails
Good much of the year

Old donkey

Overtopped by devil's club

60 MIKE LAKE CIRCUIT

If you are sated with mountain and lake views, you may find this forest walk a restful change, for even if it does begin and end by Mike Lake, that is an unobtrusive body of water, itself dominated by tall trees. An advantage for the anti-social is that this section of Golden Ears Provincial Park is relatively peaceful, only a few picknickers, canoeists, and those heading for Alouette Mountain or Blanshard's Needle making use of the the lakeside parking lot.

To reach the start of this hike, drive to Golden Ears Park following the signs from Haney. From the entrance, drive 2.8 miles on the main access road, then turn off left at the sign for Park Headquarters. Go left again a few yards in and travel on a dirt road for just over a mile to the parking place at the lake, about 200 yards beyond the point where Incline Trail to Alouette Mountain goes off right. Just west of the car-park a locked gate bars the road to vehicles, thereby ensuring peace for your walk along it.

Almost immediately you lose the lake and you are among trees, good sized conifers for the most part, belonging to U.B.C. Research Forest in which you are now walking. Continue along this unfrequented road, staying right where another comes uphill to join it after some 15

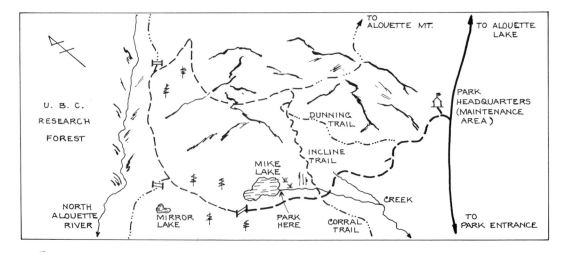

minutes, a process you repeat at the next fork with its locked gate left. As you walk this stretch, you become aware of the insistent sound of water far below you and on your left; this is the North Alouette River.

Finally, your route turns sharp right at a point where you see Mount Blanshard towering above trees (the only mountain view you have). Now you are heading back east, rising a little as you go until you come to a Parks Branch sign for Alouette Mountain and you see your return route, Incline Trail, dropping sharp right downhill. If you do have a craving for vistas, you may walk some 200 yards beyond the junction to where a break in the trees lets you look over the Fraser Lowlands back towards Haney and Port Hammond.

Back on your route downhill, you speedily lose the height that you gained so gently in the course of your sylvan stroll. The only point to watch for on this trail is its junction with Eric Dunning Trail, which comes up from the left; you may, in fact, have seen the sign marking the latter's lower end as you drove in. As you near your destination, you come on an interesting example of drowned forest just on your right as you cross the lake outlet and return to the road a short distance left from where you parked.

Thus your woodland walk ends, having shown you the stately trees and the shrubs that make up the B.C. coastal forest environment.

Round trip 3.5 miles (5.6 km)
Allow 2 hours
Highpoint 1,400 feet (460 m)
Elevation gain 600 feet (180 m)
Dirt roads and park trail
Good March to November

Burke Falls (Walk 61)

61   GOLD CREEK

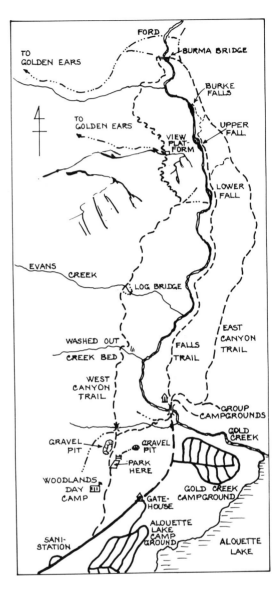

Since Golden Ears Provincial Park became autonomous instead of being a neglected appendage of Garibaldi Park, the Parks Branch has worked hard to provide a trail system for both walkers and climbers, an urgent need in view of this scenic area's proximity to the province's urban population centres. Among a number of outings beginning at the hikers' parking lot, the walk along Gold Creek to its falls is undoubtedly the most popular.

The route from Haney is well signposted, beginning with a turn off the Lougheed Highway at 228th Street and continuing roughly north, crossing the South Alouette River en route, for about 4.5 miles to the park entrance. From here a good road continues for nearly 7 miles further, until a sign, HIKER PARKING, directs you half left on a narrow dirt road which ends in a cleared space after about half a mile. Stop as close as you can to the southwest corner because it is from here, by a large gravel pit, that the trail system commences.

At first you rise on the east side of the pit until, where trails divide at its north end, you take the right-hand one for Gold Creek. This descends gradually, following a small stream to emerge at a wide dirt road just south of the bridge over Gold Creek. Cross the creek and at the fork on its north bank, follow the path marked LOWER FALL. Your route, pleasantly timbered, runs parallel to the creek, with tantalising glimpses of its waters through the trees. Eventually you do come close to it at a small beach where the flow is peaceful and the limpid stream a temptation for a dip on hot days.

But again you lose sight of it for a little; then, as you wend your way between trees, you become aware that the sound of the water is changing from a gentle swishing to a strong rushing. And there is the lower fall, spray enshrouded and powerful. The view to the west is overawing too, for you are looking directly at the great cirque formed by the mountain wall between Blanshard Peak and Edge, with Evans Peak as a lonely sentinel to the south.

If you are proceeding beyond, follow the rather rough track upwards for another quarter mile to the even more spectacular upper falls where, safe behind a wooden rail, you look straight down into boiling waters in the canyon below a vertical drop over which the creek hurls itself headlong. And here comes the true moment of decision. It is possible to continue further up a rough route marked with yellow squares; you should, however, be careful if you have youngsters with you for the drop-off is steep in places. Your alternative: a leisurely return by your outward route, perhaps pausing by one of the quiet stretches for a rest.

If you do continue, you may have to negotiate the occasional fallen tree, but this poses no great difficulty; you emerge finally on the bench some 200 feet above the creek on a path that soon joins the East Canyon Trail. Before doing so, however, you may make a short detour to yet a third cascade, Burke Fall. At the canyon trail, you must again decide: turn right and follow the rough old road back to the main bridge, or go left upstream to the Burma Bridge. This structure, if you can traverse its single wire, gives access to the West Canyon Trail and return by that route. But a caution here: do not follow this suggestion unless you are fit and reasonably active.

There you are, then, presented with a series of decisions. For most, one or both of the falls will be sufficient, particularly for those groups walking with young children. Those of you who do continue north and essay the crossing, turn left at the T-junction on the creek's west side. This path takes you across a tributary creek but then starts rising over 200 feet to bypass a vertical cliff above the upper falls; however, the view upstream spreads the whole upper Gold Creek valley out in front of you.

Thereafter, the trail works its way along the foot of a rock slide (be careful not to lose it here); it then descends, and a right turn at the junction once you are again on the level sets you on your way back to camp or transportation. This route is further back from the creek than the Falls Trail; therefore, you have time to enjoy the rich early summer growth of yellow violets and bleeding heart or, if you prefer the macabre, you may admire the healthy-looking devil's club, some of it over seven feet tall.

Now comes your last obstacle of the day: Evans Creek. In late summer, you may ford it; during high water, however, make a short detour downstream and cross on a roughly scalloped log. From here you simply follow a gentle downward gradient; in fact, if you guessed that this might once have been a logging railway, you would have been correct, though the sound of the last locomotive has long been absent from these woods. On your right you pass the start of the

Burma bridge

trail to the lake lookout, then comes an old logging bridge; in a few more minutes you are back at the original junction near the top of the gravel pit from which you set out.

Round trip to Upper Falls 4.5 miles (7.2 km)
Allow 2 hours
High Point 800 feet (280 m)
Elevation gain 300 feet (110 m)

With return via West Canyon Trail
**   7 miles (11.2 km)**
Allow 5 hours
High point 1200 feet (360 m)
Elevation gain 700 feet (220 m)
Good April to October

62 ALOUETTE LAKE VIEWPOINT

This walk provides a nice late-afternoon appetite rouser for those of you staying in one of the Golden Ears Park campgrounds. Once again, it starts at the hikers' parking lot and for the first ten minutes it is identical with the West Canyon Trail (See p. 116) to the point where, after crossing the decayed logging bridge, you come on a marker to the left of the trail indicating a footpath that heads uphill.

The trail, though rising steadily, is a pleasant one for a hot day, lying as it does in the shade of tall trees. The grade, too, is easy as the route swings gently from one side to the other, the creek that you crossed on the main trail forming the southern boundary. As you climb you begin to get occasional fugitive glimpses of the lake through the trees, but not till you have reached 1,000 feet do you have your first uninterrupted view. Here, just after the track has swung away from a large rock, a small level stretch, wired for protection, looks out over Gold Creek and allows you to see part of the lake. A pause here gives you a chance to get your breath back.

Proceeding upward, you next cross the creek that you saw earlier. By now the steepness of the slope above and the steep rock walls make it a perfect sun-trap, another pleasant stopping point for a short rest. After the rest, the route first rises then levels off on a kind of bench among trees so that it is well back from the steep edge with its drop-off. Finally, you reach the viewpoint, a clearing on a small rounded rock from which the southern half of the lake is laid out in front of you as far as the dam that controls its outflow to the South Alouette River, allowing diversion of its waters via a tunnel to Stave Lake with its hydro power stations. Away to the southwest, faint in the distance, are the outlines of the San Juan Islands of Puget Sound; across the lake, the logged-off ridge — best viewed when its raw nakedness is hidden under snow — that culminates in Mount Crickmer.

Round trip 3 miles (5 km)
Allow 2 hours
High point 1,300 feet (400 m)
Elevation gain 800 feet (240 m)
Park trail
Good March to November

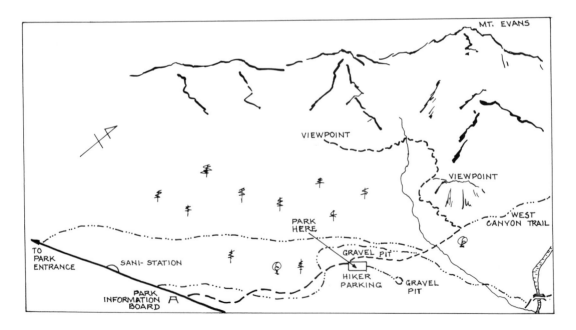

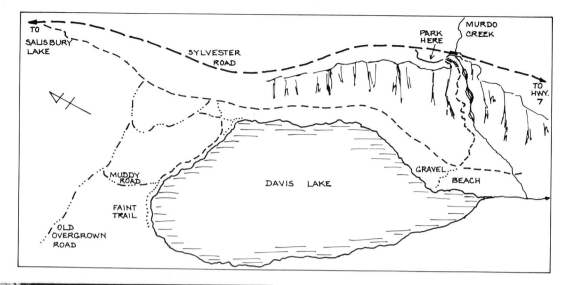

63   DAVIS LAKE

Though this attractive body of water is listed as a Provincial Park, it remains virtually undeveloped and is reached only by a road, gravel for its last few miles and used by logging trucks. Those of you who drive the 11 miles or so along Sylvester Road from Lougheed Highway are, however, well rewarded for your trouble. Not only is there the lake; you also have the Macdonald Falls to visit, where the waters of Murdo Creek tumble down into a deep plunge pool, then continue to the valley floor in a series of small rapids.

Coming east from Mission City, you drive 4.1 miles beyond the main traffic light at the junction where Highway 11 meets Highway 7. Just before a small grocery store your branch of Sylvester Road turns off sharp left, heading north a little to the east of Hatzic Lake, on the flat at first but later hugging the side of the valley past farms and occasional houses. Some building is going on along Sylvester Road, which may account for the road improvements that are cutting off a number of its bends and altering slightly the total distance. On your travels you pass Allan Lake, the name of which some enterprising developer is attempting to change to Alpen, and thereafter your blacktop ends and you drive forward on gravel.

About 9 miles along you cross Cascade Creek which has a pretty little Forest Service picnic site to your left on its north bank, a possible stopping place for you on your return journey. After the creek, the road starts rising, the hills close in on either side, and finally, just after crossing Murdo Creek, you have a parking area on the left of the road from which a trail follows the creek down quite steeply. On your descent you come to the falls — quite spectacular in late spring — then, 300 feet below your starting point, you find yourself by the gravel shores at the south end of the lake.

From here, you may simply decide to struggle back up the trail you descended. It is probably more rewarding, though — and less strenuous — for you to follow an old logging road along the east side of the lake to near its north end. From here the route angles uphill, eventually rejoining Sylvester Road some distance north of where you left your vehicle. Fortunately the road is not busy and you do have pleasant views as you look down on the lake in its tree-surrounded basin, so that return this way is well worth while. Note that some people have driven down the old logging road to near the lake and this may become the approach if the area is ever developed as a park. At present, however, it is not recommended because of its roughness.

Round trip 2 miles (3.2 km)
Allow 1 hour
High point 900 feet (280 m)
Elevation loss 300 feet (90 m)
Trail and logging road
Good much of the year

Mossy tree

64   HATZIC DYKE

One of the most attractive dyke walks along the Fraser River lies south of the Lougheed Highway between Nicomen Slough and Hatzic. Here farmland and the brown flood of the river supply the foreground while some of the finest of the mountain ranges around the valley provide romantic contrasts to the quiet pastoral scene.

Drive east on Highway 7 to Sylvester Road, 4.1 miles beyond the light controlling traffic at Mission City bridge. Turn right on Sylvester and cross the Canadian Pacific Railway tracks, then go left on McKamie Road, the first fork. Contine to the dyke and drive 1.6 miles from the main highway to where a gate bars further vehicle traffic. Park here and continue west on foot using the narrow dirt road atop the dyke.

As you proceed, your route turns from southwest to northwest, giving plenty of variety. Particularly enjoyable are views towards Golden Ears and Mount Robie Reid, especially in spring sunshine. Nor is the dyke totally isolated; two roads intersect it, one after about 30 minutes, the second some 20 minutes later. Finally your further progress is barred by the outlet of Hatzic Lake and it is time to retrace your steps. Actually, though, you may vary your return somewhat by dropping from the dyke top to the river bank, which you can follow pretty well back to the gate.

On your return trip you have a nice variety of views too. Across the river are the treed slopes of Sumas Mountain, and away to the east are the majestic peaks of the Cheam Range: Cheam itself, Lady Peak, Baby Munday — some infant that — and Welch. These, too, look particularly good in spring with their winter snow gleaming on them; added attractions are the willows coming into leaf and the fragrance of cottonwood.

A last thought, as you enjoy this walk: ponder the implication of this defence line against the potential power of the river, power that has shown itself as recently as 1948 to man's sorrow, and may do so again given the appropriate conditions. A sobering thought for you to contemplate, perhaps while waiting for a C.P.R. freight to drag its interminable length past the crossing at the highway.

Round trip 7.5 miles (12 km)
Allow 4 hours
Dyke and river path
Good all year

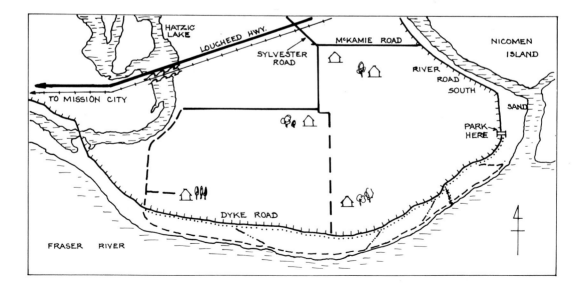

View over Long Island

65   HARRISON LOOKOUT

Anyone staying in one of the campsites in the Weaver Creek recreational area who does not make this trip is missing a really good thing. In fact, it is worth driving a much greater distance to enjoy an adventure road and a delightful ascent to a Forest Service lookout perched atop a 2300 foot knob of rock. Admittedly, the road has a gravel surface for the last 18 miles and it carries near its beginning the ominous notice: USE AT YOUR OWN RISK. Still, it is wide and its surface is well-graded while the views it provides over Harrison Lake are breathtaking.

Driving east on Highway 7 after Lake Errock, turn left on the road signposted for Hemlock Valley just before the Sasquatch Inn. Follow this road north across the Chehalis River, and less than a mile further on stay right where the road to Hemlock Valley ski area (gated in summer) branches off. Here blacktop ends and you are on gravel for the rest of the way. Another two miles brings you to Weaver Creek spawning channel, a scene of wild activity in October of every fourth year when almost half a million sockeye return to spawn and die. Just beyond this feature are the campgrounds at Wolfe Lake and Weaver Lake, and then — as the road sweeps over the crest of a hill — Harrison Lake from Echo Island to the north is spread out before you.

For the next few miles you enjoy a roller-coaster run along the lake, dropping down to cross Cartmell Creek, with Coral Falls on your left just a little beyond, then swinging up and over the next ridge. Finally, about 20 miles from the turnoff you pass the sign for Wood Lake Camp, then comes Hale Creek, and just over a mile beyond is a sign pointing right for Harrison Lookout. At this point you realise that it must be on top of the very steep bump that you have seen off and on as you travelled along the lake.

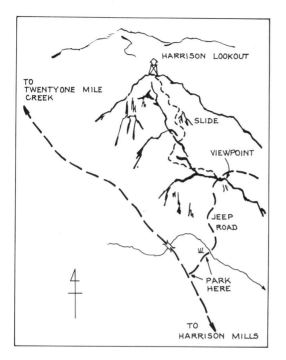

group of snow-clad summits, and north, beyond the lake, are more towering giants. Surely the impious thought must cross your mind that to pay someone for stopping here is all wrong; people lay out great sums of money for far less than this mountain retreat.

Your return trip is just as enjoyable. Now you have the Cheam group ahead of you as you drive south with Harrison Hot Springs at the end of its lake closer at hand. Just one caution; logging may be going on, so obey posted signs and remember that logging trucks have right-of-way, as if their sheer size did not ensure that!

Round trip 3 miles (4.8 km)
Allow 3 hours
High point 2300 feet (720 m)
Elevation gain 1100 feet (320 m)
Forest path
Best June to October

Harrison Lookout

Parking by the road is limited but you may, if you wish, drive on for a few hundred yards to a clearing. Beyond this point the track is too rough for vehicles, so here you take to your feet.

First you cross a small stream, then you rise quite steeply out of your little valley, gradually swinging north in the process. Finally, at the high point of the road, you view the lake on your right, while just opposite, the taped trail with its Forest Service sign rises quite steeply uphill. Soon, however, the grade eases and from now to your destination you are on a delightful little path among the tall trees of an open forest. As you climb you have occasional views of the lake, until you breast the last rise and there in front of you is the lookout with its friendly occupant.

Adjectives are inadequate to describe the panorama. Harrison Lake, 2000 feet below you, is here split by Long Island, complete with its own smaller lakes. To the east are the ridges culminating in The Old Settler, while south are the majestic peaks of the Cheam range with the great white peak, Mount Baker, beyond and to the right. Looking west you face another fine

66   MOUNT WOODSIDE

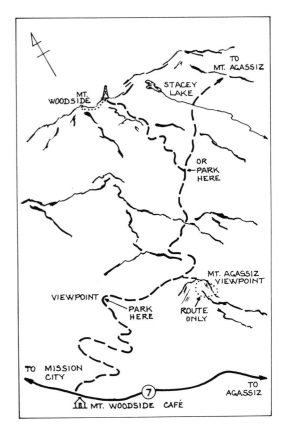

Mount Woodside and Mount Agassiz are two summits on the long ridge that rises to just over 3000 feet between the Harrison River and Highway 9 north from Agassiz, with the Lougheed Highway running along its southern boundary. The ridge also has an approach road that allows you to give your vehicle an amount of exercise inversely proportional to what you get yourself. Whether or not you take this road depends on your attitude to the car's well-being and, of course, the power of its motor. Indeed, if you do want to drive all the way, you probably need a four-wheel drive car or a truck with plenty of clearance, for the route is rough in places. If you can, though, you will want to drive some distance to avoid having to slog over an open logging road on a warm day.

Travelling east on Highway 7, drive some three miles beyond Harrison River Bridge until, almost opposite a cafe-motel on a considerable uphill stretch, you see a gravel road on your left, a metal shed near its start providing another marker. If there is weekday activity round it, check in case trucks are using the road, in which event it will not be open to you. The route rises in a series of S-bends and the surface is not the best, especially in steep sections; so go carefully, remembering that you may drive almost 4 miles if your transportation — and your nerve — holds out. If not, parking spots are available earlier, one of the first occurs after 1.9 miles, at the sixth S-bend, from which you have a fine view down the main valley of the Fraser.

If you do drive as far as the fork, your route to the objective lies to the left through the old gate, while the other continues north along the ridge for a long way. In any case, park here with one mile and 500 feet left to reach your goal, the summit of Mount Woodside, a little to the west of a cleared area with its B.C. Telephone repeater station and the garbage left by its builders.

At the start of your walk you are among trees, but soon you find yourself traversing a logged-over stretch, its only saving grace being the views that it affords across the Fraser Valley to Mount Cheam. As you rise, the route turns first north, then west, passing above a pretty little lake. Finally, you have the unkempt relay station, but fortunately you need not stop at it; a drop into a small dip on its west side followed by a short scramble brings you to an eminence overlooking Harrison River to the west, and giving an unexpected view northward to the lake. South of west the main Fraser Valley stretches off into the distance with the mountains along it vanishing into the haze that is Vancouver's unfortunate contribution to the atmospheric conditions of the lower mainland of British Columbia.

And what of Mount Agassiz? The fork leading to it goes on for several miles and the last stretch is trailless, so you will do quite well with its neighbour to the south, Mount Woodside. Actually, if you are an experienced walker and have had to leave your car low down on the mountain, there is a 2100-foot viewpoint a short distance off to the right of the road; badly overgrown, however, on its approach. To reach it, take the overgrown logging road right at about the 2.5 mile mark, that is, about ½-mile along the stretch above the sixth hairpin bend. This soon brings you out at the foot of a rock slide before a 100-foot high cliff. A faint trail rises gently east round this slide, and finally you are beyond it on a fairly easy route up to the knoll with a striking view of Mount Agassiz and across to the Rosedale-Agassiz road bridge and the peaks of the Cascade Mountains beyond. Remember, though, this is for experienced walkers only and masochists who enjoy bushwhacking.

Round trip 2 miles (3.2 km)
Allow 1.5 hours
High point 3000 feet (910 m)
Elevation gain 500 feet (152 m)
Gravel Road
Good May to October

Mount Cheam from Agassiz viewpoint

67   WHIPPOORWILL POINT

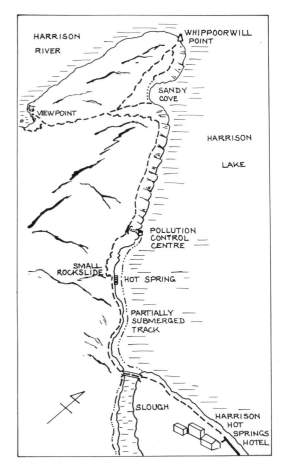

Next time you are at Harrison Hot Springs, take this short walk to put some space between the crowds and yourself. You may even find a swimsuit useful, for the route features a secluded beach, Sandy Cove, accessible only from this trail or by boat.

As a beginning, walk westwards along the esplanade fronting the beach and past the Hotel in the direction of the hot springs. Here, where the naturally hot water (83° C), smelling strongly of sulphur, is collected in a great steaming tank to be piped to the village, the trail — somewhat rough at its beginning because of a small washout — starts rising uphill. Do not descend to the track on the beach, it is partly submerged at high water and goes only as far as the Pollution Unit (Sewage Disposal) anyway.

The drop-off on your right is quite steep at first, though the trail is perfectly good and you are in no danger if you take a little care. At one point, in fact, where the route goes round a rock bluff, it runs on wooden staging, something like a small-scale replica of the old road in the Fraser Canyon. Finally, however, you level off over 100 feet above the surface of the lake and soon you find yourself walking into a valley, apparently away from the water.

Next comes the parting of the ways. If you go straight forward on the left-hand trail, you find yourself in a short time beside the Harrison River at an interesting spot but one that is a little short on space. The main route goes right, descending gently into the valley and finally emerging on a beautiful little beach, the Sandy Cove already mentioned. Here you may relax at leisure if you wish or proceed the further short distance to the point. To do so, walk along the beach to its western end and pick up the continuation of the trail as it runs into the trees, rising a little as it goes.

From the beach to the river outlet is only a few hundred yards, so you soon emerge from trees on to the picturesque rock point adorned with a beacon and triangular navigation markers, and providing you with striking lake and mountain views as you look northwards. Above Harrison Lake's eastern shore line is The Old Settler, a mountain more interestingly named

than many others. Further north is Mount Breakenridge with its surrounding glaciers, and away in the extreme distance is Cairn Needle, pointing skyward. West of the lake, logging has removed much of the mountain tree cover but in this instance economics may well advance a stronger claim than aesthetics in the face of so many compensating views.

Round trip 3 miles (5 km)
Allow 2 hours
Trail
Good most of the year

68   BARNSTON ISLAND

One of Shakespeare's characters claimed that he could "call spirits from the vasty deep"; well, so can the would-be visitor to Barnston Island. Merely by sounding a car horn, you may summon a ferry — the modern equivalent of a magic charm, if not so euphonious. In any event, this is how to reach the island, set in the Fraser River northwest of Langley.

To reach the sounding-off point from Highway 1, turn off on 178th Street North at Clover Valley Interchange located about 4.5 miles east of the Port Mann Bridge. After a mile, turn east on Hjorth Road, cross the C.N. Railway tracks, and drive to the ferry stage. Actually, you will not need your car on the island itself; so you may travel over as a foot-passenger on the free ferry.

On disembarking, turn right and follow the road past some nondescript farm buildings where river access is barred by NO TRESPASSING signs. Following this you proceed for some 30 minutes till you reach a swampy area in its wild state, an indication of what much of the island must have been like before dyking and draining. In turn, this gives way to a neater stretch of farmland and after another 20 minutes or so you come to a beach at the island's eastern extremity.

Here is a pleasant spot to rest and partake of refreshment before resuming your circumambulation, this time on the river bank. On the bank you may remain as you walk back along the island's north side, the muddy waters of the Fraser sliding silently by in almost sinister fashion on your right. There is one small break in this pattern to avoid a farm; otherwise, you remain by the river, enjoying the airy perfume of the cottonwoods if you undertake this walk in spring.

From the northwest corner back to the ferry, you are on the road again, this part of the island being settled right to the bank. It is just as well, however, that you do not need to watch your footing, for you are now facing directly to Mount Baker and you have Three Sisters on its right and the great peaks of the Cascades on the left, right round to the Lucky Four and the Mount Cheam Range.

Round trip 6 miles (9.6 km)
Allow 4 hours
Road and River-bank
Good all year

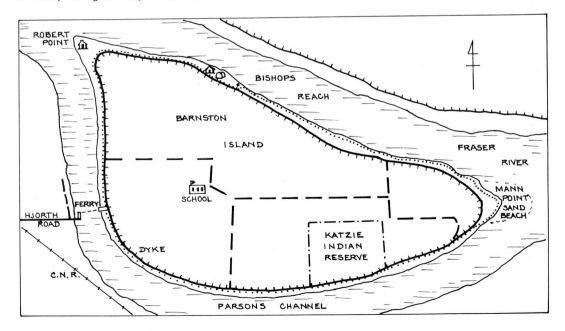

69 FORT LANGLEY

Those who leave their cars, enter the fort, visit its buildings, then depart are missing a number of interesting features that this national historic park has to offer. To get the full sense of what living in such a situation was like, you should look at the surroundings as well, since these, down to the river frontage, put the fort in its context: a once-important trading post on a high bank above the Fraser River from establishment of the original settlement in 1827 by the Hudson's Bay Company.

The approach from Highway 1 is simple, with direction signs pointing the shortest route from Carvolth Road Interchange. However, if you wish to get into the spirit of research, continue north on Carvolth Road instead of going right at the sign, and do not turn right till you come to Wilson Townline Road after about three-quarters of a mile. Go left on 208th Street and, finally, right on Allard Crescent, a thoroughfare that follows the bend of the river and leads to the cairn on its bank marking the site of the original fort, abandoned in 1839, nearly 3 miles downstream from the existing one.

Continue east from here, picking up Wilson Townline Road again, which gives access to Glover Road in the centre of Fort Langley Village. A left turn, a short drive along the main street, and a right turn bring you to the parking lot just by the park administration building.

As you look slightly right towards the fort, you see the upper entrance guarded by an ancient tree. Instead of going in immediately, however, continue to the right following the outside of the stockade. By doing so, you arrive on the top of a high bank from which you look up the river and over the level farmland below. Actually, you may go as far as the northeast corner, just below the reconstructed bastion, at which point the ground drops away so steeply as to bar further progress. Now retrace your steps and enter the fort.

To your right as you enter is the Big House, once the officers' quarters, now a museum; and don't forget the Southdown sheep in their little pen behind. Half left as you emerge is the refurbished workshop, an interesting old cart by its door. Thereafter, diagonally across the grounds stands the store, the one original structure left standing. Enter it to marvel for yourself at the great mass of nineteenth-century trade goods it carries. Last of all, the little bastion with its nine-pound cannon, which you have already seen from outside. These are all described in the excellent booklet issued by the federal parks branch and available in the Big House.

If you leave by the lower gate, you return to the parking lot close to the edge of the bank, with road and railway below you and between you and the river. Follow the path down the bank to a gate that takes you to the road, and you will see a footpath leading across the C.N. line to the river bank park. Looking downstream you see the bridge that carries the road to Albion Ferry across Bedford Reach; straight across, the little white church of the Indian Reservation on McMillan Island gleams in the sun. Now you may walk along the bank of what was once a harbour before the upper limit of navigation moved upstream in 1858, the year which, ironically, saw Fort Langley's brief moment of political glory

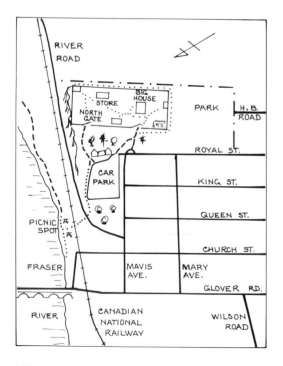

Fort from the river

when the colony of British Columbia was pro-claimed there.

Finally, since you are in an exploring mood, why not begin your return to the city by turning right on Glover Road, cross McMillan Island to Albion Ferry, and make for the Lougheed Highway? You will have an interesting round trip.

Round trip 1.5 miles or more (2.5 km)
Allow 2 hours at least
Grass or paths
Good all year

129

70 MATSQUI DYKE

If you wish, you may stretch this into a there-and-back trip of some 8 miles; there are, however, a number of intermediate points at which you may turn around when you feel that you have had enough exercise along this section of the Centennial Trail in the Abbotsford area.

To reach the western end of this walk, leave Highway 1 at Mount Lehman Road Interchange and drive north about three miles to Harris Road. Turn right, travel almost two miles to Glenmore Road where you go left and, after a few hundred yards, park at the end of the river dyke. As you look across the Fraser, you see Matsqui Island ahead of you, with Mission City on the opposite bank, the bell tower of its religious institution, Westminster Abbey, dominating the urban area.

Travel northeast at first along the dyke until after some fifteen minutes you arrive at the mouth of Matsqui Slough with its flood-control pumping station. From here you may use the road on the river bank as you head towards the new Abbotsford-Mission road bridge, which you reach after about an hour's walking. The bridge approach is, of course, above you as you walk beneath the span, but just beyond, you come on the old highway which used the C.P. rail bridge as a right-of-way.

If you continue beyond this point, your route may alternate between a track on the bank and on the roadway behind as the curve of the river causes you to change direction from northeast to southeast, and brings Sumas Mountain directly into view. Finally, four miles from your starting point, this dyke section ends at its intersection with Page Road, shortly after passing a small lake on your right.

Thus your outward journey ends and unless you have been able to organize two cars, one at either end, you have the same distance to return. Incidentally, if this suggests a portage, it will be entirely appropriate since *Matsqui* means "portage." The walking is not difficult, the dyke being virtually flat; it is nearly all in the open, however, and may be somewhat warm going on a summer's day.

Round trip 8 miles (12.8 km)
Allow 5 hours
Dyke and roadway
Good all year

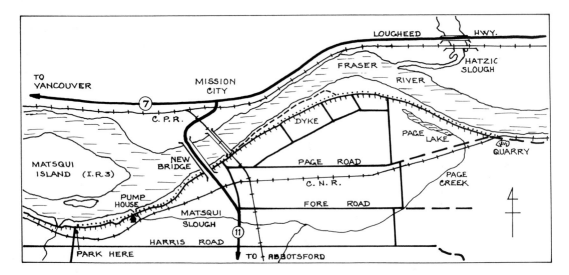

New road bridge at Mission City

71   SUMAS PEAK

For an easy ascent with all sorts of bonuses, try this mountain set in the middle of the Fraser Valley and known to everyone who drives eastward from Abbotsford along Highway 1. Not only do you start high, so reducing the amount of climbing you must do, but you also go through beautiful forest — except for one litter-strewn picnic area — and by Chadsey Lake, embowered in trees. Then you have the views from the summit over the whole lower valley, more or less, with a particularly grand sight of Mount Baker dominating the southern horizon.

From Highway 1, after travelling east from Abbotsford for 3.5 miles, turn left and drive north for about five miles on Sumas Mountain Road, passing Kilgard with its brick and tile ovens, then the small settlement of Straiton. Actually, part of the road is being reconstructed, the object being to remove some of the pleasant little bends, so the distance may be a little off;

you should, however, have no difficulty in spotting the sign, SUMAS MOUNTAIN PARK, pointing off to the right. This road switchbacks eastwards for more than 5 miles until, at a hairpin bend, you will see one wooden sign indicating a trail for Chadsey Lake, while another points upwards.

Since you are going to walk, not drive, to the peak, this is where you stop, pulling off the road and into the small parking area on the left. Do not be dismayed that the trail to the lake descends instead of climbing. Chadsey *is* below the level where you parked and you will have plenty of opportunity to regain height later. After a walk through stately forest, you reach the picturesque little body of water and come on a Parks Branch sign pointing the way and announcing that Sumas Peak is 1.5 hours away, a liberal estimate.

Follow the trail round the south side of the lake to its southeastern corner; only then does it start to rise. From this point, though, it climbs steadily in a number of wide S-bends on a

Mount Baker from Sumas Peak

reasonably gentle gradient. Still you are among trees and as this is a north-facing slope, snow lingers till well on in May, so be prepared for it or save this outing till June when there should be no difficulty in following the route. Finally, 800 feet above the lake, the trees thin out, you break into the open — and there are your views: a panorama of mountain and valley.

Over to your right on the other peak is a microwave relay tower, with a rough road leading to it. Follow a trail across towards it and join the road for your return journey. Stay on it as it turns west, then north, and it is only a short distance to your car.

Round trip 3.25 miles (5 km)
Allow 3 hours
High point 2,950 feet (900 m)
Elevation gain 800 feet (240 m)
Forest paths and dirt road
Good May to November

72   CHADSEY LAKE

In 1967 and again in 1971, the Canadian Youth Hostel Association celebrated Centennials, Canada's and B.C.'s, by constructing a trail east from Vancouver up the Fraser Valley and into the interior of the province. Some parts of this route you would traverse only if you wished to cover the whole of it, but other stretches are self-contained walks in their own right. Such a one runs from near the north end of the road over Sumas Mountain to Chadsey Lake, with interesting creek crossings and stately trees along the way; look for (but leave!) the trillium if you come this way in May.

Of the two possible approach roads, the Sumas Mountain highway is the more direct. So, from Highway 1, some 3.5 miles east of Abbotsford, drive north almost 6 miles, passing the Sumas Mountain Park signs about a mile before your stopping place. This comes after you have descended some way towards the Fraser at a point where the road bends westwards just as a narrow dirt lane joins it from the right. A little above the junction, limited parking is available on a wide shoulder from which you should be able to see one of the 1971 Centennial Trail markers.

Follow this dirt road to the right (Smith Road, though you would not know it without a map) as it curves towards a creek crossing, using an elderly wooden bridge that consists of two planks laid parallel on ties, more easily negotiated on foot than in a wheeled vehicle. Very shortly after, the road turns off right while your marked trail goes straight ahead along a little ridge and then, in a series of steep zig-zags, descends to another creek. This time you make the best of your way across on whatever stepping stones are handy before climbing out of the gully on its other side.

From now on your route rises steadily, picking up an overgrown logging road, turning right, and following it for about three-quarters of a mile, crossing over your creek again some 900 feet higher than you did originally. Next comes a relatively flat stretch, but soon you experience an abrupt change of direction; ninety degrees left, and uphill once more. You will note also that the markers are now those of the '67 trail,

the explanation being that the original route was cut off by private development so that what you have been on to this point is the '71 rerouting, actually an improvement in many ways over its predecessor, being more scenic and more challenging.

The path now rises in a series of easy switchbacks, re-enters the valley of the creek, and contours into it before crossing yet again the friendly little waterway. Your next point of interest is a bluff with fine views to the north and up-river; then follows a stretch on quite a steep sidehill, with something of a drop-off as you head into another valley and encounter a fast-flowing mountain stream complete with small rapids. After you traverse this creek, a few more minutes gives you the sight of water glinting between the trees; your objective, Chadsey Lake, is attractive at all seasons with

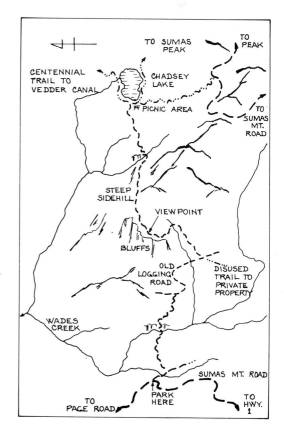

its surround of trees but particularly appealing in fall with its beds of water lilies.

For your return walk, take care to follow the correct line of markers from the lake. The Centennial Trail itself continues eastwards, emerging near the mouth of the Sumas River, miles from your starting point unless you have arranged for someone to meet you there. Your route is the left-hand one as you leave the Provincial Parks Branch picnic site on the lake's northwest corner. Once turned in the correct direction, you should have no trouble in following the route back to your transport, arriving well breathed and exercised.

You may even make your drive back a circular one by continuing to descend the hill, crossing the C.N. tracks, and going westward on Page Road to its junction with Highway 11 just south of Mission Bridge. From here, Highway 1 lies to the south, and Highway 7 is on the north bank of the Fraser.

Round trip 6 miles (9.6 km)
Allow 5 hours
High point 2,200 feet (680 m)
Elevation gain 1,700 feet (520 m)
Trail
Good May to October

73 VEDDER MOUNTAIN

Here is one of those accommodating walks that is capable of expansion or contraction as you please, both with respect to distance to be covered and elevation to be gained. For purists who have to do things the hard way there is the trail beginning just above Cultus Lake, involving a vertical gain of nearly 3,000 feet and some 11 miles of walking. Lesser mortals seeking exercise may drive to 1,300 feet and join the trail at that level, cutting the distance to less than 8 miles. Those who unashamedly prefer to take the easy way may proceed by car for nearly another mile and take off from the 2,000 foot level, with the prospect of a nice civilized outing of less than 7 miles and with only a thousand feet of climbing left.

You approach the trail via a gravel road that turns right off the main Chilliwack-Cultus Lake highway, just at the Forest Ranger Station about 2 miles south of the bridge over the Chilliwack River at Vedder Crossing. As you head on to this road you see the trail pointer on your left just north of the forest station office, so you should have no difficulty. Drive it for a little less than a half mile to the point where it forks at a sign for a Canadian Armed Forces establishment, with one branch going straight on while the other, a

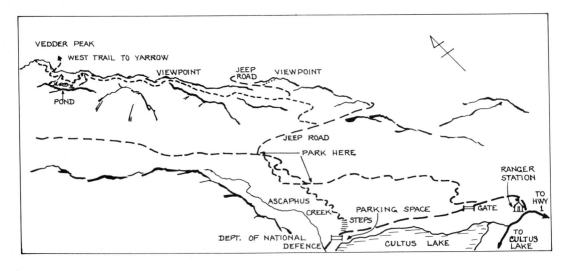

little narrower but still perfectly good, rises to the right.

At the fork, purists will drive straight along the military road (providing the gate is open), dropping to just above the lake a little over a mile from the fork. Here, at a parking lot just before a second gate, the long trail goes off uphill to the right in a series of steps. All others take the right fork uphill, the road rising in a series of S-bends though not steeply enough to pose any problems for drivers. At 1.3 miles beyond the fork, where there is a small quarry on the right for parking, a sign on the left of the road points to the trail, here at the 1,300 foot level. Those of you who start from this point will find that your route first contours for a short distance on an old logging road before rising steadily in thick bush till it intersects the road again at 2000 feet.

If you have driven the extra 0.8 mile to this last point, you will see the Vedder Peak sign pointing right up a rough narrow road, with the down trail dropping off in the bush to the left. Follow this old road for just under a half mile to where another trail marker points you left on a very overgrown track. This route soon turns right again, heading uphill in the midst of pleasant open forest and, since it has now acquired distance markers for each half mile, you may tell how far you have progressed along it. Near the one-mile marker, a pointer indicates the first viewpoint — a not particularly rewarding one along the Vedder Canal and over the rich lowlands of what was once Sumas Lake.

Instead of leaving the trail here, you would do better to continue along it since you get the same view a little further on without leaving your route at all. As you proceed you realize why this is called Ridge Trail for the track takes you along in a series of undulations towards the rocky knoll, your objective, that you see occasionally from viewpoints along the way. The path runs mainly in small timber but in June it has many yellow violets along it; and here and there, a number of beautiful trillium, a remarkable proportion being twins.

The further you proceed, the more the different vistas open out around you. Above International Ridge to your left looms Mount Baker with its lesser satellites around it. On your right you have the Fraser with the Harrison

River joining it, while a little further west, Sumas Mountain fills the centre of the scene. Now, however, you undergo your final trial before the scramble to the summit. Your trail drops steeply down to a little lake, well furnished with lily pads and some marshy ground, before it turns back in a draw to regain the height you lost.

Here, just before the final rise, you come to the junction with West Trail, one that comes up from the Yarrow side, and now you may have to use your hands on the final few yards. The reward, however, is worth the effort; you now enjoy without interruption all the views that you had in part up to now. And as you sit and feast your eyes on the panorama, you have as counter-attraction the entertainment provided by those cheery panhandlers, the whisky-jacks. One other item is less pleasing: trailbikes are messing up the route, gouging great ruts in it. That nuisance apart, this walk is a pleasant diversion for the visitor to Cultus Lake; remember, you can get away with only 1000 feet of climbing!

Round trip 7 miles (11.2 km)
High point 3,000 feet (910 m)
Allow 4 hours
Good April to October

Lily pond near the summit

74   TEAPOT HILL

When does one walk become two? When you can reach the same destination from entirely different starting points — either of which gives a satisfactory outing in its own right — though the two may be combined by adroit manipulation of transport. Such is the case with Teapot Hill, the 1000-foot-high bump located just to the east of Cultus Lake near its southwest end, and situated in the provincial park of the same name some 7 miles from Chilliwack.

The first approach, entirely within the park boundaries, goes off to the left 1.6 miles beyond Lakeside Lodge as you drive south along Columbia Valley Highway. Here an old logging road (Road 918), a barrier at its beginning blocking off vehicle traffic, leads uphill from a spot where there is parking space by the lake for several cars. The route rises steadily but on a fairly gentle grade, close to a creek at first but later in mixed forest, dense here and there, with the lush growth of fern and moss indicating a plentiful rainfall. After a half mile, a horse trail comes in from the left; then, in another ten minutes, the Parks Branch sign for the footpath to Teapot Hill appears on the right, a large garbage can beside it so that you may dispose of discards on your return trip from the top.

This path, well graded and easily ascended except for one series of steep steps, soon brings you on to the summit ridge along which you walk to its south end, where the slope drops right off and wire cables mark the viewpoint. From here, you see in one direction the western end of the lake with the long ridge of Vedder Mountain rising behind it. Looking southwards, your eye follows the line of Columbia Valley as it disappears into the blue south of the U.S. border, the line of International Ridge on its left.

Your return is by the same route, but before you leave the summit note a narrow trail from the east with a sign announcing that you use it at your own risk. This is the end of the other approach, a somewhat more sporting proposition than the one just described which is so good that it tends to lack challenge.

For this second route, continue on Columbia Valley Highway for 3.4 miles beyond the lodge to a left fork on Frost Road at the sign for the Columbia Bible Camp. This road rises to the bench level and heads towards International Ridge, finally splitting at a T-junction where you go left on Watt Road. Very soon you come to the entrance to the Bible Camp, so drive carefully round the sports field to the parking lot by the buildings and let the camp manager know that you are making for Teapot Hill. The trail

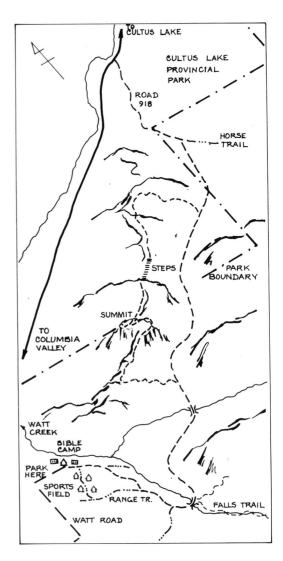

begins at the camp's northeast corner, looking uphill among tall trees on the south side of Watt Creek.

After 400 yards, follow the Watt Ridge Trail sign right but continue straight ahead at the next junction where Range Trail goes off to the right. Next, take the left fork down towards the creek, actually the other end of Road 918. This road crosses the water to its north side, but here you are faced not with two possible routes, but three. Of these, the right hand one going up the creek may be speedily discarded. It does lead in a short distance to picturesque rapids and falls but at time of high water it is likely to be submerged and its crossing impassable.

Of the other two roads, yours is the one on the left. This follows the creek a short way downstream, then gradually turns to the right away from it. Ignore one left fork, cross another creek — note the barrier marking the park boundary — and, where a tree on the left has the numeral 7 incised in its trunk, look for a narrow trail going off left. This is the other end of the trail which, at the top of the hill, you are told that you use at your own risk. It *is* steep, but in June it is adorned with honeysuckle and tiny starflowers and really the only difficulty is a small washout near the summit.

If you do not like the sound of this, you simply stay on the road for another half mile and go up on the Parks Branch trail when you come to it, returning the same way.

Round trip (route 1) 2 miles (3.2 km)
Allow 1 hour
High point 1000 feet (300 m)
Elevation gain 700 feet (220 m)

(route 2) 3 miles (4.8 km)
Allow 2 hours
Elevation gain 400 feet (120 m)
Good much of the year

75   ELK MOUNTAIN MEADOWS

Even if you feel that the summit of Elk Mountain (4,700 feet) is beyond you, there is no reason why you should not be able to get above the trees on its approach ridge so as to enjoy the views, south over the Chilliwack River to the Border Peaks and west along the Fraser. And you have the flowers as well, these meadow optimists that grow so lavishly during their short season once the snow has gone. If these are not inducements enough, perhaps mention of wild strawberries will tempt you; they grow in profusion during August, a well-nigh irresistible temptation to even dedicated ridge walkers.

The approach to this garden of delights is a trifle complicated, perhaps as a test of your perseverance, but the drive is a pleasant one as it wanders through the upland country between

Big leaf maple (Acer macrophyllum)

the main valley and the Chilliwack River. From Highway 1 going east, turn right on Prest Road, a short distance beyond the railway crossing; then, after 2.5 miles go left on Bailey. Where it forks 0.3 mile along, follow Elk View Road right and uphill in a series of roller-coasting switchbacks. Stay left where Ryder Lake Road branches off, pass the community hall and public park and continue uphill on the gravel road from the end of blacktop. As you rise, ignore all roads leading off until you go right at the final fork, following the sign for Sky High Ranch. Finally, about 7.5 miles from the beginning of Elk View, your odyssey comes to an end at a small quarry on the left where you leave your car.

At this point, you are at 2,000 feet as you set off on the trail, clearly marked with aluminum squares, which rises just behind the quarry, heading left. Your start is among trees which provide welcome shade on a hot day as first of all you go north to approach the prominent ridge that you saw towering above the trees on the last part of your approach road. When you do finally reach it, at 2,700 feet, you turn east and set your face heavenward while you ascend, steadily but not too steeply, with open slopes on your right and trees to the left until, as you progress, you come into the sub-alpine meadow country.

From now on you should be revelling in the midst of flowers or stuffing yourself with strawberries so it matters little if you do not reach the summit. It is only the first one on a ridge anyway: thus, all you see ahead from it is the next crest, Mount Thurston, some two miles further ahead and 600 feet higher. In fact, this is a walk on which it is better to travel hopefully than to arrive, so your destination can simply be whatever point you happen to be at when you decide to return.

Just one final caution: these meadows are fragile and already are showing signs of wear and tear. Please leave them for others to enjoy by causing as little disturbance to plant life as you can.

Round trip up to 9 miles (14.4 km)
Allow all day
Trail
Best July to September

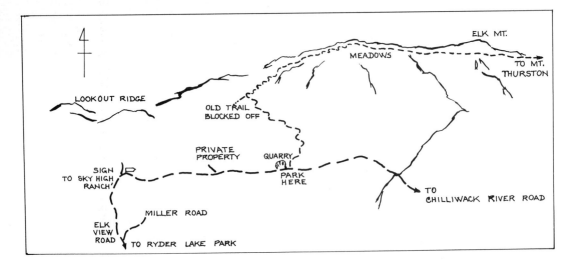

Liumchen Ridge from Elk Mountain

76 McNULTY FALLS (CHEAM TRAIL)

The unwary climber who is misled by the sign at the highway and sets out for Mount Cheam by this route is going to be disappointed. The way to that mountain lies 3 miles back at Popkum, and this trail peters out far below the summit with no obvious means of approach. On the other hand, it does provide a variety of spectacular mountain and valley views for a moderate expenditure of effort as it zig-zags up a ridge to a fine lookout point at the 2100 foot level, a satisfactory destination.

The trail takes off from the south side of Highway 1 three miles east of Popkum with its gas stations and cafes. A little before you come to it, a warning sign,"Mt. Cheam Trail," indicates its existence, its beginning being an old road on the right as you drive east. You may either park here just off the highway or drive in a little way, turning right on a good dirt road after 100 yards, then proceeding for another 300 to a spot just before a creek. From here the trail goes off upwards through a lush growth of thimbleberry, rising quite steeply to a campsite, which you reach in about 20 minutes.

From here, continue right, ignoring a path to the left, and start zig-zagging up the spine of the ridge. As you proceed, note how the vegetation quickly thins out, indicating the increasing poverty of the soil caused by its inability to retain moisture which, seeping down to lower levels, accounts for the luxuriance there. On your way up, you will be glad to stop for a breather from time to time and, by choosing your spot carefully, you may combine these pauses with glimpses of the Fraser Valley.

At 1200 feet you will want a longer halt, however. Here the trail swings back to the west and, from a high commanding rock spur, you have your first real view of the falls, a striking sight particularly at high water. Those of you who wish to proceed further will find that the trail continues to rise steeply in a series of dog-legs for another 900 vertical feet to the lookout, from which the whole valley to the west, including the confluence of the Fraser and the Harrison, is spread out before you.

The lookout point will be the destination for all but those intrepid souls who must follow every trail to its ending. If you belong to this latter category, you will find little change from what you have already experienced. The views of the valley open out, you get a glimpse of Harrison Lake, then at 3,300 feet you reach the foot of a rock-slide. From this point, the route continues seemingly ever upwards, not to end till it has reached 5,500 feet, above which towers the great eastern ridge of Cheam, an awe-inspiring sight. It should be pointed out that snow stays late on the upper part of the trail, even into late June and July. Particularly is this true of the gullies; traverse of these may give some difficulty.

Even those of you who do not go high can see the effect of winter avalanches on the steep slopes in the scars on the hill face. Some of the scars, however, have a human cause: cutting corners on the trail is causing severe erosion in several sections below the 2,100 foot level. Please

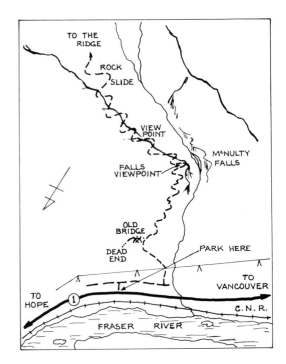

do not aid and abet this destruction; all people show by leaving the made route is thoughtlessness, not boldness.

Round trip to 2100 feet (640 m)
    4 miles (6.4 km)
Allow 3 hours
Trail
Good June to October

77 LINDEMAN LAKE

This reasonably short walk takes you up to one of the most beautiful lakes in the Chilliwack Valley region, that stretch of country which is now so popular for boating and fishing despite its distance from main centres of population. Actually, both the Provincial Parks Branch and B.C. Forest Service now have campsites conveniently located for this and other outings near Chilliwack Lake, the new Provincial Park being at the northwest end of that fine body of water where the Chilliwack River emerges from it as a broad, fast flowing stream. The Forest Service goes one better, having a small camping area right at the trail's beginning.

Going east on Highway 1, turn south at the Chilliwack-Sardis intersection and continue past the Armed Forces base to the Chilliwack River at Vedder Crossing. At the bridge go left on the road to Chilliwack Lake. This road crosses Post Creek 24 miles in from the bridge, but the best parking for this hike is actually reached by going north 0.3 mile before this point where a road leads you into the Forest Service parking lot by the creek and about 400 yards upstream of the main road. Just on the east side of the bridge, the trail goes off upstream with the creek hurrying along on your left as you ascend. Actually this is part of the Centennial Trail but you would not know it, so active have the vandals been in removing signs; fortunately, the route is well-trodden and clear so you should have no difficulty.

After some 20 minutes, you cross to the east bank, using a partly flattened log as a bridge. (Note: another log, a little downstream, is also used but the approach to the higher one is better.) Now you climb steadily, the creek seeming to mock you as you toil upwards, a warm business on a sunny day, even if the pleasantly treed route does offer shade. This uphill pull continues for another 15 minutes before you find the grade easing off, while the creek's impetuous rush changes to a gentle gliding motion. As you advance, you see great rocks that have tumbled from steep slopes, perhaps helping to dam up the valley and create

the lake which is your objective.

Finally, you emerge from trees and there it is in front of you, confined in its narrow trough with craggy pinnacles rising from the ridge on the east, while the side you are on culminates in another ridge, invisible somewhere above you. Almost any spot along the banks will do for rest and rumination — plus a little fishing if your taste lies that way. As you look north along the steep slopes just above the water, you see the line of the Centennial trail continuing, en route

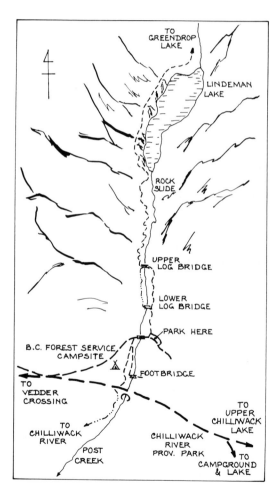

to Greendrop Lake and, eventually, to the Skagit Valley. You who are satisfied with this modest achievement, however, have the comfort of knowing that Lindeman is the more attractive of the two; in fact, it ranks high in any list of beautiful mountain lakes.

Round trip 2.5 miles (4 km)
Allow 2 hours
High point 2700 feet (820 m)
Elevation gain 700 feet (260 m)
Best June to October

Log jam on Lindeman Lake

78   LOWER POST CREEK

Like the hike to Lindeman Lake, this outing starts where the B.C. Centennial Trail crosses the Chilliwack Valley Road 24 miles east of Vedder Crossing and about a half mile west of the entrance to the newly developed Provincial Park at the outlet end of Chilliwack Lake. This time, though, instead of heading upstream on Post Creek, you go to the south side of the road and, almost directly opposite the lay-by at the trail sign into the Forest Service camp site, find the trail's beginning a little way down the bank a short distance west of the creek.

Though your route, identified by Centennial Trail markers, parallels the course of the stream, you are sufficiently far from it on most of your walk to be able to give your attention to the forest through which you pass. The forest has quite large Douglas firs and spindly lodgepole pine, the dense clumps of the latter contrasting with the relative isolation of the former. The density of the lodgepoles suggests that these are survivors of the forest fires that have favoured this tree with its fire-resistant cones, which open to deposit seeds after a conflagration, a striking instance of adaptability. Ground level, too, has its attractions with the bunchberry flower in June carpeting either side of the path.

After a little more than a mile, you turn back left to the creek and cross it on a somewhat ramshackle footbridge, minus handrails, one that may involve a little manoeuvring if any member of your group needs assistance during periods of high water. Thereafter, you stay on the left (east) bank for a short distance till you emerge on a logging road. Here you will see a Centennial Trail sign facing you on its opposite side; however, you do better to go left for a few yards on the road for, by so doing, you come to a wide bridge across the main river. The old trail crossed it a short distance downstream on what now looks like an extremely unsafe log, passage by which is not recommended except for those who wish to show off their prowess as tightrope walkers.

The open spot by the river is pleasant for lazing on a warm day. If you wish a viewpoint for your destination, however, look towards the rockfall south of the river and just to the right of the bridge crossing. Here you will see the trail angling up the rockfall towards the left. It is easy to explain why it seems to be heading in the wrong direction: a rock bluff dropping sheer into the river prevents direct access to its south bank; hence the route must rise 180 feet and go over the top of the obstacle. By following this path up for a short distance, you come on an open rock platform just left of the trail with an outlook southeast towards the lake, giving views of the mountains, particularly to the east where Paleface Peak (6300 feet) lords it over the landscape. Coming back down, too, you look across the wide main valley to the narrow cleft of Post Creek where it emerges from below the eastern slopes of Williams Peak (6985 feet).

If you do follow the Centennial Trail west from here, you start by losing a good part of the height you made to get over the bluff, and there-

Nurse tree over the creek

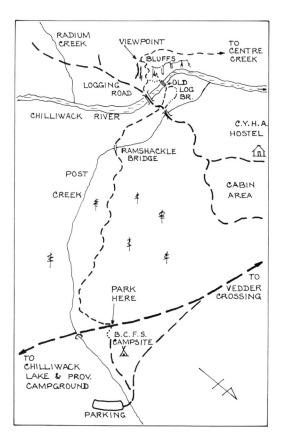

after you follow the river downstream on its south side, not to recross it for several miles. Perhaps, therefore, you are best to content yourself with your viewpoint, a rest by the river, and a return to the main road.

Round trip 2 miles (3.2 km) or more
Allow 2 hours
High point 2100 feet (640 m)
Elevation loss 150 feet (46 m)
B.C. Centennial Trail
Good May to October

79   UPPER CHILLIWACK RIVER

This is a walk for the venturesome camper-hiker, involving as it does a drive along the whole length of Chilliwack Lake (open weekends and holidays only) where the beauty of the scenery is, unfortunately, not matched by the quality of the road. This is single-track for a good part of the way and pot-holey for most of its 8 miles, especially the last two from Depot Creek. At the road's far end, Victoria Bridge spans the upper river where it enters the lake, and it is from near the east side of this structure that you begin your walk upstream.

Work your way along the muddy bank southeast for about 100 yards towards the trees. As you approach this grove, you should see the marker indicating the actual trail beginning, and

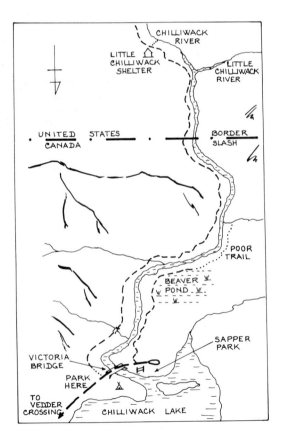

from here on you should have little trouble despite the occasional open stretch where the lush vegetation does its best to overgrow the path. On tree-shaded sections no such difficulty exists, and the trees along this trail are worth mention; giant cedars, many clad in moss, leave you awed by their majesty, and also saddened by the casualties among them, their roots undermined by the river in its periods of high water. But the trees have other enemies that take their toll: beaver. Here and there you will come on trunks gnawed by these industrious engineers, even though they cannot rival man for destructiveness.

Thus you progress, crossing sloughs on footbridges or over logs, occasionally working your way along the river bank itself, then traversing a beaver swamp. On your way, keep an eye out for a long cleared line on either side of the valley; it is the International Boundary, but you would hardly know it, except that the trail is a little better on the American side. Actually, your foray into the U.S.A. is going to be a very minor one, a mere half mile or so to a primitive trail shelter, Chilliwack Hut. This makes a satisfying destination with large stumps to sit on and a convenient watering place down at the stream.

Now that you know the country a little, you may look about you on your way back, marvelling at the prolific growth of shrubs and flowers: bunchberry and salmonberry, foam flower and false solomon's seal, plus some exceedingly healthy looking devil's club. The open stretches of trail by the river bank give glimpses of high peaks like Mount Lindeman (7578 feet), bare rock on its exposed slopes with even a small glacier in a sheltered section. But the river itself remains the chief attraction: now wave-capped and impetuous, now clear and placid as it flows north towards its lake, a journey which ends after it passes beneath the bridge by which you started.

This bridge itself — or a predecessor — plus the surrounding area is interesting historically; here in 1860, the Royal Engineers established a base while surveying the 49th parallel for the boundary between Canada and the U.S.A. For this reason, the south end of the lake has been set aside as Sapper Park in commemoration of that example of long-ago international cooperation. Since you are on the spot, then, cross to the west side of the river and look at the unusual memorial with its commemorative tablet. While you are at it, you may even walk a short distance upstream on this bank, for an overgrown trail starting almost opposite the monument takes you to a beaver pond. Don't tarry too long, though, remember the road you have to drive back on.

Round trip 4.5 miles (7.2 km)
Allow 3 hours
Good mid-July to September

Chilliwack Lake from south

80 SWANEE CREEK FALLS

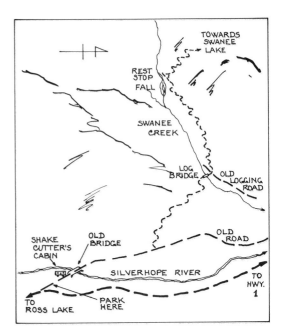

If you feel that the 2900 foot climb to Eaton Lake is beyond your powers, try this sporting walk instead; not only does it have a clear trail, recently put in by the Attorney-General's Department, its vertical rise is only some 900 feet, and the falls themselves are completely unspoiled.

Though Swanee Creek flows — rushes would be a better word — into Silverhope Creek almost opposite the mouth of Eaton Creek, the trail approach is fully a mile south of the Forest Service sign for the turnoff to Eaton Lake, and 11.5 miles south of Highway 1 on the Silver-Skagit road which leaves it two miles west of Hope. Here a sharp turn right takes you on to an old road with a bridge over the main creek a short distance along it. DO NOT DRIVE ACROSS. The bridge is in a poor state of repair.

Crossing the creek

While you are at it, leave the road clear by drawing well to the side.

Actually, you are only going to stay with this old track for a quarter mile, at which point the trail goes off left, plunging into the bush and angling a little uphill amid tall trees until you become aware of Swanee Creek ahead of you. You realize that you must cross it by a squared-off log, involving a little bit of a balancing act. Just beyond, you cross an old logging road that comes up to the creek, then you start rising quite steeply until you are high above the racing water.

Now your grade eases off; soon you see white water on your left marking the falls, and finally you come out on its bank just above them. This is your destination. The trail does go higher but it does not approach the creek again, staying in the forest instead and, in its present unfinished state, it does not give access to Swanee Lake.

Round trip 2.5 miles (4 km)
Allow 2 hours
High point 2400 feet (725 m)
Good June to October

81   HICKS CREEK

This walk may be as short or as long as you wish since its route lies in a fairly shallow valley that rises at its divide to just over 3700 feet before dropping over to the Chilliwack River side. In fact, it is used by the Centennial Trail to get from the one major river system to the other; but this involves a walk of 11 miles one way, so something a little less strenuous will do if you are visiting the Silver-Skagit valley. The creek does have one or two pleasant spots for picnics, fishing, or just lazing around without the necessity of any elaborate organization.

Vehicle approach, like that for Swanee Creek, is via the gravel Silver-Skagit road, 15.2 miles in from Highway 1 and some 10 miles south of the campground at Silver Lake. Here an old logging road goes off westwards, its end adorned with Forest Service litter barrels. A Centennial Trail sign provides another marker — that is, if it has not been torn down by vandals. You may, if you wish, drive a short distance along the track but the surface is not the best, turnarounds are few, and the distance you save is negligible. In any case, whatever you do, follow the old track past the point where the

Hicks Creek

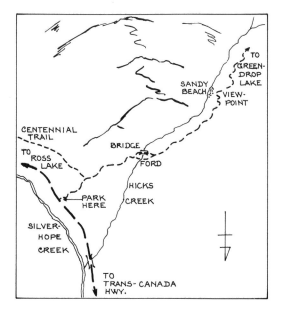

Centennial Trail to Ross Lake goes off left and continue towards the creek with its little wilderness campsite, complete with Forest Service outhouse.

Your first concern is how to get across, the obvious means being to ford; a little searching, however, discloses the existence of an old bridge a few yards upstream, enabling you to avoid wet feet. On the north bank, continue upstream through bush and across the foot of a large sandbank before coming back to the creek at a pleasant open gravel bar where you may settle down to do whatever pleases you. Here, then, is a suitable destination. If you do go further, stay with the trail; there's a lot of country to get lost in.

Round trip 1.5 miles (2. 4 km)
Allow 1 hour or more
High point 2100 feet (640 m)
Elevation gain 200 feet (60 m)
Good May to October

83 RHODODENDRON TRAIL (SKAGIT RIVER)

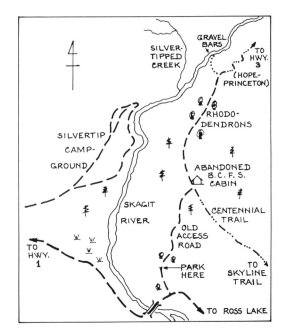

If during the latter part of June you are staying in the new Silvertip Campground, just west of where the road to Ross Lake crosses the Skagit River, you should not miss the chance to enjoy the flowering of the red rhododendrons. These plants are not often seen in B.C. except under cultivation, though C.P. Lyons does record their appearance along a two-mile stretch of the Hope-Princeton Highway some seven miles north of here. For this display, however, you have to walk, because the bushes are over two miles from the Silver-Skagit Road. An additional source of interest connected with this trail is its historic significance; it is, in fact, part of an old route to the interior, the Whatcom Trail, created in 1858 for immigrants to use in order to avoid the tax imposed by Governor Douglas on immigrants arriving via the Fraser River.

From the campground (some 27 miles from Highway 1), cross the river and drive 0.1 mile to where a trail sign on your left indicates access to both the Centennial Trail and the one to the Hope-Princeton Highway. You may drive in on the old road a short distance, if only to get clear of the highway and its dust. After about a mile this track comes to an abandoned Forest Service cabin; just before it, the foot-trail goes at right angles to your line of travel. Before you turn off on the left-hand branch, note the Centennial Trail marker to the right, for that path uses the old trail southwards.

But you are heading back towards the river where it emerges from its deep valley. You begin by wandering gently along on virtually flat terrain amid lodgepole pine that gradually changes to more luxuriant growth as you descend from one old terrace to another. Then, at about the two-mile mark, you find yourself among the rhododendrons, a display that continues almost to the point where the trail starts to rise. Since you are not heading for the Hope-Princeton Highway, this is probably far enough, especially as a very short detour left brings you out above the river close to a large gravel bank, though its actual state depends on the amount of runoff water.

Here you may fish, sprawl, or contemplate the glacier high on the northeast side of Silvertip Mountain while remaining always conscious of the Skagit hurrying by as though anxious to reach Ross Lake; it is a spot you won't want to hurry away from.

Round trip 4 miles (6.4 km)
Allow 2 hours
High point 2000 feet (610 m)
Elevation gain small
Best in June

83   SKYLINE TRAIL

Once again, this is a sampling, the full cross-over being far beyond the scope of the person looking for a short outing. Actually, this walk is part of the Centennial Trail as well, the route by which it leaves the Skagit for Manning Park, rising to over 5000 feet in the process.

From the Silver-Skagit Road, 35 miles from Highway 1 and about 3 miles north of where Ross Lake ends at present, the trail goes in on the left, its entrance signposted. Presumably, if the scheme for raising the lake level goes ahead, this important recreational amenity will have to be re-routed, with a possible change of distance. Note that parking is limited at the trail end; all you can do is to get as far off the travelled portion of the road as possible. Once afoot, you strike into open forest, the trees small but the route giving pleasant walking with shelter from the sun and the chance to see the occasional deer.

Less than a quarter mile in, the Centennial Trail from Hicks Creek comes in from the left, and shortly thereafter you cross a small creek — your last water for two miles. After leaving it you rise on a series of gravel benches heading east and south until, at 2400 feet and a mile from your start, you come to two or three clearings that give you views over Ross Lake and the mountains surrounding it, with perhaps a glimpse of Mount Hozameen to the left.

This you may make your destination if you wish, especially if you have been enjoying the numerous interesting flowers and shrubs en route: lupin, queen cup, twin flowers, pipsissewa, bunchberry, and vetch, to name a few.

If you do go further, your next viewpoint is a mile further on and 800 feet higher, by which time you are entering the valley of a second creek, towards which the trail descends as a prelude to crossing it. From here your view is of Mount Hozameen pointing heavenward, an unforgettable sight. This too may be a destination or you may go the extra half mile for the sake of water.

Round trip 2 miles (3.2 km), or more
Allow 2 hours at least
High point (at Hozameen viewpoint) 3200 feet (980 m)
Elevation gain 1300 feet (360 m)
Good June to October

Rhododendron in seed

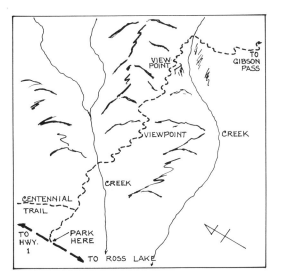

Booming grounds

84   BRISTOL ISLAND

This interesting short beach walk along the south bank of the Fraser is feasible except when the river is high during the run-off season in early summer. The return, along a quiet country road, is particularly appealing in May when the trees round the small houses and riding stables are snow white with blossom.

Leave Highway 1 at the Hope Airport sign on Yale Road almost directly opposite the Silver Skagit Road indicator. Continue north to the C.N.R. crossing, staying right at the fork just before it and following the sign for Hope Riding Ring. Drive 0.2 mile beyond the railway, pass one track going left, then one going right before you park at the second right fork just short of the causeway that links the "island" to the mainland.

From here, drop down to the river beach east of the road and turn north towards the river over alternating sand and pebble beaches. As you proceed along the shoreline, you are aware of the horse riding trail on the sand, just below, or at the vegetation line. You may see Pebble Beach right across the water, with Devil's Hump (900 feet) behind it and the scars made by the C.P.R. track and Highway 7 on the steep slope to the left.

About two-thirds of the way along, you must negotiate one tricky little stretch where space is lacking between the bank with its rounded stones and the dense vegetation; all you can do here is to scramble for a few yards till the beach opens out again towards the island's western point. Here you come upon a small log-towing operation, one which uses the still water between the island and the river-bank for booming its timber before its transportation to downstream sawmills, and this is where you leave the beach for your return by road.

Just before the dock, climb the bank to a dirt road and go left along it enjoying the pleasant rustic scene with its trees, its fields, and paddocks, the home of numerous riding horses. Then you have bush on your left for a short distance till the road bends south and you cross the causeway back to your waiting car.

Round trip 1.75 miles (3 km)
Allow 1 hour
Beach and dirt road
Good except at high water

85   PEBBLE BEACH

If you wish, combine this walk along the north bank of the Fraser River with a search for agates, or even a little panning for gold on one of the sandy stretches. Whatever your activity, though, you should enjoy this outing on clean white pebbles and fine river sand, surrounded as you are by high mountains in a delightfully romantic setting.

After driving on Highway 1 north along the river front at Hope, cross the Fraser and 0.1 mile beyond the bridge, turn sharp left at a sign reading NO THRU ROAD. This route leads downhill past some new homes as well as old cabins, crosses a disused railway grade, and forks a little more than half a mile from the highway. Take the left fork on the dirt road and park just beyond, where a wide stretch of stream bed, dry much of the time, separates you from Croft "Island" (Private).

Follow the track down the right side to the great pebble beds fronting the river. Across its waters you are looking towards the entrance of Silverhope Valley, guarded by towering sentinel peaks; westwards and downstream are the spurs

of other ranges receding from sight as the lowlands open out. To your right front are the main C.P.R. tracks and the new highway; as you work your way round, you pick up the old railway embankment a little lower than its successor with a track down from it to the beach.

The further west you go, the more you find yourself being forced towards the north bank by the curve of the river, and at last your onward progress is barred by the mouth of a creek. To vary your return, work your way on to the disused railway embankment and proceed east along it, the slope of Devil's Hump on your left. Now you view the river through a screen of trees with, downstream, the natural-gas pipeline span. Soon you have houses below you on your right and, finally, where road and railbed come close together, you leave your friendly bank for the short road walk back to your car.

Round trip 2 miles (3.2 km)
Allow 2 hours
River beach and railbed
Good except during high water

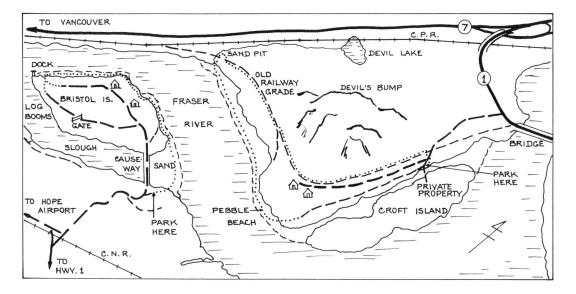

86 THACKER MOUNTAIN

Don't be put off by the impressive title of this walk. Thacker Mountain is a nice pocket-sized little peak all of 850 feet above sea-level. It does, nonetheless, give fine views: from Manson Ridge in the east, to Hope Mountain due south, with the town of Hope nestling beneath its frowning battlements; thence southward to Silver Peak and Holy Cross, in front of which flows the Fraser on its way to the Gulf of Georgia; turning next to northwest you have Zofka Ridge with again the Fraser emerging from its canyon; finally, to the north rises Mount Ogilvie, near whose eastern foot lies Kawkawa Lake.

To reach this panoramic viewpoint from the Hope-Princeton Highway, turn north off it 0.6 mile east of its junction with Highway 1 on 6th Avenue at the sign pointing to Hope Golf Course. Take the first right on Kawkawa Lake road, past Coquihalla Campground, and just beyond the river crossing go sharp left. Cross a small creek and park by a burned-out cabin beside a sign, "Thacker Mountain Ecological Reserve," close to where a rough road goes left uphill.

While the road is drivable if you have no concern for your car, the walk up this miniature mountain is part of the pleasure because, almost from its beginning, you have views over Hope and its surroundings, from the Coquihalla River flowing just beneath you to the widening valley westwards. Your route winds round the hill, with various tracks going off on either side. Stay with the road, however; after an hour or so of gentle walking emerge on the summit, which is adorned — if not exactly beautified — by the presence of a C.N.-C.P. telecommunications tower and installation. Ignore these as much as possible; instead, give your attention to the various prospects that open before you. And don't forget in spring the riches that lie at your feet: chocolate lilies, Oregon grape, paint brush, and ocean spray.

To vary your return, pay a visit to the site of the one-time Thacker home on the mountain. After descending for a short distance, take the second overgrown trail to the right after the road has turned westwards. In a few minutes you come to a ruined cabin on your left by a trail intersection. Go left here, and a short walk brings you in sight of an old power-line, in front

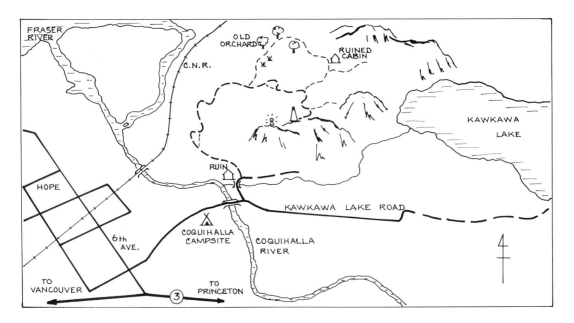

of which are the fruit trees of a one-time orchard and what remains of a drained area. From here back to the road is only a few yards so you now continue downhill to your car by the burnt building.

The story of this picturesque area is a rather sad one. In 1959, Mr. L. T. Thacker left it to University of British Columbia as an ecological reserve. The institution has, however, made singularly little use of the bequest, some of which is suffering damage from trail bikes. The residence and its surrounding gardens have reverted to the wild state, and the ruin by which you parked was, in fact, the last habitable structure of the estate. Perhaps some day the reserve will be put to its proper use, with visitors limited to travellers on foot.

Round trip 3 miles (5 km)
Allow 2 hours
High point 850 feet (230 m)
Elevation gain 800 feet (220 m)
Dirt road
Good all year; best in May

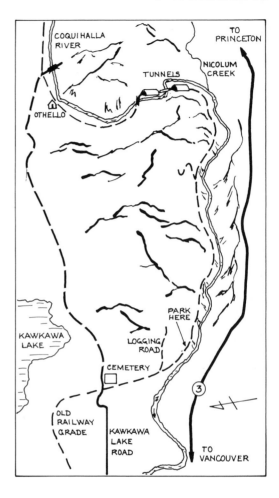

87   COQUIHALLA RIVER

Here's a walk with a difference; it lies along an abandoned railway grade and culminates at the far end of a tunnel in the middle of an awe-inspiring canyon. The distance you walk is adjustable too; you may start where the right-of-way leaves the Kawkawa Lake Road, drive 0.6 mile to where you first become aware of the river below, or even further if you wish; it's more fun to walk, though, and less nerve-wracking. It seems better, too, to use renewable human energy rather than dwindling fossil fuels.

From the Hope-Princeton Highway, 0.6 mile beyond its junction with Highway 1, turn left on to 6th Avenue at a sign for Hope Golf Course, then take the first right on to Kawkawa Lake Road, pass the Coquihalla campground, cross the Coquihalla River, and stay on the blacktop at the junction just beyond. Drive this road for another 0.6 mile to just below the pleasantly-situated cemetery where you see a track crossing it at right angles. Turn right on it and drive to some convenient lay-by.

If you begin walking where the old railbed begins to parallel the swift-flowing water, you frequently find yourself with only the width of

153

Old railway trestle over the Coquihalla

Make this walk in spring if you can, when you are regaled with the balsam scent in the air. You can also enjoy the plants that have established themselves anew where freight trains once panted their way upwards from Hope towards Merritt or Princeton, passing en route the small way-stations, quaintly named after Shakespeare's characters: Othello, Lear, Jessica, even a villain like Iago. Now all is peaceful along the track except for the rush of white water, particularly impressive at spring run-off but spectacular at almost any season.

Finally, at a point where rockfall from above is beginning to obliterate the track, you come to the first of what is a series of tunnels; impressively dark, this one. In fact, you might do well to have a torch in your pocket for the rock-fall in the great tube. Then you emerge on a small platform beyond which further progress is impossible since the first section of the trestle that spanned the canyon has been removed. The scene is awe-inspiring; below is the river pent in its narrow gorge and on its far side straight across you see one tunnel following another, indicative of the difficulties faced by the rail-road builders.

A faint track on your right as you emerge from the tunnel leads downwards to a pebbly beach, and it is worth your while to scramble down to appreciate the full grandeur of the scene. Here the water boils furiously as it is forced to turn this way and that by the canyon walls, even forming a considerable cave just opposite your vantage point so that the river seems to be flowing into a natural tunnel. To turn from the sublime to more mundane matters, this is a favourite fishing spot, so if you have the means, you might try a cast or two.

Once back on the track, you may retrace your steps, marvelling at the ingenuity used to push this railway line through such difficult terrain, coupled with regret, perhaps, that it is now a thing of the past.

the track between the rock walls rising on one side and the river far below on the other. Then come stretches that are less steep, where moss-covered trees testify to the dampness of the atmosphere in the deep gorge. Meanwhile, if you look across to the other side of the valley you become aware of traffic on the Hope-Princeton Highway speeding along beneath the beetling crags of Hope Mountain.

Round trip 3.75 miles (6 km)
Allow 3 hours
Dirt road
Good most of the year

88   SPIRIT CAVES

This walk, on a trail created by recipients of a 1973 summer employment grant, is not for the faint-hearted or the ill-conditioned, rising as it does some 1700 feet in less than two and a half miles. However, the rewards, views along the Fraser Canyon, are more than compensation for energy expended by those who go the whole distance; even those who make it only part way have ample recompense, both aesthetic and physical.

For those travelling north on Highway 1 towards Yale, the trail is on the left of the roadway opposite a marker pointing out the site of the old graveyard, and just beyond a sign

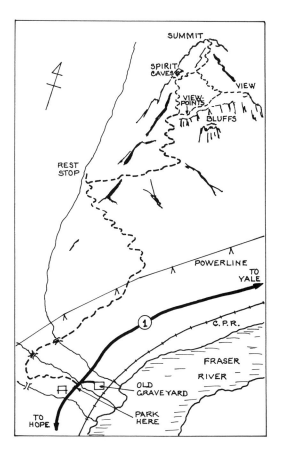

welcoming live visitors to the community. At its beginning, the trail travels upwards between two creeks, finally swinging right and crossing one of them near the lower margin of a B.C. Hydro right-of-way. A little later, it crosses a third creek, one which you will meet again if you get to the 1,200 foot level. Because the timber has been cleared off this area, you have a choice of striking views, upstream to Yale and beyond where the road vanishes into a tunnel that pierces the prominent rock dome, Mount Lincoln, with Lady Franklin Rock a river feature just below.

This stretch of trail is a naturalist's delight in spring, with yarrow, wild strawberry, red-flower currant, bleeding heart, yellow violet, Oregon grape, and cherry all blossoming, and with the balmy scent of cottonwood perfuming the air. But as you rise above the power-line, you enter forest and climb steadily as the markers inform you: 900 feet, 1000 feet, 1100 feet, 1200 feet. At this contour, however, comes respite with a small side trail leading to a rest area by the creek where you may recruit your reserves of energy for what lies ahead.

What does lie ahead is, first of all, a fairly level section along a steepish hill face with a short slide area to negotiate. Then come zig-zags until the trail crests at just under 1900 feet with a breathtaking view down the Fraser River, parallelled by the highway and two railway tracks; even the power-lines do not look too incongruous from this height in this picture of a major traffic artery created by natural forces and adapted by man for his own purposes.

But the eye also catches the outlines of high mountains and ridges. Prominent among the latter is Zofka Ridge, named after the pioneer who prospected the Giant Mascot Mine near Hope. Here many will be content to stop, but if you wish to continue you have a choice: to follow the signposted route left direct to the caves, or to continue along the edge to another viewpoint, this time of Silver Peak. From this spot, the trail cuts back a little left into the forest to a fork where a short jog to the right gives yet one more view, while the forward continuation takes you uphill again and towards another junction. Here the trail to the left heads back to the caves while the one on the right goes to the summit.

If you choose the latter alternative, stay right when you return to the intersection mentioned above; this gives you the caves as well. These consist of great hollows in shattered rock, but they are not particularly deep and after the surfeit of views are apt to be a little anticlimactic; nevertheless, their situation does offer another outlook over the Coast and Lillooet ranges, and it is a solemn remoteness that is inspiring.

To complete the circuit, continue down the trail to the original viewpoint, and from there to Highway 1.

Round trip 4.75 miles (7.6 km)
Allow 4 hours
High point 2000 feet (610 m)
Elevation gain 1700 feet (520 m)
Trail
Good May to October

Routes to the coast, by river, rail and road

89   HISTORIC YALE

Next time you are driving north through Yale on the Fraser Canyon section of Highway 1, stop to read the message of the historical markers on the right of the road just south of the Canyon Inn Hotel. Better still, get out of your car for an hour or so and take a walk into the past; you'll find plenty to interest you if you get away from the main road, saunter through the quiet streets of the old settlement, and look out on the river. Try to recreate the scene when this was a busy port with the Hudson's Bay Company fort dominating the landing area, and with freight wagons setting off northwards, not as today via a tunnel through a mountain, but by a track that went up and over.

Having parked close to the markers, drop downhill for one short block and turn left just before the C.P.R. tracks. Immediately behind the hotel you experience your first segment of history, the cairn commemorating the Cariboo Wagon Road, that feat of nineteenth-century civil engineering which opened up B.C.'s interior. Next, having passed the little railway depot, you come to the province's oldest church, the simple wooden St. John's the Divine with its single small bell to call the faithful as it has done since 1861.

You are not finished with old churches yet, however, strange as it may seem in view of Yale's reputation for sin in gold rush days — or maybe because of it. Immediately after St. John's, then, cross the railway tracks and, turning left again, continue your stroll northwards. In a small cluster of Indian houses just south of Yale Creek stands St. Joseph's Roman Catholic church, founded by the Oblate Father, Charles Grandidier OMI, in 1861 though the actual building is somewhat younger than its Anglican neighbour, dating as it does from 1880.

Returning through the village, go one block east of your outward route to follow the river on what was called, appropriately enough, Front Street, now peaceful and mainly deserted, with only a few of its buildings left, and these by no means the originals like those of the Barnard Express depot. Standing on the bank by what was once the steamer landing, you look across to the C.N.R. settlement opposite and, if lucky, you may see one of its inhabitants cross the fast-flowing, turbulent waters in his small boat. At this point the Fraser is flowing roughly east and west, the start of its bend to the north being marked by a large rock in the midst of its channel. Lady Franklin Rock, its unlikely name, commemorates the visit to Yale in 1861 of the British polar explorer's widow.

Actually, this landmark is in interesting juxtaposition with Mount Lincoln, whose name presumably reflects the strong American influence during gold-rush days. Today, though, its splendour is much diminished with the highway tunnel through it and the local TV aerial on its summit. Thought of the tunnel, however, may remind you of the miles still to go; so, perforce, you turn uphill and recross the tracks into the present once more.

Round trip 1 mile (1.6 km)
Allow 1 hour
Roads
Good all year

St. Joseph's Church

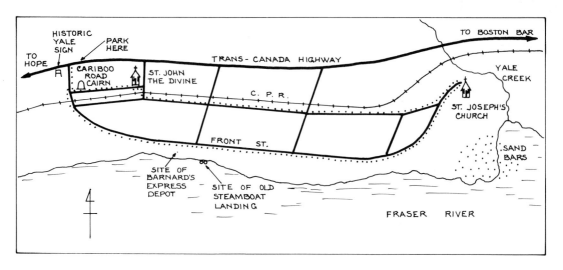

90   OLD ALEXANDRA BRIDGE

Some time when you're driving north through the Fraser Canyon, retire from the rat-race for an hour, step back into B.C.'s recent past, and discover what that stretch of the Trans-Canada Highway signified for your parents and grandparents; you may find it revealing.

The starting point for this short walk is the south end of Alexandra Bridge where the present road crosses both main railway lines and the Fraser in swinging from the west bank to the east. Park in the viewpoint lot, drop down to the C.P.R. track, and cross it to the old road. Now you have the bridge structure overhead and you get some sense of its height above the one-time highway.

After passing beneath the bridge, you come in a short time to a washed-out section where the river boils below in a fashion more awe-inspiring than comforting. A little later you find yourself walking along old wooden stages, now somewhat the worse for wear, and you realise how narrow the old road was. Ask some old-timer what it was like to meet a truck or bus on one of these stretches; his account may be a little lurid.

By now you are getting down towards the old bridge with its simple lines, and you swing back from the river a little to cross a tributary stream over an old wooden trestle — without guardrails, naturally. Next a small aqueduct carries a creek across the road above your head before letting its waters arc down to mingle with the Fraser's muddy flood, and just by the bridge,

remains of a small orchard indicate what was once a homesite.

From the bridge you look downstream to its upstart neighbour; you may, however, also look straight down through the open mesh of metalwork that is the surface, providing you do not suffer from vertigo at the sight of the smooth chocolate-coloured water slipping by below. Incidentally, if you have a dog with you, you will have to carry him over since his paws are not adapted to walking on such a footing. Take time at the eastern end, though, to admire the bold pine-topped promontory rising sheer from the water and creating a great eddy at its foot.

Now you follow the old road as it swings upwards in a series of S-bends towards the line of the new highway. From here, you must walk the new highway for two or three hundred yards back to the bridge to cross it on its sidewalk. Back near your point of departure, pause to read the message on the commemorative cairn which honours not only those who built the original structure in 1863 but also the creators of the 1929 bridge which you have just traversed on your journey into the past. Examine also the carvings of sockeye salmon commemorating the great fish run up the Fraser that ends in the spawning grounds of the Interior tributaries.

Round trip 2 miles (3.2 km)
Allow at least an hour
Roadway (mostly disused)
Good April to November

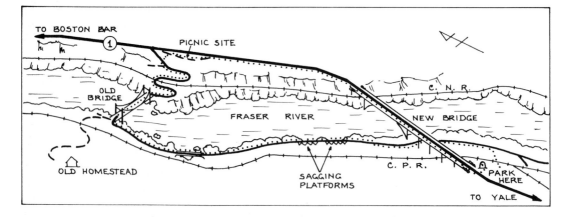

Goat's beard along the roadside

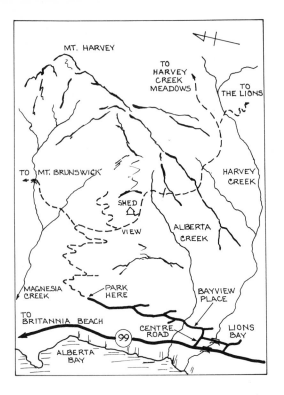

91   HARVEY CREEK

This walk has a number of possible terminal points; which one you choose will depend on your fitness and your desire for variety in scenery. One thing is certain: you can have no better views over Howe Sound than from this old logging road as it twists and turns upwards to 2,000 feet or more from its starting point, 800 feet above Lions Bay.

To reach its beginning, drive the Squamish Highway north seven miles from Horseshoe Bay junction, crossing Harvey Creek and then turning sharp right on Centre Road in Lions Bay village. Go left at the intersection with Bayview and, ignoring the turnoff for Stewart, left again at two successive T-junctions. Shortly after the second of these and about a mile from the highway, the pavement ends while the partly overgrown logging road continues upwards. Start your walk here.

The rough track rises in a series of big and little S-bends with its first major junction coming after about an hour's walking. At this stage, if you have had enough of climbing and wish to enjoy the fruits of your labours, you may proceed along the level section of the left fork, marked TO MOUNT BRUNSWICK, for about 700 yards to where the road crosses Magnesia Creek. Here you may relax in a perfect sun-trap, looking directly across the sound to Mount Elphinstone, with equally attractive views of the islands, from Bowen to Keats. Above and behind you, rising almost perpendicularly from the creek gorge are Mount Harvey and its smaller appendage, Harvey's Pup.

Those of you who take the right fork should continue rising for an other 400 yards or so to a second separation, this one with a superb view over the water and along the coast to Horseshoe Bay; some hikers may be content with this. If you are still eager to walk, however, continue right, the route levelling off and contouring towards the basin of Harvey Creek. Stay right again at the next junction; shortly after, negotiate a small rockfall that blocks the road. Even into May you will come on gullies choked with snow beyond this point and only if you are properly shod should you try to cross these, since the drop-off is steep and a slip could have serious consequences.

As you proceed, you gradually change direction left to round the flank of Mount Harvey and, as you do, you experience a dramatic change of scenery. In place of islands you have the great headwall of the Lions ridge before your eyes, with the West Lion pointing skywards in dramatic fashion. Here, at 2,700 feet, the B.C. Mountaineering Club trail to the Lions veers off to the right, dropping gently to cross the creek as a prelude to some real climbing.

This is probably as far as most will wish to go; remember, you are now almost 3 miles from your transportation. If you do continue, you may reach the sub-alpine meadows above Harvey Creek, but that is a major hike, and the return itself is not lacking in interest. Upper Howe Sound may be more sombre than its southern reaches, but it is beautiful too. Indeed, nature does its best for you on this walk; more than can be said for humankind, from the logging company that has clear-cut the slopes, aiding their erosion, to the inevitable trail-cyclist with his stench and din.

Round trip, up to 5.5 miles (9 km)
Allow 3 hours
High point 2,700 feet (820 m)
Elevation gain 1,900 feet (580 m)
Disused logging road
Good May to October

92   FURRY CREEK VALLEY

Though the entrance to this valley has a locked gate plus NO TRESPASSING signs, these deterrents are not directed at the hiker who stays on the roads and trails, but rather at unauthorised vehicular traffic that may create difficulties for the logging equipment that uses this route for access to the operating area. If prepared to travel on foot, then, you may indulge in one of other of the walks that range from short and easy to lengthy and steep.

The approach is simple. Some 17.5 miles north of the Highway 99 turnoff above Horseshoe Bay, the road passes a large gravel pit, then starts ascending a long straight hill. A little more than halfway up this hill, your route turns sharp back on the right, the gate a few yards in. Some limited parking is available clear of the travelled portion; but if you are in doubt, it is probably better to stop on the other side of the highway in the space above the Hydro sub-station.

At first you stay north of the creek rising on an S-bend to gain height. After little more than a half mile of walking comes a major fork; stay right here, following the lower road, the other leading to logging operations on the north side of the valley. You now stay fairly level as the rush of water announces your approach to Furry Creek, whose crossing you come to after a mile. Up to here is the least rewarding part of the road but perhaps a few of you may wish to stop here, especially in winter. If you come this way in fall, you have a fairly gentle stream splashing in a boulder-strewn bed; early summer,

however, is a different story — a rushing torrent, whose violence perhaps supports the theory that "Furry" is a corruption of "Fury."

The road now swings southwards briefly, bridges Phyllis Creek, then ascends in a long switchback before pointing east into a wide valley flanked with power lines. By now you have risen to over 1000 feet, and, looking back over Howe Sound, you see Mount Sedgwick's great eastern shoulder pointing directly to its summit, a narrow line of rock flanked on either side with snow fields. As you continue, the grade levels off, you re-cross Phyllis Creek and, finally, arrive at Marion Lake, another possible destination for your walk, one that may involve you in a little fishing if you have the necessary gear. But the road continues, and those of you with curiosity and stamina may go some distance further to yet another lake, Phyllis, from which your tributary creek got its name. This, however,

is the end. Beyond is Vancouver Watershed territory, the headwaters of the Capilano River.

One other possibility, but only for strong, experienced hikers, takes you off the road about ½ mile beyond the first crossing of Phyllis Creek at a point where the centre wire of the line carried on wooden poles is directly overhead. Here, an overgrown old logging road goes off left into the bush, recrosses the creek, and, now shrouded in over-arching alder, serves as a highway for bear.

As you proceed, you realize that you are turning back into the main Furry Creek valley but now high above the stream. The trail becomes more rugged, going over washouts and finally emerging into the open where a small creek splashes over a rock and makes a refreshing pool. You are now at 1900 feet and three miles from your start, but the next possible destination, Beth Lake, is a good hour further on and 1500 feet up, over what is little more than a marked route in places, one that rises very steeply even if it does provide fine views of Howe Sound and Mount Habrich and is rich in summer flowers: queencup, bunchberry, fireweed, and false azalea — first comers in the new succession following the logging of the area — with hellebore on the edge of the forest.

These, then, are possible choices, the last described being the most difficult, and one that should not be undertaken before July because of late lying snow.

Marion Lake
Round trip up to 10 miles (16 km)
Allow up to 7 hours
High point (Marion Lake) 1700 feet (520 m)
Elevation gain 1500 feet (460 m)
Good June to November
Mainly logging road

Beth Lake
Round trip up to 10 miles (16 km)
Allow up to 7 hours
High point 3450 feet (1050 m)
Elevation gain 3250 feet (990 m)
Good July to November

STAWAMUS CHIEF (SOUTH PEAK)

Though the face of this great rock mass is strictly for climbers, the summit with its views is not unattainable by those who prefer solid ground under their feet. In fact, some private individuals have created a signposted trail system that takes much of the guesswork out of the walk though the ascent is still steep enough to give a sense of accomplishment — and an appetite.

From Highway 99 a mile north of Shannon Falls Park turn right on what remains of the old road; go right again after a few yards then turn left on a dirt road for about a quarter mile to the quarry where it ends just to the south of the Chief. The trail itself, well used and clearly

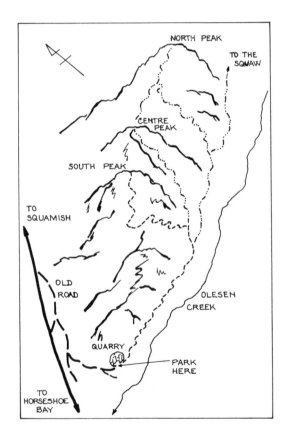

South Peak from Centre Peak

visible though somewhat rocky, takes off from the east end, rising steeply and following the line of Olesen Creek. Aluminum markers on trees also help to provide guides, useful in wet or misty weather.

Behind the mountain, the trail continues upward in an impressive ravine, the creek remaining on your right and below you as you ascend. After about 45 minutes you come to the parting of the ways; the path that goes a little right leads to Centre and North Peaks while you turn off sharp left following the markers and continue uphill in a series of switchbacks. Next you come to an impressive rock bluff, and here you swing south to make your way over a shoulder towards your goal, the open flat rock of the summit.

From this vantage point you have views galore. Howe Sound lies spread out almost at your feet, from the Municipality of Squamish at its head to the islands that dot its south end.

Across the water lies the Tantalus Range with its towers and glaciers, while round to the north is the great mass of Mount Garibaldi, a fairly recent volcano, geologically speaking, and considerably younger than the granodiorite batholith on which you are standing.

One caution: keep youngsters away from the outer edge of the rock. Its apparently rounded slope soon steepens precipitately and becomes the forehead of the great rock face. The same applies to the lower part of the approach trail which may involve some scrambling and the occasional assist on some of the larger rock steps.

Round trip 4 miles (6.4 km)
Allow 3 hours
High point 2,000 feet (610 m)
Elevation gain 1,900 feet (580 m)
Rough trail
Good April to October

94 SKOOKUMCHUK NARROWS

Anyone who visits the Sechelt Peninsula and fails to pay his respects to this natural wonder is missing an unforgettable experience; and it's free in return for expenditure of the small amount of energy required to walk five miles on good, virtually level trails. The shoreline by the great tidal race is provincial parkland too, so that you are free of attempts at exploitation of a scene of great beauty.

To reach the beginning of the trail, turn right off Highway 101 at the Egmont signpost, a little short of the Powell River ferry terminal at Earl's Cove. Drive 3.3 miles on this roller-coaster of a road, passing two lakes, North and Waugh,

before coming on the Parks Branch parking lot just short of Bousfield's store. Follow the trail down a small creek which it eventually crosses on a footbridge before climbing uphill behind some cabins whose water-lines share the right-of-way. Soon, however, signs of human settlement disappear and you are alone with the forest, a healthy second-growth, its floor carpeted with salal, red-flowering currant, and a variety of ferns.

After about a mile you see water through the trees, but as you come closer, you recognise it for the surface of another lake, not the inlet you are seeking. Still among trees, the trail follows its southern shoreline, then leaves it behind. Next, some 1.75 miles from the start of your walk, you come to the first dividing of the ways with the left-hand trail leading to boat-

Tide race at North Point

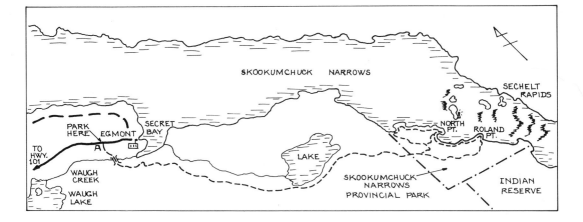

moorings, toilets, and North Point while its right-hand fork is anonymous as it goes off a little uphill. Nevertheless, following it may be the more rewarding choice.

If you do so, you eventually come to a notice announcing the proximity of The Narrows, and soon you emerge on a brow of rock overlooking the great race. Then, as you follow the coast trail back, you have varied opportunities to watch the tide flowing into or out of Sechelt Inlet, noting its great whirlpools and eddies as well as the tremendous rush of white water. Two points, Rowland and North, give grandstand views of the spectacle from the inlet to its mountain background, but the great attraction is the unresisting flow of water over the submarine rock ledges.

On resuming your journey from North Point, continue along the rocky bluffs on the edge of the forest to the boat moorings, a sheltered cove, where the still water contrasts with the violence of the inlet. From here to the trail junction is only a matter of minutes and thence you simply retrace your steps.

Finally, a word on names. It would be inspiring if the person who named Egmont did so with the chords of Beethoven's great overture ringing in his ears as an aural counterpart to the visible grandeur of the scene. In contrast, Skookumchuck is the Chinook term for "powerful water," though it is interesting that "skookum" in Salishan originally meant "demon," a not unlikely connotation.

Round trip 5 miles (8 km)
Allow 3 hours
Forest trail
Good all year

95   GRAY CREEK FALLS

This trail may be short on distance; nonetheless, it is long on points of interest and is well worth the drive out from Sechelt if you have a spare hour or so. It is particularly rewarding in spring during the snow-melt when the water is high and the rapids and falls are at their most scenic.

To reach its beginning, drive north from Sechelt on the Inlet Road 5.2 miles from the Forest Ranger Station (by the traffic light in the village) to just beyond the point where blacktop ends before the bridge over Gray Creek. Parking space is on the north side of the bridge but the trail itself, a little overgrown at its beginning, goes in on the south bank, heading upstream from the road. Unfortunately, the high water that provides the best spectacle also tends to wash out the trail; you may have a little tricky navigating on its early stretches where the bank has been undermined, so that you cannot see the route for water.

As you proceed, however, the path ascends to higher rock banks with the creek some fifty feet below you. And now you find yourself in a miniature example of coastal rain forest, the trees dense and many of them moss-covered, their extended branches looking eerily like outstretched arms. But the creek too is worthy of your notice, especially the third fall where a real cascade pours over a rock ledge in a cloud of white spray. By this time, though, the trail has become very faint indeed; so even if there does seem to be more interesting water upstream ahead, you had better set about retracing your steps before you become too bushed.

Both going in and returning, watch how you negotiate the side creeks that tumble down the banks to join the main flow. While these probably dry up as summer advances, they are healthy little rivulets in the month of May, demanding some cunning and agility to negotiate dryshod.

On the return journey, look in if you have time at Porpoise Bay Provincial Campsite with

its mountain views and beach walks on the shores of Sechelt Inlet. From here, looking westward you may see how close this long crooked finger of water has come to linking up with Georgia Strait and forming another island.

Round trip 1 mile (1.6 km)
Allow 1 hour
Faint trail
Good most of the year

96   CHAPMAN CREEK FALLS

If you want to find out where Sechelt gets its water supply, pay a visit to these falls; you will not be disappointed, particularly if you can make the outing in May when the water-flow is greatest and the falls most spectacular, especially the third — the highest one. One unfortunate feature — from the walker's point of view — is the recent widening of the pipeline road because this has created, beyond the reservoir, a long straight stretch that is rather uninteresting. However, you may get over that difficulty by driving part way along it, if you don't mind a bumpy ride.

For the approach by car, leave Highway 101 at a point 0.2 mile east of Sechelt Hospital beside a quarry and by the hospital warning sign. Travel east on an old road, staying left at one fork, and arriving at a Hydro power-line right-of-way in a wide cleared stretch, one possible parking spot if you don't relish rough roads. Continue right, up a steep little hill, and arrive on its top quite close to a reservoir, another potential place to leave your car. At this point, veer half left into a screen of trees by the water tank's west side. From here the recently cleared road stretches out straight ahead for over half a mile; so if you are still carborne, you may drive this stretch as well till you come close to a trail crossing of the pipeline road where your walk definitely should begin.

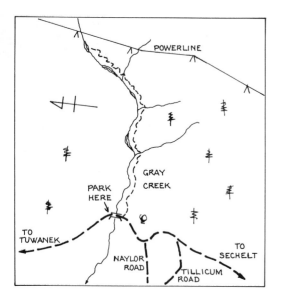

Go ahead from this intersection on roughly the same line, but using the old pipeline route with its interesting curve till you come to road end. From here the old wooden pipe runs above ground on a trestle; follow this along, dodging as best you can the water jets from punctures in the pipe, and becoming more and more aware of the roar of water. And then, there is the creek and its lowest falls. Shortly thereafter, you pass a second cascade. From here it is not far to where the pipe ends just above the highest fall, over which the water plunges fifty feet into a dark gorge spanned here and there by precariously perched trunks of fallen trees. Most mortals will

Approaching the falls

be glad to keep back from the edge while venturing timid glances into the chasm.

It is a pity that the approach road is so wide and straight. Perhaps in time it will become overgrown and shady like its predecessor; in that case you may enjoy the longer walk from the reservoir and obtain the benefit of added exercise.

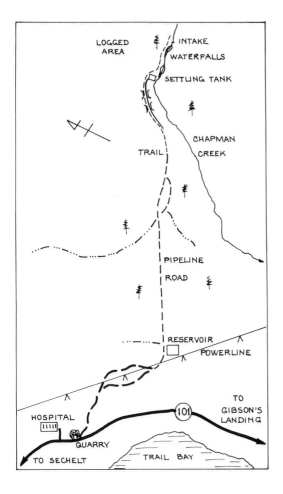

Round trip 1 to 3 miles (1.6 to 5 km)
Allow up to 2 hours
Dirt road and trail
Good most of the year

97 SUNSHINE COAST RECREATION CENTRE

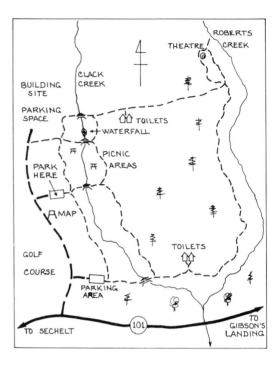

At first sight this may seem a strange location for a walk. The explanation, though, is simple once you learn that this tract of land was set aside for indoor-outdoor recreation, but that the local voters turned down the plan for a sports complex when it was put to them in referendum. Nevertheless, there is a system of trails covering the ground between two creeks, with bridges over one of them and with picnic tables set here and there for *al fresco* dining.

This walk has its beginning six miles west of the Gibsons Super-Valu shopping centre along Highway 101 on the right-hand side of the road just before the local golf course. At the recreation centre sign, a road goes off uphill among the trees. After driving along it for a few hundred yards, you come to a large directional sign on the right showing trails and parking areas, one of which is located just a little way beyond, also on the right of the road.

For a start to your walk, you may first follow Clack Creek upstream, crossing it on the highest bridge and travelling eastwards in forest. By so doing, you come to a small open-air amphi-theatre by the banks of Roberts Creek and here, perforce, you turn south following the water

Oregon grape

downstream. Finally, as the hum of traffic announces the proximity of the main highway, you come on a trail going right, one which brings you back to your original creek somewhat lower down than you were to start with. At this point you may cross, or not, as you please; paths ascend on both sides more or less parallel with the water back to the middle bridge of the three. From it to your parked vehicle is no distance at all.

Some trees and plants have identifying marks so this walk may be a botany trip as well as a pleasant forest hike. As is often the case in late spring, the creeks are attractions in themselves. Because of the high water levels their rapids and falls are in full flow, a pleasing sight. So, for a short outing close to a main road, the Sunshine Coast Recreation Centre is well worth considering.

Round trip 1.5 miles (2.4 km)
Allow 1 hour
Forest paths
Good all year

98   SOAMES HILL

As you approach Langdale by B.C. Government Ferry from Horseshoe Bay, you are aware, if you remain on the boat deck instead of joining the stampede below, of what Dr. Samuel Johnson might have called a considerable protuberance right on the coast and south a short distance from the landing stage. This is the 900-foot Soames Hill, whose summits provide a variety of views: south along the Sunshine Coast to Shoal Channel and Keats Island, or west to Mount Elphinstone and Sechelt Ridge, or east along the island-dotted waters of Howe Sound to the great mountain chain along its eastern shoreline.

The hike starts, at present, at the top of a rise on Highway 101 just a mile south of the ferry terminal. Here a lay-by on the seaward side by a garden with a wire fence provides parking space, with the trail itself angling off from the opposite side of the road. (Note that a new subdivision is going in just below this access road, which may lead to changes.) Walk up this track as it heads towards a quarry; just before that feature, however, a lower fork angles off left. This takes you further round the flank of

Dogwood

the hill and into forest before it starts its steep ascent among the trees. Eventually, just a short distance below the top of a small rock bluff on your right, you see a trail leading off left; keep it in mind but save it for your return and continue right on to the open rock. Here, on top of the bluff, you may enjoy the view to the south with its pleasing variety of land and sea. Continue upwards (but more gently now) staying in the open on the south side of the hill till you reach its high point. From here you have your previous outlook with the addition of the Sechelt benchland outstretching south and west towards Roberts Creek.

On your descent don't forget the fork you passed on your way up. A short walk along it brings you to another viewpoint, facing west this time to the mountains. While you are at it, go to the southwest summit knoll for the sake of touching all bases. Now, finally, you are ready to return to the flat, but keep your brakes on; the trail is just as steep going down as it was coming up, so take your time even if you do feel a little heady after your experience. And in spring don't forget to admire the forest vegetation; the dogwoods are notable with their huge white flowers, while arbutuses range from quite small shrubs to large trees.

Round trip 1.9 miles (3 km)
Allow 1.5 hours
High point 900 feet (280 m)
Elevation gain 600 feet (180 m)
Good all year

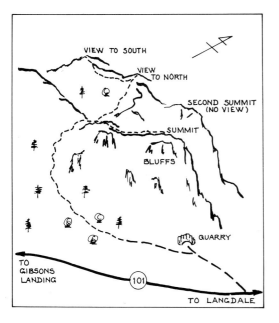

99   PAUL RIDGE

This walk in the very popular Diamond Head recreation area has an advantage over the hike all the way in to the old lodge: though only half as far, it sacrifices none of the magnificent views, nor do you have the descent to Elfin Lakes with the corresponding rise on the return trip. The panorama from the high point on the ridge, Round Mountain, is unsurpassed almost anywhere. To the north, Mount Garibaldi reaches skyward; in the northeast, Mount Mamquam

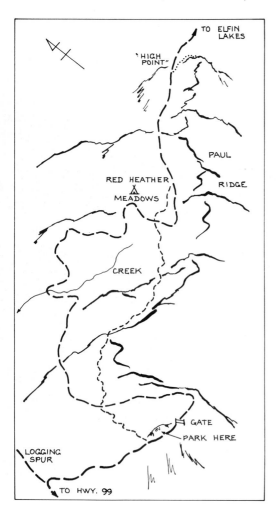

with its great glaciers broods over the lake and river that bear its name; south and east rise the graceful spires of the Sky Pilot group; and across Howe Sound the majestic range of the Tantalus stretches westward; completing the circle, you have the valleys of the Squamish and Cheakamus, the high country between them with, finally, the sweeping western ridges of the Garibaldi Massif pointing towards the peak.

To reach the start of this walk, turn east off Highway 99 a little less than a half mile north of its crossing of the Mamquam River; a large sign, DIAMOND HEAD RECREATION AREA, by the road indicates the exact point. From the turnoff, the road rises about 3,300 feet in approximately 9.5 miles, all but the first mile or so unsurfaced. Though rough in places, it is quite drivable with reasonable care; the first 6.4 miles, in fact, are on a good logging road that heads east. At that point a signpost directs the driver to the left (uphill) fork and now the direction changes to mainly north until the last mile, where it turns back east again.

At the parking lot, a locked gate bars further progress by car. There is a visitors' book in which hikers should register. From here you may walk up the main access road; there is, however, an old trail to tempt the venturesome. This takes off from a few yards west of the lot, going up on the bank to the right. It then meets the main road after about twenty minutes and continues as a well-marked path among tall trees, leaving the road below and on your left. Besides being shorter, this route is more picturesque than the main access. In fact, it was the old packhorse trail to the back-country in the days before motorized vehicles.

As you rise, the trees thin out and the country becomes sub-alpine in the tract known as Red Heather Meadows, the Park Branch's recreation area. Just above the wilderness campsite here the trail intersects the road again and at this point some may feel that they have gone far enough. Even so, there are rewards in the views afforded and in the stillness of the surroundings.

But if you are going on, continue on the trail, which cuts across one bend of the road, then joins it for the last 40 minutes or so of climbing to its high point. From here, the road drops gently towards the old Diamond Head

Lodge, just visible afar off. Rather than lose the height you have gained, though, you are going a little higher still, so turn uphill and angle round the knob above to gain the ridge crest with the views already mentioned. One note: there is no trail in this last little bit, but the country is clear and the road below serves as a marker.

For the return, you may retrace your steps or follow the main access road; the latter has no advantages except, perhaps, novelty. Therefore, the trail is preferable as it winds downwards through great trees to the everyday world. Incidentally, did you note how the fragile terrain beyond the Red Heather Meadows has suffered from wheeled and tracked vehicles? This fact alone ought to be sufficient argument for keeping *all* traffic out.

Round trip 7 miles by trail (11.2 km)
Allow 5 hours
High point 5300 feet (1620 m)
Elevation gain 2,000 feet (610 m)
Forest trail or dirt road
Good June to October

Mt. Garibaldi from Paul Ridge

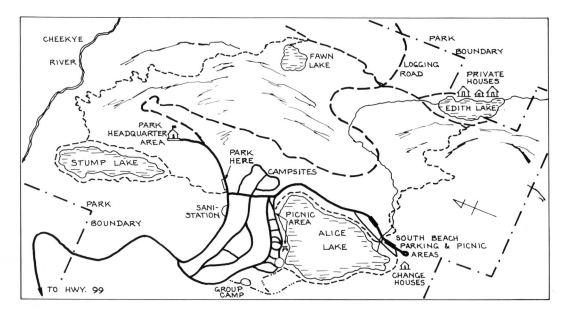

100 FOUR LAKES TRAIL

As in other areas administered by the Provincial Parks Branch, Alice Lake Park has a well-developed system of hiking trails. There are short ones like those round Alice Lake and Stump Lake, and long ones — Four Lakes Trail being the main example. This trail includes the paths already mentioned and adds to them the connecting links of a circuit involving Fawn Lake and Edith Lake, even though the latter is not, strictly speaking, in the park.

So well known is Alice Lake Park that it is scarcely necessary to say that you reach it by turning off Highway 99 some 9 miles north of Squamish, and driving to one of the parking lots, preferably the one just east of the sani-station, which is reached by staying left and driving uphill at the park entrance instead of making for the lake. Here, in an open space north of the road and just beyond the right turnoff into the campsite location, you have the pointer for Stump Lake Trail to your left, and from it you start your walk.

At first you are in thick bush but this thins

out when you reach the fork where the arms of the Stump Lake Circuit separate, leaving you free to choose whichever you wish. The right arm gives views over De Beck Hill; from the left arm you see Mount Garibaldi and Alice Ridge; each gives glimpses of the lake and its cluster of water lilies. At the far end, beyond a little island, the trails join and here you fork right again.

Back in deep forest, you become aware of the increased rush of water and soon you find yourself just above the Cheekye River, which flows down from Mount Garibaldi, its valley separating Brohm Ridge and Alice Ridge. On this stretch the influence of the stream is manifest in the near rain-forest effect that is produced, quite a bit different from the vegetation elsewhere. The difference soon becomes obvious as you climb steadily eastwards, rising to 900 feet as you near Fawn Lake; lush skunk cabbage gives way to salal, and alder to miniature conifers.

Fawn Lake is a little off the trail to the right. Where the spur road goes off to it, the foot trail you have been on develops into a logging road, a status it is to maintain till you reach lake number three, Edith Lake.

Indeed, when you come to a major inter-section, the route crossing yours is the main approach to Alice (Cheekye) Ridge, one which antedated creation of the park so that it must remain in being because it gives access to some cabins by Edith Lake.

At this lake, go right at the first turn-off, then right again, leaving the logging road for the footpath again as a prelude to your descent to Alice Lake on the last three-quarter mile stretch. For a good part of this section, the trail jostles Dryden Creek in an attractive little valley with lush vegetation, and finally path and watercourse together arrive at the south end of the lake. From here you may use either shore to return to your transport. Each is pleasant, but perhaps the one on the east side is the prettier with its views of De Beck Hill across the water; it is also a little shorter.

At the north end you must return to pavement again, but only for a short distance as you walk up through the campsites to the intersection with the Park Headquarters road where your car is parked.

This low-level walk on well made trails, carefully signposted, is good for those times of the year when more ambitious outings are out of reach because of weather. The only difficulty is that individuals vandalise the signs, tearing some of them down or reversing them so that they are not always completely accurate; on the whole, though, common sense will indicate which way to go despite such activity.

Round trip 3.5 miles (5.6 km)
Allow 2 hours
High point 950 feet (290 m)
Elevation gain 300 feet (91 m)
Trail
Good April to November

101   DeBECK HILL

This miniature mountain, stretching along the southwest side of Alice Lake, provides an interesting walk on a highly unofficial route (at time of printing), one that may supply a useful corrective to the blasé feelings engendered by hikes on carefully maintained and signposted Parks Branch trails round the lakes in the Provincial Park; the walk involves carefully following directions with the aid of only a few orange tapes on the upper stretches to guide you.

The start of the hike is the South Beach parking lot in Alice Lake Park, from which you walk south via the turnaround for cars and make your way over or under the barrier that blocks off the maintenance yard. Just inside this yard on your right as you enter it, an overgrown logging road angles back uphill in the direction of the lake. After a few minutes, however, you find yourself at a sand pit and your road seems to vanish; but if you look carefully left at the foot of the loose sand, you will find it again rising gently in a southwesterly direction.

After some 20 minutes, take the right fork uphill where the road splits and continue till you have another sharp turn right at a point where going straight seems to promise a viewpoint — a promise that isn't kept. Now you are travelling east with some quite impressive bluffs above you on your left, but the second-growth forest quickly reasserts itself and soon you find yourself in a kind of tunnel of alder. As you progress, signs of bygone logging activities show themselves; lengths of rusted cable, an old power winch abandoned and forlorn, even an occasional railroad tie. But nature is active in undoing the works of man, and in June the roadside is strewn with beds of bunchberry, the flowers looking for all the world like small-scale dogwood — which indeed they are.

Again your track swings and now you pass a large sawdust pile on your left. Finally, below some bare rock, your route, taped, takes off uphill right leaving the old road you have followed to this point. A few minutes on this track bring you into the open just below the summit ridge with its line of trees, and here it is that you have your reward in the form of views: views of

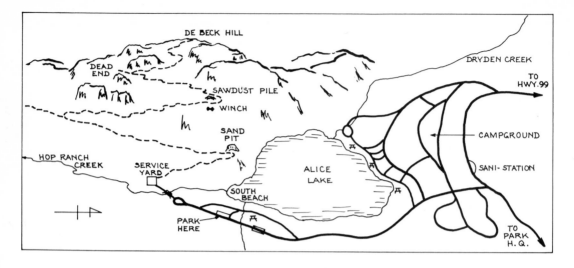

Mount Garibaldi rearing itself above Alice (Cheekye) Ridge to the east and, equally striking, the Tantalus Range away to the west above the Squamish River. But the nearer scene has its charms also: the park, densely treed, on one side of you, the Cheakamus valley stretching north with Cloudburst Mountain to the left of it, and the flat delta lands round Squamish to the southwest.

Now you retrace your steps; to your campsite if you are having a holiday in Alice Lake Park, to your car otherwise.

Round trip 2.5 miles (4 km)
Allow 2 hours
High point 1350 feet (420 m)
Elevation 650 feet (200 m)
Old logging road
Good April to November

Mt. Tantalus from Hut Lake road

102 LEVETTE LAKE

This small body of water, set in a rock basin surrounded by tall Douglas firs, does not have to rely on its own undoubted attractions to commend it as the destination of a walk, for it has, as a magnificent backdrop, the peaks of the Tantalus Range with their snowfields and glaciers. Wherever you cast your eye, there is beauty. Yet this spot is not far from Squamish, and the whole trip need take as little as four hours if you can bring yourself to leave the lake after only a short pause on its shore.

To reach your starting point, drive north through Brackendale and go straight on where Highway 99 forks right for Alta Lake at the little graveyard. Cross the Cheakamus River at Fergie's Fishing Lodge and then, immediately after the bridge, turn right on Paradise Valley Road. Drive for 1.3 miles to a left turn just opposite the North Vancouver Outdoor School; follow this road uphill for 0.8 mile to a junction where a left fork (private) leads to Evans Lake Forest Camp, a summer centre for young people, and the right fork is your way to Levette Lake.

The old logging road from here is very rough, suitable only for 4-wheel drive vehicles, so park off the road at the fork. You will have a walk of 1.75 miles to your destination on a route that begins deep in second-growth forest but later opens out as you rise steadily, providing you with a variety of mountain scenery. To the south, behind you, are the peaks of the Sky

Pilot group; to your right you have glimpses of Mount Garibaldi; to the left you have what are only the first views of the Tantalus. After about 45 minutes, stay right where the road forks, a procedure that you repeat some five minutes later where a road, marked private, leads to cabins. You make a left turn about ten minutes thereafter, and soon the sight of water through the trees indicates your destination. A little tree-clad rock bluff some 30 feet above the lake overlooks its calm surface framed against an alpine background which has few equals.

But suppose you had stayed right at that last fork. Well, if you want to explore, you may continue on the old road as it rises to almost 2,000 feet, the views becoming more awesome as you advance till, at one point, you have the three mountain groups mentioned earlier vying for your attention. Proceeding further, you pass a small lake on your left, descend a little as you swing gradually to the west, then suddenly the whole view opens out before you: Mount Tantalus itself with its glaciers towering above the valley of the Squamish River far below. Only the most dedicated walkers will wish to continue past this viewpoint. If you do belong to that category, you arrive eventually, and unexpectedly, at pretty little Hut Lake (also Hud), the only trouble being the height you must regain on the return. Actually this would make a pleasant overnight back-pack trip so that you have your return ascent first thing in the morning.

One caution: the upper stretches of the trail to Levette Lake have been logged and burnt over recently so the bare rock of the bluffs can give hot walking on a summer day.

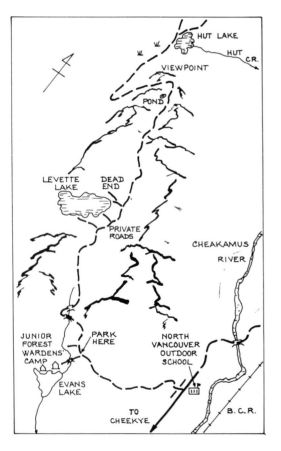

Round trip 3.5 miles (5.6 km)
Allow 3 hours
High point 1400 feet (425 m)
Elevation gain 800 feet (240 m)
Old logging road
Good April to October

103   CULLITON CREEK

For anyone who has time to spare en route to Alta Lake and Whistler Mountain, this walk gives a break of two hours or so coupled with some interesting views of distant glaciers, nearby lava cliffs, and a spectacular waterfall with a sheer drop of nearly 500 feet.

From the Alice Lake turnoff on Highway 99, drive 6.4 miles to a point just before a sign warning of a steep descent, a spot where the power-line right-of-way is just on the east side of the road. Here a logging road diverges right at quite a narrow angle, remaining on the contour while the main road drops away to cross the creek a half mile further on.

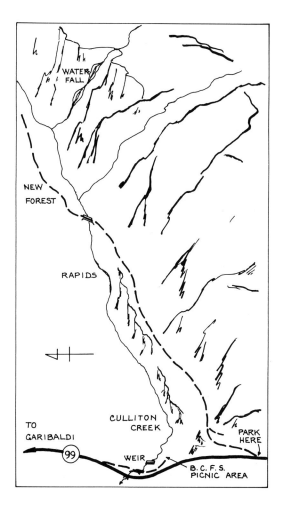

After a little more than a mile, the rush of water announces that the creek is not far off — indeed, two or three hundred feet below the track and parallel with it as it boils down headlong on its way to join the Cheakamus River. Gradually the road levels off, turns toward the stream, and crosses to its north side. Here you may stop to rest in the coolness; it is more rewarding, however, to continue up the valley for another quarter mile or so past a Forest Service sign announcing the date of the area's replanting. A little beyond comes the great surprise; from the sheer cliff on the south side of the valley a jet of water hurls itself down in two great steps. In summer when the glacier melt is greatest, the spray forms great clouds, a sight of naked power.

This is really far enough. Up the valley are high lava cliffs but these are at their best when viewed from a distance where their rawness is not so evident. And the return trip, too, has its points of interest: the glaciers and peaks of the mighty Tantalus rising in their majesty across the valley of the Squamish River.

Otherwise, the walk back is through forest till the wires of the powerline stretch across the view, the logging road swings south, and cars on the highway become audible once more. Another point: the B.C. Forest Service picnic site where the road crosses the creek is a pleasant spot to while away a little time as well.

Round trip 4.25 miles (7 km)
Allow 2.5 hours
High point 2,000 feet (610 m)
Altitude gain 1,000 feet (300 m)
Logging road
Good May to October

A locked gate bars vehicle access but there is room for parking clear of the thoroughfare. The logging road makes pleasant walking as it heads into tall trees and rounds a shoulder into the main valley of Culliton Creek. After ten minutes or so, the road starts rising quite steeply, heading eastward towards some spectacular slopes, the result of past igneous activity. Some logging has been going on but it is hoped that a screen of trees will be left to hide the bare slopes. It is worth mentioning that in summer the fireweed is a blaze of colour, and in fall the rich gold of the shrubs is a delight to the eye.

104   NO-NAME LAKE
(TRICOUNI TRAIL)

The route you follow on this walk is one created by climbers making for the alpine country between the Cheakamus and Squamish rivers, hence its unofficial title, Tricouni Trail. Obviously, the climbers' destination is far beyond the scope of a hike suitable for this book, but the little lake — anonymous on maps of the area, though bearing a number of unofficial titles such as Gilders and Cedar — does provide a satisfactory turnaround for what may be considered an adventure outing into quite wild terrain. The path itself is narrow and a little overgrown in spots, but it is quite well marked with red paint and aluminum squares so that it is easily enough followed once you are embarked on it; in fact, your greatest difficulty may be in finding its beginning.

Travelling north on Highway 99, some 13 miles beyond Alice Lake Park turnoff, you come on a sign for Alpine Lodge pointing to the left. Take this road (private) which crosses the Cheakamus River and the B.C. Railway, then follow the signs for Lucille Lake camping and recreation area. Where the final pointer indicates a left turn to the lake, however, stay right for a few yards then turn half left, dodging a large log that blocks part of the road. Drive to the far end of the open area just left of some old concrete foundations, now almost hidden from sight by bush. These probably date from the mid-1950's when B.C. Hydro was cutting its underground aqueduct from Daisy Lake to the Squamish River; indeed, one of the shafts, the Talking Tunnel, is a little to their right.

The trail itself begins in a tunnel of alder, heading quite steeply uphill for the first few hundred feet. It begins to level off as it approaches the first of a number of rockfalls where great blocks of basalt have tumbled from cliffs above. Your route, however, carefully stays along the lower edge of these devil's brickyards so that you do not have to scramble over rocks; indeed, you have time to admire the great vertical stacks of columnar basalt, especially at the third one, the most spectacular. Next you head into a draw with tall timber which is apparently to be spared from the nearby logging to maintain the access corridor to the high country.

All this time you have been rising steadily to over the 2000 foot mark and you are almost at your destination, the little lake with its cedar-shake cabin. The main trail branches off right a few yards before the lake and you may follow this route round to the east side of the water. From that point your view is back towards The Barrier, with a small knoll adorned with a microwave installation indicating roughly the point from which you started. Another viewpoint is the low rounded bluff just south of the cabin. From here you have a view of Cloudburst Mountain to the south with glimpses of the Tantalus range in the southwest.

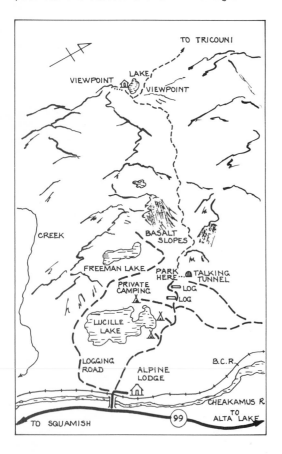

105 THE BARRIER

Indian pipe

Round trip 3 miles (5 km)
Allow 3 hours
High point 2,400 feet (730 m)
Elevation gain 1,100 feet (340 m)
Marked route
Good June to October

Anyone who has driven north on Highway 99 past the little settlement of Garibaldi must have cast at least a passing glance upwards to the right in the direction of the great lava cliffs that make up the ramparts of The Barrier. Though their awesome height and stark barrenness may suggest a difficult approach, they are, in fact, easily reached by a well-constructed Provincial Parks trail that takes you quite gently from 2,000 feet to 4,500 feet.

From the junction with the road into Alice Lake Provincial Park, drive on Highway 99 nearly 14 miles till, almost opposite the sign for Garibaldi Lodge, a pointer on the right indicates the fork leading to Black Tusk parking lot, located some 1.5 miles off the main highway. Here, notices indicate the state of the trail, an important matter where snow may lie into July on its upper stretches. In front of you, Rubble Creek rushes down its boulder-strewn bed from its source, the subterranean seepage from Barrier Lake. Barrier Lake and the two Garibaldi Lakes were created by the volcanic forces that blocked the upper part of the valley, preventing the normal escape of run-off water.

As you set off, note the lack of vegetation on the great rock wall ahead of you, and contrast that bareness with the thriving forest on either side of the valley. Soon, however, the rock is out of sight as you start rising steadily among stately trees, mainly fir and cedar, with a flight of steps at one point providing passage over a rocky stretch. After almost a mile, your route swings to the left into a tributary valley, crosses two creeks — one on a bridge, one on stepping-stones — then makes height in a series of long and short zig-zags where notices warn of the dangers involved in cutting corners, which causes slides. Thus you progress until, at 3.5 miles, you reach the parting of the ways. Here the trail to Taylor Meadows and Black Tusk goes off left and uphill while the route to the lakes and the Park Headquarters lies straight ahead.

Just beyond this junction is a short spur track right leading to a superb view of the Upper Barrier from a rocky bluff. If you decide to combine lunch with sightseeing here, spare a crust

179

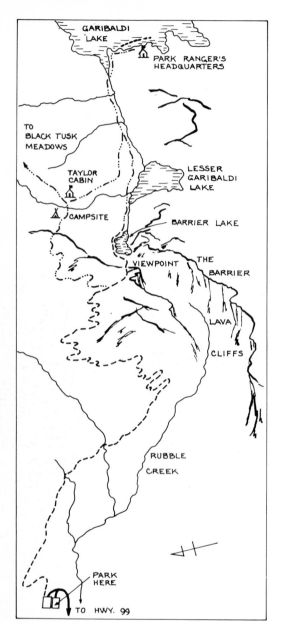

for the whiskeyjacks and the chipmunks; a little largesse satisfies them and their antics provide ample recompense. On returning to the main lake trail, you may walk the short distance to Barrier Lake or, if you don't mind adding a mile or two to your outing, you may continue to the main Garibaldi Lake, passing its smaller namesake en route.

Your return, of course, is easy on such a well graded trail and you may find it appropriate to give a silent vote of thanks to the Parks Branch for its attention to the access route into such scenically attractive country, so bringing it within the range of even moderately active walkers.

Round trip 8 miles (13 km)
Allow 5 hours
High point 4,500 feet (1,375 m)
Park trail
Good July to October

106 BRANDYWINE FALLS

Though the B.C. Provincial Parks Branch has plans for developing this scenic area as a day-use park, it has so far made only minimal improvements at the former Brandywine Falls Resort, with the result that many may pass by on their way to Alta Lake unaware of what they are missing: the waters of the creek pouring headlong over a great basalt sill into the cauldron below, where the spray-cloud resembles steam rising from the depths. The views below the falls have their attractions too, from the creek's narrow gorge to its outflow into Daisy Lake.

As you drive north on Highway 99 from Garibaldi to Alta Lake, you cross the B.C. Railway track from right to left and, very shortly after, you are aware of three A-frame buildings on your right by a large open space adorned at present with two chemical toilets and several litter barrels. Close to the far end of this, by a sign pointing to the falls, a road with a locked

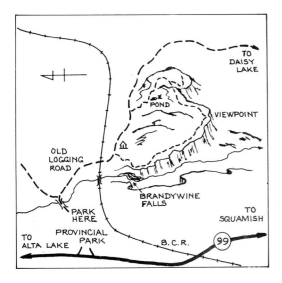

to your junction point. Follow the trail back upstream to the bridge and your car.

Actually, you may walk a little further on the north side instead of crossing back right away. By so doing you have the chance of looking at the dykes of columnar basalt that stand up above the general surface level, silent witness to the igneous activity that helped to shape the landform of this area of British Columbia.

Round trip 1 mile (1.6 km) or more
Allow 1 hour
Good May to October

Brandywine Falls

gate leads to a crossing of the creek. Follow the creek downstream, recross the railway, and just beyond, by an old cabin, fork right on a footpath. This track speedily brings you to a viewing platform and your first sight of the spectacular leap of water into space.

After such a sight as this, you may feel that anything else has to be anticlimactic and certainly you are not easily going to come on another instance of sheer natural power on such a scale; however, gentler vistas are available to you if you continue along the cliff edge, still with the odd glimpse of the falls as you proceed downstream. Now you arrive at a second viewpoint from which your view is south over Daisy Lake, the man-created storage reservoir, dammed at its south end, which impounds the waters of this Brandywine Creek as well as of the Cheakamus River.

Now turn north, still following the rim of what was presumably the onetime Cheakamus River gorge, though that stream is no longer visible, having cut a course for itself some distance further east so that the edge on which you are walking simply slopes down to another tree-clad lower level. Eventually your route draws back a little and you meet the road that you left originally just at the railway crossing. Go left on this towards the tracks, finally returning

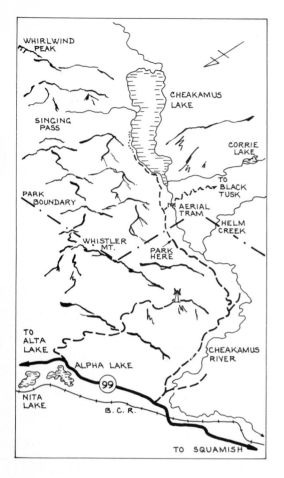

107   CHEAKAMUS LAKE

This fine body of water, situated just two miles inside the western boundary of Garibaldi Park, provides all sorts of picturesque picnic sites along its north shore, with views over the lake to the McBride Range and the glaciers of the park's high country. Two cautions, though: the five-mile approach road gets only minimal upkeep and can be rough in spots; and snow lies long in this country, so save this hike for high summer or fall.

The approach road (signposted) turns off to the right from Highway 99 about 28 miles north of the Alice Lake intersection and 0.3 mile beyond the railroad crossing that rejoices in the appellation of Function Junction. This gravel road passes the Department of Highways yard, then forks. Here you go left, following the sign, and begin to rise a little as you traverse a logged-off stretch that has been replanted in the last few years, though the results are as yet scarcely visible. At two miles, fork left again and once more you rise somewhat towards the road end in a small turn-around area.

From the road end the trail takes off into the trees, crossing two small creeks before reaching the park boundary with its register for hikers and wilderness campers. Now the route continues eastward in tall timber, an indication of what this whole area must have been like before so much of it was logged. Progress is easy for the trail remains virtually level as it converges with the Cheakamus River, which is heard before it is seen. About a mile along, a sign points right for Helm Lake Trail, one of the routes into the high country to the south. But it is worth taking a short side trip along this as far as the river-crossing to view the humanpowered aerial tramway — an interesting method of transportation, though somewhat hard on the arms and hands.

On rejoining the main trail, continue through the forest which obviously provides a suitable habitat for some healthy-looking devil's club, especially where the road is parallel to the river and close to its bank. Gradually the current slackens, the water becomes a deeper green, and the lake begins to open out ahead amid tall mountains, some with impressive glaciers on their slopes.

Any spot along the lakeshore may be the location for a picnic stop. The trail itself continues for a good distance along the lake's north shore, growing gradually less distinct the further you go. In fact, young children may need assistance in one or two spots where the path traverses a rocky face about fifty feet above some dark and deep-looking water. On this stretch, the alternation of treed areas with avalanche-created open spaces gives nice contrasts in vegetation, the clear forest floor contrasting with the lush ground cover of grass and flowers where the sun asserts its power.

Wherever you stop, the views are rewarding;

fishing, too, is a possibility if you have come prepared to make a cast or two. You won't be disturbed by noisy power boats either; there aren't any, and one can only hope that the peace will be allowed to continue.

Return poses no problem, either. It is pleasant to wander along the trail through the forest, this time watching it thin out at the park boundary. Across the river, too, an interesting lava flow shows itself where logging has cleared the vegetation cover and further away rises Metaldome Mountain, with Sproatt over on its right. Even with the threat of a roughish drive, this trip is a satisfying experience.

Round trip 4 miles (6.5 km)
Allow 3 hours
High point 2,725 feet (840 m)
Forest path
Good June to October

Aerial tram over Cheakamus River

Rainbow Falls

108 RAINBOW FALLS

If you are staying at Whistler and have a spare hour some evening before dinner, try this short walk as an aperitif.

To reach the start of this outing, take the road that branches west off Highway 99 about three fourths of a mile south of the skilift parking lot, and signposted for Rainbow Lodge and the west side of Alta Lake. First you pass some barrack-like condominiums before crossing the B.C. Railway track, then, after little Nita Lake, you come to the main lake with its youth hostel sign. Continue for a mile beyond this, passing

Rainbow Lodge on your right and, finally, just where the road crosses the creek, park on its south bank to the left.

The trail, its beginning marked with tape, ascends the bank on the left where the road has been cut through the natural slope of the hill. The grade, however, soon evens off, and you find yourself ascending parallel with the course of the stream, among second-growth for a start, but later among tall shade-giving trees. The rush of water below you on the right alone breaks the stillness until, after some 15 minutes, you find your track converging with the creek and you come upon the lower falls, set in a cool and shady valley.

Continue a short distance further upstream to emerge at the foot of the upper falls where the creek plunges over a rock sill into a fine pool before regaining momentum for its next dash. On this last stretch, you may have noticed a trail angling uphill to the left; if you want a little more exercise, you may retrace your steps a short distance and ascend it once you have

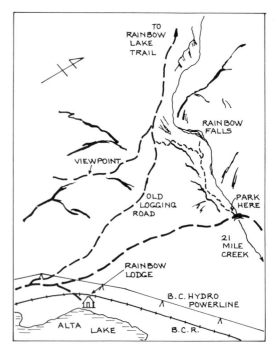

Devil's club berries

enjoyed your view of the falls. This track rises 200 feet out of the ravine towards a logged-over stretch, finally converging with an old somewhat eroded logging road from which views open out dramatically.

Ahead, and a little right, other rapids and falls stretch some distance upstream while behind and above rises a shoulder of Rainbow Mountain. More spectacular, though, is the prospect out across the valley to the east. Spread out before you is Green Lake, aptly named when you see the shimmer of its glacial water; behind it are the glaciers of Wedge Mountain and Weart shining in the evening sun, rendering Whistler Mountain to the southwest somewhat puny by contrast. Between these two areas of high country lies the deep valley of Fitzsimmons Creek, with the mountain country round its head just visible in the distance.

Now comes return down the trail and back to the road. If you want to turn this into a longer walk, you may continue on the old road till it splits a little further up the hill with the left branch heading south a short distance along the lower slopes of Mount Sproatt. From here views open out even more, so your extra expenditure of energy is amply rewarded.

As for the right fork, it supplies hikers and climbers with access to the alpine country between Sproatt and Rainbow, country that contains two small lakes named — believe it or not — Gin and Tonic, as well as Rainbow Lake itself.

Round trip 1.5 miles (2.4 km)
Allow 1 hour
High point 2700 feet (820 m)
Elevation gain 500 feet (152 m)
Good May to October

109   NAIRN FALLS

Because of their distance from Vancouver —
they lie a few miles south of Pemberton and
twenty north of Mount Whistler — these falls
are perhaps not as well known as they ought to
be. That may be all to the good, however; viewpoints are limited, and the Parks Branch warning
at the beginning of the trail is not to be taken
lightly since a slip on the rocks could be serious.
Indeed, the appropriate adjective from this
sample of the unleashed power of nature is
"sublime" in its original sense of "inspiring
admiration and terror," and few visitors will return from a visit to the falls with senses unstirred.

To reach the start of the trail, turn sharp off
the highway at the Nairn Falls Park sign and
drive into the camping area for about a fifth of a
mile, staying right at each intersection. The trail
sign itself is on the right just by a campsite, so
park as close to it as possible without blocking
access. Note also that dogs are to be kept on
leash, a necessary precaution in view of the
narrow trail's proximity to the river.

From its start at a viewpoint about 70 feet
above the water where the Green River makes a
turn to the east, the trail heads south, gradually
approaching the water till after about half a mile
it is just above the current and separated from it
by only a narrow beach. Along the way, tall
conifers provide shade, welcome in summer, as

Caution: low clearance

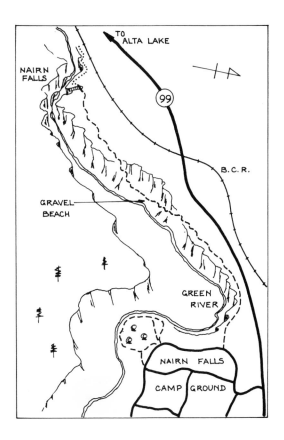

Top of Upper Falls

the route begins to rise to the ever-louder rush of falling water. After crossing a narrow footbridge, you emerge finally on a platform of water-smoothed rock with its dramatic view of the upper fall where the river launches itself head-long into a narrow abyss amid a cloud of boiling spray. Just as spectacular is the way it turns at right angles to its original course to get round the rock barrier in its path before going over the lower fall.

This latter is more difficult to see clearly, its full majesty being visible only from a rocky outcrop to which the visitor must descend as best he can, with the necessity of getting back up again. To continue further along the trail is difficult too, as you have to scramble for a short distance to reach an upper level space. And after this excitement comes anti-climax because

once you have scrambled to the top of the falls, all you see is a mountain stream hurrying on its way with little hint of the drama to come.

Besides the falls, this setting is worth a word. To the east Mount Currie rises above a wild wooded gorge, while to the south are steep slopes from which the right-of-way of both road and railway have had to be carved. Indeed, sight of a B.C. Railway freight crawling uphill is quite dramatic as a contrast to the onward rush of the river.

Don't hurry this trip. Besides using the falls trail, sample the other paths in the park that stretch along the river lower down, where it resumes its northward journey to mingle its waters with the Lillooet River below Pemberton.

Round trip 3 miles (5 km)
Allow 2 hours
Park trails
Good May to November

MORE WALKS

ROUND VANCOUVER

BELCARRA PARK. From loco continue west past Sasamat Lake (regional park) to Burrard Inlet

BUNTZEN RIDGE. Start just east of the Belcarra-Anmore road junction. See "103 Hikes".

GRAVESEND REACH. Go east on Steveston Highway after leaving Highway 99 just north of the Massey Tunnel. Turn right past the gravel works on a road (sign-posted Garbage Dump) that swings back along the river dyke.

IONA ISLAND. From the Sea Island exit of Highway 99 go right on Airport, left on Grauer, right again on McDonald and left on Ferguson.

PEACE ARCH PARK. Just off Highway 99 (north of Blaine) on the border between Canada and the U.S.A.

QUEEN'S PARK. From 12th Street in New Westminster turn east on 6th Avenue.

SERPENTINE FEN. This recently established wildlife management area lies in the triangle between King George Highway and Highway 99 in Surrey. Park off King George just south of the Serpentine River and follow the dyke west.

VAN DUSEN GARDENS. Parking is on the side of Oak Street at West 37th Avenue.

U.B.C. BOTANICAL GARDENS. Still in process of creation, these lie on the north side of West 16th Avenue about a quarter of a mile west of the Wesbrook Crescent intersection.

FRASER VALLEY

ALDERGROVE LAKE. Leave Highway 1 at County Line Road interchange and drive south on Highway 13. Go left on Fraser Highway into Aldergrove then right on Jackman Road for nearly 3 miles to this new regional park.

BRIDAL VEIL FALLS. Turn right off Highway 1 about a mile east of Agassiz-Rosedale turnoff.

CHILLIWACK MOUNTAIN VIEWPOINT. From Highway 1 after crossing the Vedder Canal, go north on Lickman Road till it turns right. Walk left uphill, cross a clearing and pick up the trail to the left of an old building.

CLIFF PARK. Turn south from Dewdney Trunk Road on 252nd Street about 3.5 miles east of Haney for this picturesque park on Kanaka Creek.

KILBY MUSEUM AND PARK. Just east of where Highway 7 crosses Harrison River, turn south at the Historic Park marker and follow signs that bring you back towards the riverbank close to the C.P.R. bridge at Harrison Mills.

LIUMCHEN FALLS. At Sleepy Hollow turnoff on the road south to Cultus Lake from Vedder Crossing, go left. Turn right on Vance Road, then left again at the 3-way fork by the Department of Defence fence. Park at the top of the hill and follow the trail down from the top of the knoll on the left.

ROLLEY LAKE PARK. Turn north off Dewdney Trunk Road a mile west of Stave Falls.

HIGHWAY 99

ALEXANDER FALLS. From Highway 99, 2.5 miles north of Brandywine Falls, turn west for drive of five miles on dirt road to Forest Service picnic site.

ALTA LAKE PICNIC SITE. This is just to the west of Highway 99 a little north of Whistler Mountain.

BRITANNIA MINE MUSEUM. Access is from Highway 99 in Britannia Beach by a right turn at the sign.

LANGDALE CREEK. Almost directly opposite the Sechelt ferry terminal on the west side of Highway 101 at Langdale. Trail is on north side of the creek.

MURRIN PARK. On Highway 99 between Britannia Beach and Squamish you have parking space on the west side of the road at the top of the long hill.

SHANNON FALLS. These are just east of Highway 99 a little south of Squamish.

WHISTLER MOUNTAIN. From the top of the chairlift go straight ahead then swing right westward below the ridge towards the top of the T-bar lift.

Garter snake

INDEX

Agassiz Mt. Viewpoint — 124
Aldergrove Park — 188
Alexander Falls — 189
Alexandra Bridge — 158
Alice Lake — 172
Alouette Lake Viewpoint — 118
Alta Lake — 189
Ambleside — 48
Atkinson, Point — 43
Baden-Powell Centennial Trail — 60,66
Baden-Powell Trail, Deep Cove — 66
Barnston Island — 127
Barrier, The — 179
Beaver Lake — 32
Belcarra Park — 188
Beth Lake — 161
Black Mountain — 47
Blackie's Spit — 105
Blue Gentian Lake — 51
Boundary Bay — 99
Brandywine Falls — 180
Bridal Veil Falls — 188
Bristol Island — 150
Britannia Mine Museum — 189
Brockton Point — 32
Brothers Creek — 50
Brunette River — 75
Buntzen Lake — 83
Buntzen Ridge — 188
Burnaby Mountain — 71
Burnaby Lake — 73
Burns Bog — 102
Campbell River — 109
Capilano Canyon — 53
Capitol Hill — 70
Cates Park — 68
Central Park — 77
Century Park — 79
Chadsey Lake — 132
Chancellor Woods — 17
Chapman Creek Falls — 166
Cheakamus Lake — 182
Chilliwack Mountain — 188
Chilliwack River — 144

Cleveland Dam — 53
Cliff Park — 188
Clinton Trail — 20
Confederation Park — 70
Coquihalla River — 153
Council Trail — 21
Crescent Beach — 105
Culliton Creek — 176
Cypress Falls — 41
Cypress Provincial Park — 47
Davis Lake — 119
De Beck Hill — 173
Deer Lake — 79
Delta Nature Reserve — 102
Diamond Head — 170
Dog Mountain — 64
East Canyon Trail — 116
Eaton Lake — 146
Edith Lake — 172
Elk Mountain Meadows — 137
Endowment Lands Forest — 20
Fawn Lake — 172
Fort Langley — 128
Four Lakes Trail — 172
Furry Creek — 161
Garibaldi Lake — 179
George C. Reifel Bird Sanctuary — 98
Goldie Lake — 62
Gravesend Reach — 188
Gray Creek Falls — 165
Grouse Mt. Highway — 56
Haddon Park — 30
Harbourview Park — 70
Harrison Hot Springs — 126
Harrison Lookout — 122
Harrison River — 126
Harvey Creek — 160
Hatzic Dyke — 121
Hemlock Trail — 20
Heritage Village — 79
Historic Yale — 156
Hollyburn Ridge — 46
Hollyburn Skyline Trail — 44
Hut Lake — 175

Imperial Trail — 21
Iona Island — 188
Jericho Beach — 28
John Hendry Park — 36
Kilby Museum and Park — 188
Kitsilano Point — 30
Kwomais Point — 105
Ladner Harbour Park — 96
Langdale Creek — 189
Levette Lake — 175
Lighthouse Park — 43
Lindeman Lake — 141
Little Mountain — 34
Liumchen Falls — 188
Lost Lake (Hollyburn) — 51
Lost Lake (Coquitlam) — 84
Lynn Canyon — 57
Macdonald Falls — 119
McNulty Falls — 139
Marion Lake — 161
Matsqui Dyke — 130
Merilees Trail — 32
Mike Lake — 114
Minnekhada — 88
Mosquito Creek — 54
Mundy Lake — 84
Munro Lake — 89
Murrin Park — 189
Mystery Lake — 64
Nairn Falls — 186
No-Name Lake — 178
Old Alexandra Bridge — 158
Old Dollar Mill — 68
Paul Ridge — 170
Peace Arch Park — 188
Pebble Beach — 151
Phyllis Lake — 161
Pitt Lake — 111
Pitt River Dyke — 87
Poco Trail — 85
Point Roberts — 100
Post Creek — 142
Queen Elizabeth Park — 34
Queen's Park — 188
Quilchena — 24
Rainbow Falls — 184
Red Heather Meadows — 170
Redwood Park — 106
Reifel Island — 98
Renfrew Ravine — 36
Richmond Nature Walk — 94

Robert Burnaby Park — 81
Rolley Lake Park — 188
St. George's Trail — 56
Sandy Cove — 126
Sapper Park — 144
Sea Island Dyke — 92
Second Century Trail — 112
Semiahmoo Trail — 104
Serpentine River — 188
Seymour Mountain — 60
Shannon Falls — 189
Shaughnessy Heights — 26
Simon Fraser University — 72
Skagit River — 148
Skookumchuck Narrows — 164
Skyline Trail — 44
Soames Hill — 169
Southlands — 22
Spanish Banks — 16
Spirit Caves Trail — 155
Stanley Park — 32
Stawamus Chief — 162
Steveston Dyke — 93
Still Creek — 73
Stump Lake — 172
Sumas Peak — 131
Sunshine Coast Recreation Centre — 168
Swanee Creek Falls — 146
Teapot Hill — 136
Thacker Mountain — 152
Tricouni Trail — 178
Trout Lake — 36
Twentyone Mile Creek — 184
U.B.C. Botanical Gardens — 188
U.B.C. Gardens — 14
U.B.C. Research Forest — 112
Upper Chilliwack River — 143
Van Dusen Gardens — 188
Vanier Park — 14
Vedder Mountain — 134
Weaver Creek — 122
West Canyon Trail — 116
Westlake Lodge — 44
Whatcom Trail — 148
Whippoorwill Point — 126
Whistler Mountain — 189
Whyte Island — 39
Whytecliff Park — 39
Woodside Mountain — 124
Wreck Beach — 16
Yale — 156

About The Mountaineers

Organized in Seattle in 1906, The Mountaineers is for those who enjoy the out-of-doors and who would preserve the small remaining wilderness. With more than 8,000 members, The Mountaineers is the third largest outdoor club in the United States, and has members all over the world. The purposes of the organization are:

To explore and study the mountains, forest and watercourses of the Northwest;

To gather into permanent form the history and traditions of this region;

To preserve by the encouragement of protective legislation or otherwise the natural beauty of northwest America.

To make expeditions into these regions in fulfillment of the above purposes;

To encourage a spirit of good fellowship among all lovers of outdoor life.

Other books from The Mountaineers

50 Hikes in Mt. Rainier National Park

101 Hikes in the North Cascades

102 Hikes in the Alpine Lakes, South Cascades and Olympics

103 Hikes in Southwestern British Columbia

Trips and Trails, 1: Family Camps, Short Hikes and View Roads in the North Cascades and Olympics

Trips and Trails, 2: Family Camps, Short Hikes and View Roads in the South Cascades and Mt. Rainier

Bicycling the Back Roads Around Puget Sound

Footloose Around Puget Sound: 100 Walks on Beaches, Lowlands and Foothills

Discover Southeast Alaska with Pack and Paddle

55 Ways to the Wilderness in Southcentral Alaska

Hikers' Map to the North Cascades: Routes and Rocks in the Mt. Challenger Quad

Guide to the Leavenworth Rock Climbing Areas

Darrington & Index: Rock Climbing Guide

Climbers Guide to the Olympic Mountains

Cascade Alpine Guide: Climbing and High Routes, Columbia River to Stevens Pass

Snow Trails: Ski and Snowshoe Routes in the Cascades

Mountaineering: The Freedom of the Hills

Mountaineering First Aid

Snowshoeing

The Alpine Lakes

The North Cascades

The South Cascades: The Gifford Pinchot National Forest

Challenge of Mount Rainier

The Unknown Mountain

Fire and Ice: The Cascade Volcanoes